BLESSINGS FROM BEIJING

Greg C. Bruno

BLESSINGS FROM BEIJING

INSIDE CHINA'S SOFT-POWER WAR ON TIBET

ForeEdge

ForeEdge

An imprint of University Press of New England

www.upne.com

© 2018 Greg C. Bruno

All rights reserved

Manufactured in the United States of America

Designed by Mindy Basinger Hill

Typeset in Minion Pro

Library of Congress Cataloging-in-Publication Data available
upon request

Hardcover ISBN: 978–1-61168–978–5

Ebook ISBN: 978-1-5126–0185–5

5   4   3   2   1

FOR MY FAMILY.

You've taught me the meaning of empathy and pushed me

to practice it with every breath. I love you.

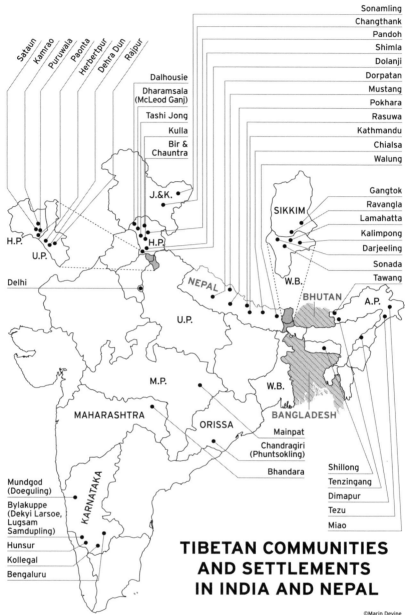

Sataun
Kamrao
Puruwala
Paonta
Herbertpur
Dehra Dun
Rajpur

Dalhousie
Dharamsala (McLeod Ganj)
Tashi Jong
Kulla
Bir & Chauntra

Sonamling
Changthank
Pandoh
Shimla
Dolanji
Dorpatan
Mustang
Pokhara
Rasuwa
Kathmandu
Chialsa
Walung

J.&K.

SIKKIM

Gangtok
Ravangla
Lamahatta
Kalimpong
Darjeeling
Sonada
Tawang

H.P.
U.P.
H.P.

Delhi

NEPAL
W.B.
BHUTAN
A.P.

U.P.

M.P.

MAHARASHTRA

ORISSA

W.B.

BANGLADESH

Mainpat
Chandragiri (Phuntsokling)
Bhandara

Shillong
Tenzingang
Dimapur
Tezu
Miao

Mundgod (Doeguling)
Bylakuppe (Dekyi Larsoe, Lugsam Samdupling)
Hunsur
Kollegal
Bengaluru

KARNATAKA

TIBETAN COMMUNITIES AND SETTLEMENTS IN INDIA AND NEPAL

©Marin Devine

Sources: Central Tibetan Relief Committee; Planning Commission – Central Tibetan Administration; Department of Home – Central Tibetan Administration

CONTENTS

THE TIBET AUTONOMOUS REGION AND GREATER TIBET

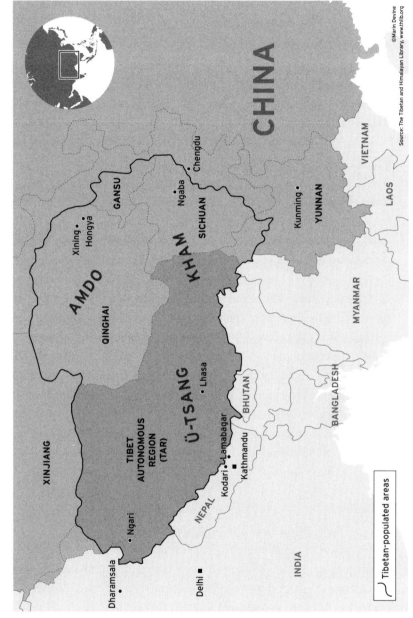

PREFACE

The flag-lined footpath that circles the Dalai Lama's current home and monastery in northern India has been a congested route of faith and fealty for decades. Hewn from the rooted and rocky side of a former British hill station, the undulating trail of gravel, dirt, and devotion has been trodden by Tibetan refugees, Hollywood actors, lawmakers, seekers, hippies, and settlers since the 1960s. On most mornings the only sounds on the trail around the Tsuglagkhang Temple—modeled after similar routes of devotion in Tibet—are those of fluttering meditation flags, circling crows, and the muttered mantras of elderly Tibetans praying for the long life of their "Ocean of Wisdom."

These days, though, the prayers on this path of pilgrimage are growing faint. Once a busy barometer of exiled history, traffic on the footpath that locals call the *kora*—which roughly translates to "circumambulation" or "revolution"—is slowing down. Many Tibetan refugees, pushed away by time, boredom, globalization, and a soft-power war with China, are moving on. *Blessings from Beijing* is the story of this evolution.

As the sixtieth anniversary, in 2019, of the Tibetan exile community approaches, the freedom in exile that His Holiness once heralded is under siege. Beijing, buoyed by a more assertive foreign policy in the last decade, is taking its war with the Tibetan exile government to the source as never before. And the refugee families who have made their homes outside China—in the mountains of Nepal, the jungles of India, or the cold concrete houses high above the kora—are increasingly caught in the middle.

Blessings from Beijing untangles the ribbons of power China ties to Tibetans beyond its borders, and examines the political, cultural, social, and economic pressures that are changing Tibet's refugee communities. Reported over eight years and inspired by two decades of living, studying, and working with Tibetan refugees, *Blessings from Beijing* journeys to the front lines of this fight, into the high Himalayas of Nepal, where Chinese agents reportedly pay off Nepali villagers to inform on Tibetan asylum seekers; to the monasteries of southern India, where pro-China monks wish the Dalai Lama dead; inside Asia's meditation caves, where dedicated souls ponder the fine line between love and war; and to the streets of New York City, London, and Paris, where the next generation of Tibetan refugees reconsiders its freedom fight.

But *Blessings from Beijing* does not stop at the well-worn tales of Chinese political meddling and economic statecraft. It goes beyond them, and within them, to explore how China's relationship with the Tibetan exile community—and Tibetans' relationship with themselves—are changing, most likely forever. Unlike past efforts to chronicle Tibetans' modern-day struggles and triumphs, the stories laid out within these pages do not shy away from Tibetans' own, self-made obstacles. Rather, they lift a proverbial curtain to reveal a people still struggling to make sense of their now-six decade displacement.

What follows are chronicles of China's efforts to weaken and shape the Tibetan diaspora, through direct and indirect means, and Tibetans' own battles to keep their communities vibrant, purposeful, and energized amid the onslaught. Tibetans have been called one of history's most successful refugee populations, and they very well may be (although no Tibetan I've ever met would consider that an honor worth earning). And yet, for all their success in capturing the world's collective imagination, Tibetans of the diaspora are also a community under enormous pressure and growing division. Their young, like refugees anywhere, are tempted by drugs and alcohol; political and religious differences are growing caustic and bloody; and their modern democracy, a product of exile itself, is a messy, oft noninclusive, affair. The Communist Party of China is the source of Tibetan malaise, but Tibetans' self-inflicted wounds have made China's strategy more effective.

Blessings from Beijing is a story of change, both within the Tibetan refugee community, but also within myself. One family in particular features prominently in this journey, that of a former nomad named Purang, whom I know better simply as Pala (which means "father" in the Tibetan tongue).

When I was first introduced to the Tibetan people, as a college student in 1997, I was captivated, horrified, and eventually motivated by the stories of suffering that I heard. I've studied their language, traveled to their villages on both sides of the border, practiced their faith, recorded their suffering, and, as a journalist and a writer, written about their struggles. In the early days of my infatuation, time seemed on their side. In the late 1990s, enlightened and idealistic youth were following the Beastie Boys' lead—hosting concerts, printing T-shirts, and raising cash for the global "Free Tibet" movement. When I returned home to the United States from Asia for the first time, in 1997, I sold "Free Tibet" hoodies near the Skidmore College bookstore, lectured in front of the local Students for a Free Tibet chapter, and raised funds for a Tibetan high school student named Ugyen. One of the last times my college band ever played in public was at a charity event to benefit Tibetan schoolkids. We raised over $1,000 on ticket sales and beer.

More than anything, though, I was angered by what was then, to my mind at least, a black-and-white tale of evil over good: In 1950, China's forced takeover of a self-governed Tibet eventually pushed a simple Buddhist monk and his faithful flock over the Himalayas into exile. With their compassionate smiles and infectious sense of optimism, these exiles worked diligently to save their people and advocate for their freedom. In the process, they captured the world's imagination.

But over time, the longer I lived and worked in Asia, the more I saw the margins of Tibetan suffering (displacement, unemployment, addiction, statelessness) in shades of gray. To fill in the gaps and find clarity in the murkiness I traveled throughout South Asia, visiting with Tibetans in refugee camps in India and Nepal; I toured Tibetan communities in Europe and North America; I relocated to China for a year to teach English to students of petroleum geology in a rural Chinese backwater; and at forty-one I quit my job as the head of communications at New York University Abu Dhabi to study for a master's degree in Chinese studies at the London School of Economics and Political Science. Along the way I discovered that Beijing's "blessings"—the Dalai Lama's euphemistic way of describing the statecraft that China wages on his people—have not only caused but also exacerbated the challenges lying dormant in the Tibetan community itself.

My interest in chronicling the uncertainties facing the Tibetan diaspora is not to criticize or embarrass; I have immense respect and admiration for what has been accomplished during six decades of exile—especially the way the exiles have preserved and shared their culture, religion, art, language, and traditions. Nor is the aim to feed Beijing's narrative of a feckless population of refugees who would be better off returning to a "new" China. (Though in some instances, they might be. China today is approaching superpower status, and as I quickly learned from classmates at the LSE, Chinese young people are more open-minded and globally sophisticated than ever before.) And I certainly do not profess an expert's grasp of all the challenges facing Tibetans in exile today; though I've studied both languages vigorously, I have not attained fluency in either Tibetan or Mandarin, and therefore was forced to rely on translators throughout the reporting for this book.

Rather, my effort here—based on years of journalistic and humanistic observations with people I count as friends—is simply to refocus attention on a community of people still waiting to return to their Xanadu, and perhaps to dispel some of the myths that sixty years of displacement have brought to the fore.

In creating refugee settlements in India and Nepal, the Dalai Lama and his advisers sought to maintain cultural and religious cohesiveness during an extended period of *temporary* exile. It was a noble vision, and its execution has succeeded far beyond anyone's expectations. Tibetans and their peaceful, colorful culture captured the world's hearts and minds. In late 2016 there were some 2.5 million mentions of "Tibet" on Facebook and over 73 million web pages with the word "Tibetan" cataloged by Google; and at 13.1 million followers, the Dalai Lama was more popular on Twitter than the presidents of Turkey, France, and Israel combined. In the world of social media, this Buddhist monk, his people, and the land they call "home" are marketing demigods.

But along the way this marketing miracle hit a roadblock. A host of factors, such as time, more pressing calamities, and political missteps, formed part of the obstruction. The "blessings" bestowed by Beijing have shaped the rest. As the Tibetans' struggle for autonomy or independence moves into its seventh decade, the Tibetan diaspora—torchbearers of their people's struggle on the other side of the border—must take a long, hard look at their own strategies to ensure their efforts in exile are not in vain. I hold out hope that China will engage the Tibetan exile government to forge a negotiated solution to their predicament, before the Dalai Lama dies. But if that does not happen, and the Dalai Lama departs before the modern Tibet question is answered, the Tibetan diaspora will need unprecedented unity to weather the storms that will follow.

This is not a work of fiction, nor is it an academic undertaking in the strictest sense. It is, in the words of anthropologist Clifford Geertz, observations derived from countless hours of "deep hanging out." I alone bear responsibility for the conclusions drawn within the pages that follow, and I apologize in advance for misinterpretations or errors that have found their way into the final text. Most important, what follows is a snapshot of a community under strain. Over the course of my writing this book, many of those whom I turned to for guidance, especially longtime Tibetan settlers in India and Nepal, migrated to the West. While this trend confirms my general observation that Tibetans are experiencing a second migration, it also means that at times my more granular analysis is subject to the memories of those who have since moved on.

Finally, a note on sources: I have used real names whenever possible, but masked identities on a number occasions to protect those sharing sensitive or potentially damaging information. For example, I have changed the name and some details of a young Tibetan man to whom I was introduced in Dharamsala, India, and who retold the story of his friend's self-immolation inside Tibet. With his family still living on the other side of the border, I did not want to bring extra attention to this man's relatives. There are other instances of concealment, throughout the text, which I made for similar reasons.

What follows is a work of passion, persistence, realism, and, above all, hope. More than anything I share these stories as a reminder of why Tibetans captured the world's attention in the first place, and how much they still need our collective attention today.

ACKNOWLEDGMENTS

Every work of nonfiction owes a debt to the openness, energy, and generosity of its contributors. It is those closest to the tale—the university scholars, the humanitarian aid workers, the subjects themselves—who guide authors from the edge of fiction toward the stability of narrative fact. Books based on the lived experiences of others fail to exist without the protagonists' spirit, knowledge, and willingness to share their stories.

Hundreds of such "experts" are behind this story. Some of them appear on the pages that follow; many do not. But all of them allowed a stranger to probe their pasts, plumb their insights, and peer into their world, however briefly. I am grateful to them all.

Two scholars of contemporary Tibet merit special mention. In 1997, Hubert Decleer and Andrew Quintman were the academic guides for my study of Tibet through the School for International Training (SIT). Hubert and Andy emanate an infectious passion for the people, places, and customs of Tibet, and their love of their subject deeply influenced the life trajectories of their students, myself included. It is thanks to their mentorship that I developed an unshakable curiosity about the modern challenges facing the Tibetan diaspora.

Had it not been for SIT, this book would never have materialized, for it was through the school that I first met Purang Dorjee, the elderly shopkeeper whose life has informed many aspects of this narrative. Purang took me into his home in McLeod Ganj during the winter of 1997 and inspired me to learn more about his people. I am forever indebted to Purang, for welcoming me into his life two decades ago, and for inviting me back so many times since.

Rinchen Dharlo, the former president of the Tibet Fund in New York, and Robyn Brentano, formerly the Tibet Fund's executive director, were gracious with their deep contact lists and extensive knowledge. Each was quick to introduce me to Tibetan sources and opened more doors than I can possibly count. Without them, this book would not have been possible. For one, it was Robyn's invitation, in 2009, that led to my brief audience with the Dalai Lama. Robyn also reviewed portions of the final manuscript, providing invaluable perspective on contemporary events.

Kate Saunders, at the International Campaign for Tibet, was also incredibly generous with her time. She, too, has deepened my understanding of the challenges facing Tibetans, on both sides of the border. I am particularly grateful for her assistance in securing an interview with the Seventeenth Karmapa, one of the most important Tibetan religious figures whose place in history is still being written. Kate also connected me with Adam Koziel of the Helsinki Foundation for Human Rights, whose sharp eye helped keep a number of factual errors from entering the final manuscript.

Esther Kaplan, at the Nation Institute's Investigative Fund, was among the first to recognize the importance of this work. The institute's grant, in 2010, enabled me to conduct fieldwork in Nepal and North India, kick-starting the book's reporting process. As one of the few organizations still funding independent investigative journalism, the Nation Institute merits a special thank-you.

Because most journalists make lousy historians, I am deeply indebted to those scholars and experts who spent hours in person, on the phone, or with my manuscript printed out in front of them, steering me through the dizzying and often politicized story of Tibet's modern history. Robert Barnett, of Columbia, and the independent Tibet scholar Matthew Akester were most gracious with their time. Their combined knowledge of Tibet's past and present informed many aspects of this story, and I am forever indebted to these two masters of Tibetan history.

Additional academic insights were offered, and eagerly accepted, from Fiona McConnell of Oxford; Christopher Hughes, Stephan Feuchtwang, and Andrea Pia of the London School of Economics; and from Gary Beesley, whose knowledge of the murky world of intra-Tibetan religious rifts is unrivaled. Each of these experts kindly reviewed key sections of the text, offering expertise on topics as far-ranging as Chinese history, foreign policy, and Tibetan Buddhism.

In Nepal, two human rights activists are doing yeoman's work in protecting vulnerable Tibetan refugees from prosecution. In 2010, when I began this study, Sudip Pathak and Sambu Lhama seemed the only advocates working to protect Tibetans in Nepal from the ever-tightening grip of Chinese influence. These tireless human rights champions took me under their wing and opened doors to Nepal's legal and humanitarian communities that would have been inaccessible otherwise.

At the Council on Foreign Relations, in New York, Michael Moran and Robert McMahon were inspiring storytelling mentors, and equally inspiring bosses, permitting me to sojourn in Asia on an extended book-reporting sabbatical when I first began this project. Without their flexibility and support, I am certain this endeavor would never have gotten off the ground.

Throughout the reporting, writing, and publishing process, I leaned heavily on friends and former colleagues to review manuscript drafts, produce maps and other material, and offer moral support. Matthew Corcoran, in particular, spent hours reading and providing thoughts on pacing, structure, and flow. I am certain that without his energy, *Blessings* would be far less readable than it is today. Marin Devine, a gifted graphic designer, put together the maps that appear here, offering her expertise for little more than the cost of an overpriced gin and tonic. Edward Brachfeld provided the initial inspiration for my pursuit of this topic, while Suzanne Strempek Shea offered invaluable advice on successfully navigating the publishing process.

My agent, Carrie Pestritto, was a fantastic advocate at every juncture and saw in *Blessings* a story that needed an audience. She was relentless in finding one, and served as a constant source of optimism during what can be, for many authors, a drawn-out process of rejection. Her skillful review of proposal drafts, and persistence in pitching them, brought the search for a publisher to a positive conclusion.

My editors at UPNE—Stephen Hull and Susan Abel—and Glenn Novak shepherded multiple versions of the manuscript through the editing churn with great professionalism and grace. Their deft handling of diction and prose ensured that this project was, from start to finish, a collaborative endeavor.

Many others educated me on issues related to Tibet and the Tibetan diaspora; I am grateful to all of them, including Abanti Battacharji, Olrich Cerny, Rhoderick Chalmers, Yeshi Choedon, Tenzin Choepel, Ginger Chih, Michael Davis, Paula Dobrianski, Sonam Dorjee, Tenzin Dorjee, Thondup Dorjee, Tenzin Drakpa, Nathan Freitas, Zhu Guobin, Dorje Gyaltsen, Lobsang Gyatso, Trinlay Gyatso, Nigel Inkster, Sonam Khorlatsang, Vijay Kranti, Margaret Lau, Mary Beth Markey, Kai Meuller, Karma Namgyal, Tsewang Namgyal, Lobsang Phelgyal, Tashi Puntsok, Sophie Richardson, Jigme Lhundup Rinpoche, Kirti Rinpoche, Samdhong Rinpoche, Thupten Samphel, Lobsang Sangay, Phunchok Stobdan, Lubum Tashi, Lhadon Tethong, Tenzin Tethong, Tenzin Topten, Bhuchung K. Tsering, Tempa Tsering, Kunchok Tsundue, Tashi Wangchuk, Kalsang Wangmo, Robert Weinreb, and Tenzin Woeser.

Blessings would still be an obsession, rather than a bound text, had it not been for the support and encouragement of my family. My parents, Kenneth and Claire, were unconditional cheerleaders, funding my university travels to Tibet in the 1990s, and years later serving as eager readers of multiple drafts. Mom and Dad: I cannot thank you enough for the support you've given me, early and often. These *Blessings* are for you.

And finally, Judita, my life partner: without her love and unconditional support, the story of Tibetans' modern challenges would never have met the page. Thanks to her support I was able to temporarily step back from life's obligations and pursue with vigor the stories contained here. Writing a book is like running a very long, slow, painful marathon; friends and family are unwitting participants. Judita endured this journey as much as I did—first as a travel partner, dodging dysentery and maniacal monkeys in Nepal, and later as a mother, caring for our young daughter as I disappeared for weeks of research in South Asia. For that, and for so much more, I am eternally hers.

Pala, my Tibetan "father," was a patient patriarch. Each evening, when the family assembled for dinner in the open-air courtyard, the elderly Tibetan merchant would call for me to join him at the long wooden table beneath the household shrine. Fried bread and fruit lay neatly arranged on ivory-white prayer scarves, offerings to the Buddhist deities of enlightenment and wisdom. Photos of the Dalai Lama, the embodiment of the Tibetan god of compassion, Avalokiteshvara, smiled down at us as we ate.

Pala didn't have much English, and I even less Tibetan, so we would spend the hour or so that we slurped noodles together counting to ten in his native tongue. He would hold out his cracked and blackened fingers, worn from years of herding livestock on the high Tibetan Plateau, and sound out digits on his knuckles like a sitar player tracking beats. *Chig, nyi, sum, zhi, nga . . . chu*, he'd say, waiting for me to repeat each before moving on.

This was how I spent my evenings during the winter of 1997, when I stayed with Pala and his family off Bhagsu Road in the Tibetan refugee capital of McLeod Ganj, in northern India. It would be decades before I learned Pala's real name—*pala* means father in Tibetan—but to this day, thanks to Pala's nightly persistence, I can still count to ten in his language.

Patience has long been a survival instinct for Tibetan refugees. For much of the last six decades, these exiles, men and women who fled Tibet in March 1959, have heartened themselves by believing that one day they would all return home. Life on the torrid Indian subcontinent, far removed from the thin, snowy air of the high Himalayas, was always meant to be temporary. Exile would be endured, tolerated, and survived as an extended ethnic family.

Yet as the sixtieth anniversary of their flight approaches in March 2019, the tenuousness of that dream is increasingly apparent. As Beijing's foreign policy has grown more adventurous, particularly since a post-Olympic expansion in 2008, one of history's most successful cultural relocations is facing its greatest challenge.[1] And as time passes, the Tibetan refugee families who have made their homes outside China and Chinese-controlled Tibet are paying the heaviest price.

Though Tibetans have been in exile since the late 1950s, their prominence on the international agenda came much later. In October 1989, four months after young Chinese democracy activists in Beijing were violently put down by the People's Liberation Army in Tiananmen Square, the Dalai Lama was awarded the Nobel Peace Prize "for his consistent resistance to the use of violence in his people's struggle to regain their liberty."[2] As Nicholas Kristof wrote in the *New York Times* a few years later, the massacre in Tiananmen—against Chinese calls for greater self-determination—pushed Tibetans' plight to the fore. "Tibet has come out of nowhere," a Western diplomat in Beijing told the columnist. "There were always a small number of people interested in Tibet. But before June 4, they were drowned out by the rest of the people with their love affair for China."[3]

During these formative years of Tibetans' international rise, the Tibet problem seemed eminently solvable; like Pala, I was patiently optimistic. And for nearly a decade after returning to the United States from my initial interactions with the Tibetan people, the Christmas cards I received from my Tibetans friends were an annual reminder of the optimism surrounding the issue. China had a big bark, but when it came to protecting Tibet's refugees, the world's bite was more menacing.

The Christmas cards stopped coming in 2006; one of the last I received was from a Tibetan friend wishing my family "happiness always, in all that you do." Then, on Saturday, June 21, 2008, as the Olympic torch made its way to the Roof of the World, Tibetans' perpetual optimism was turned on its head.

Following a series of protests inside Tibet, Zhang Qingli, the top Communist Party official in the Tibet Autonomous Region at the time, vowed to hunt down the exiled activists overseas who he said were responsible for plans to "ruin the Beijing Olympic Games." It was a warning shot fired across the bow of the Tibetan villages I had come to call home. "Tibet's sky will never change, and the red flag with five stars will forever flutter high above it," Zhang said, his navy-and-white polka-dot tie shimmering in the Lhasan sun. China "will certainly be able to totally smash the splittist schemes of the Dalai Lama clique." And this smashing, Zhang added ominously, will occur "inside and outside of the nation."[4]

What amounted to a Chinese declaration of war on Tibet's exiled thousands also served as a wake-up call for my infatuation.[5] So in early 2009, a few months after China proudly and peacefully hosted the Summer Olympics (in spite of Zhang's rhetoric), I applied for an investigative reporting grant from the Nation Institute, a nonprofit media center, to help me understand the battle lines that China had drawn. That October, grant in hand and a mini six-week sabbatical negotiated, I found myself on China's southern border, and in the firing lines of one of Beijing's most aggressive transnational conflicts.

On the first of what would become nearly a dozen reporting trips over the years, I began searching for answers to two questions: What tactics was China employing to fight its burgeoning war with Tibetan refugees? And how was this war affecting my friends? The answers, as I would discover, are contained in Tibetans' unrealized dreams, crushed communities, and the fractured families spread across the Asian continent. Their collective stories are not so different from many other tales of refugee relocation. But the actors involved in this drama—the world's second-largest economy, the planet's most famous monk, and the liberal order of democratic states mediating between them—make understanding the story of China's war on Tibetan refugees all the more urgent.

Zhang's pre-Olympic pledge to target Tibetans "outside of the nation" was not aimed at Tibetans alone. Rather, it marked the opening salvo of a much broader expansion of China's foreign policy priorities coalescing in Beijing at around the same time. The following year, in July 2009, a Chinese politician and leading shaper of Communist Party policy delivered remarks that China watchers have been parsing ever since. Standing beside Secretary of State Hillary Clinton in the rotunda of the Eisenhower Executive Office Building in Washington, DC, State Councilor Dai Bingguo outlined in more detail than any Chinese official ever had what constituted China's "core interests."[6]

"To ensure that our bilateral relationship will move forward on the track of long-term and sound development," Dai began, "a very important thing is that we need to support, respect, and understand each other, and to maintain our core interests. And for China, our concern is we must uphold our basic systems, our national security; and secondly, the sovereignty and territorial integrity; and thirdly, economic and social sustained development."

China's Office of the State Council later expanded on Dai's general themes, noting that "suspicion about China, interference and countering moves against China from the outside are on the increase."[7] Most ominously for Tibetan refugees, the State Council determined that "separatist forces working for... 'Tibet independence' have inflicted serious damage on national security and social stability." A "core interest" red line, it seemed, had been crossed.

Dai did not elaborate on how these interests—such as Taiwan reunification, South China Sea navigation, unrest in Xinjiang, and Tibet—would be defended or protected. Instead, scholars inside and outside China have been left to fill in the blanks. What is clear, though, is that Beijing's tactics (both offensive and defensive) have expanded far beyond the country's national borders. One senior Chinese military official has even suggested that in the post-2008 world, Beijing's "security boundary"—what the UK-based Taiwan expert Christopher Hughes refers to as China's "security perimeter"—"could even include outer space."[8] China was now ready to circle the globe, and even blanket it, to defend its own interests.

For Tibetan refugees in particular, a group of people once dubbed poisonous by Beijing security officials,[9] China's expansion of power and pressure since 2008 has engulfed them like a cloud of toxic gas, and continues to claim victims in a global dragnet of influence. It does this in myriad ways:

First, Beijing challenges Tibetan sympathizers with an unrelenting degree of coercion, intimidation, and propaganda. No Tibet-related issue is too trivial to draw the attention of China's diplomats. Consider what happened in late 2012, when China's consulate in San Francisco waged a highly public (though ultimately unsuccessful) campaign to win the removal of a pro-Tibet mural in the small college town of Corvallis, Oregon. In a letter to the mayor, Chinese officials said the image, which was painted on a renovated storefront, "tainted" US-China relations. The mural showed Chinese police beating Tibetans, and others ablaze in protest. The town's mayor refused China's removal request, but the mural's Taiwan-born owner grew so nervous about possible reprisals by Chinese interests that he bought himself a gun for protection.[10]

Second, China works to siphon off support for the Dalai Lama within the Tibetan exile community itself, by refusing to negotiate with and constantly vilifying the Tibetan leader, or by supporting anti–Dalai Lama political and religious factions. One monastery in the South of India that I visited is home to a group of monks who have challenged the Tibetan spiritual head's ban on an esoteric devotional practice that some fear is religiously dangerous. Worship of the protector deity known as Dorje Shugden has divided Tibetan refugees so deeply that some told me only the Dalai Lama's death will bring resolution. It is a rift that Tibetans created but, as you will read, one China works hard to widen.

Third, China's state security targets individuals, both Tibetan and non-Tibetan, who use their freedom to advocate for changes inside Tibet. Chinese computer hackers pry open Tibetans' e-mails, infect their documents, and track their movements. Those who are most vocal have been kidnapped, beaten, and tortured over their ties to the Tibetan cause. An American diplomat stationed in New Delhi told me that China's anti-Tibetan espionage program in India was "one of the most aggressive efforts [of spycraft] since the Cold War." Beyond that, China also seeks to control aspects of Tibetans' own faith—by stage-managing the selection of reincarnated lamas, for instance.

But as heavy-handed as these tactics may be—publicly expressing anger over a mural in rural America, stuffing activists blindfolded into the backseats of unmarked cars, or cracking Tibetan computers around the world—they won't alter the world's opinion of Tibetans, or significantly change the pro-Tibet policies of Western nations. To achieve those goals, China deploys a fourth line of offense, one that it hopes will sway the world's major powers to see the Tibet problem Beijing's way: economic and political blackmail targeting the very governments that have aided the Tibetan exile community since its birth.

France was among the first nations to confront this devastating math following Zhang's 2008 threat. During a press conference on November 27, 2008, Chinese foreign affairs spokesman Qin Gang warned of serious consequences for Paris if French president Nicolas Sarkozy sat down with the Dalai Lama the following month. France, chair of the rotating EU presidency at the time, was courting Chinese development around Europe, but its insistence on linking human rights to investment, and giving the Tibetan leader a forum, made Beijing bristle. China had already canceled a key China-EU economic summit in protest of the Dalai Lama meeting, and threatened more, unspecified, pain.

On December 6, the French president went ahead with the Dalai Lama détente anyway, a thirty-minute meeting between the two men in the Polish port city of Gdańsk. The response from China was immediate. Talks on a planned contract for the purchase of 150 French-made Airbus passenger planes were postponed.[11] Weeks later, a Chinese trade delegation toting more than $15 billion worth of business deals for Europe intentionally avoided French businesses.

"I looked at a map of Europe on the plane," China's Prime Minister Wen Jiabao said at the time. "My trip goes around France. We all know why."[12]

In recent years China has also begun deploying a fifth method that drives some Tibetan refugees mad with frustration, despite its low-tech application: strategic silence. By refusing all overtures for dialogue with Tibetan exiles about their fate (the two sides held nine rounds of talks between September 2002 and January 2010), Beijing is giving Tibetans the equivalent of the cold shoulder in a dysfunctional marriage. As the Obama administration noted a few months before leaving office, "The death of the Dalai Lama in exile without a resolution of differences likely would increase instability in China, and we encourage China to adopt policies that would reduce the risk of unrest and resume dialogue with the current Dalai Lama while he remains healthy."[13] But for now, at least, Beijing appears willing to risk it.

Not long after China's response to France's Tibetan courtship, I paid a visit to one of the world's best-known Tibet scholars, someone who understands well what these refugees face. Robert Barnett met me at a small diner not far from his Columbia University office in Manhattan. For over an hour as we sipped bottomless cups of tea, I told Barnett what I had learned during the first of what would become many visits to the front lines of China's soft-power war on Tibet. Fear of Chinese spying on Tibetans had become obsessive, I told him. Chinese influence in the community was growing, I said.

None of it surprised him. Barnett, like most prominent Tibet experts in the West, had himself come under the gaze of Chinese diplomats. Beijing's war on Tibet's refugees also targets those who support and study the issue. "In the last twenty-four hours I've been given at least three presents by Chinese officials, quite nice ones," he said without a hint of irony. "One is a calendar, a huge, lavish kind of calendar. Another was an attractive Chinese pottery that was rather expensive. They're all the time trying, calling up and asking to meet. It happens all the time."

"What's important about it," Barnett continued, "is not that this is happening all the time to many, many people, but that it means [the Tibet issue] is important to China. In my view, this is the thing we should take away from this. We shouldn't take away an image that China is mean, or naughty, or breaking the rules. It isn't breaking the rules. It's just playing the game rather better than most people and pursuing its own interests."

In other words, to Barnett, it was the second question I had set out to answer—how China's approach to the Tibet issue is directly affecting Tibetan refugees—that was of greater consequence.

Taking another sip of tea, Barnett explained it this way: "I don't want to say that the project is crumbling. The project [of Tibetan cultural relocation] is under huge pressure. I think the center of the project, the Tibetan government, may be holding relatively well. But what we're seeing is China quite successfully driving wedges within the Tibetan community and weakening its center, while that center is largely silent: it's a quiet center, in the sense that it doesn't address its internal divisions very openly or effectively. It seems to find it hard to embrace discussions with its critics or explain its differences. And this lack of real conversation is amplified by the Internet, where, as often happens, critical voices are more expressive and active than those, probably the vast majority of Tibetans, who agree with the Dalai Lama but are largely silent. This produces some maybe skewed perceptions on what's happening. Those perceptions are very influential in terms of attitudes and critiques. But I fear they aren't leading to the kind of renewal or improvement in collective thought or strategy that many have been hoping for."

Barnett went on: "In many ways this is the result of a Chinese strategy, which says, 'Let's insult the Dalai Lama, and let's deny him any concessions, so he will (a) appear to be a problem, (b) be hated by Chinese, and (c) appear to get nothing for all his efforts.' As a result, among people who follow him, some people will say, 'He's a failure. He hasn't gotten anything for his policy.' It seems to be one objective of China's strategy to frustrate a sector of the less patient Tibetan exiles, which it hopes will then undermine the Dalai Lama, especially if it can get it to turn to violence, and then undermine the government in exile and reduce its effectiveness.

"This is a classic way to weaken an opponent," he added.

By January 2016, China had all but declared victory. An opinion piece published by the *Global Times*, a Communist Party–linked paper, announced that the "Dalai Lama's clique is falling apart." Reincarnation "cronyism," the de facto ban on Shugden worship, internal conflicts, and corruption were pushing Tibetan refugees to the brink of collapse, the paper declared.[14]

Left unmentioned was the role China was playing in helping to expedite the free fall.

I'd been in the company of the man China calls a "wolf in monk's robes" on numerous occasions—during public teachings at his monastery in McLeod Ganj, and at a lecture in New York City. But it wasn't until I began investigating China's treatment of his Tibetan brethren abroad that I had the opportunity to speak with him.

In the fall of 2009, a few weeks after the grant from the Nation Institute had landed in my bank account, I set out for North India, my first foray into China's war on Little Lhasa. Friends from the Tibet Fund in New York City had invited me to join them on a visit to McLeod Ganj for meetings. A sit-down with the Tibetan leader was on the agenda.

I awoke early on the morning of our meeting with the Dalai Lama, well before the portable space heater in my room had kicked on. The invitation was not for a personal audience, but as a member of a group; there would be about twenty other people in the room listening to him speak to fellow Nobel laureates on the topic of religious tolerance. "Questions," I was told, were "likely. Come prepared."

Sitting at a small wooden desk at the Chonor House, a few hundred yards from the Dalai Lama's front door, I pored over notes from recent conversations I had had with Tibetan refugees on the streets and in the homes outside my window. A self-immolation crisis was beginning to brew across the border that fall, and residents of the normally placid village of eleven thousand were growing frustrated with how slowly the world was responding to the pleas of their desperate relatives. A young Tibetan businessman told me he was increasingly doubtful that the Dalai Lama had the political skills to push China to change. Others spoke cryptically of the ubiquitous presence of Chinese spies in the Indian village that Tibetans have called home since the 1960s.

One Tibetan man, a former Indian-army-soldier-turned-mystic whom I had met in a meditation cave a few days earlier, told me how he wanted to kill the people occupying his ancestral homeland. It was likely little more than bluster—his shaggy mane of black hair, soft eyes, and weak handshake said to me he was more monk than mercenary. But the sentiment was nonetheless being repeated that winter by a growing segment of young Tibetans.

As I recalled these conversations, I jotted down questions for His Holiness in my notepad.

By eleven that morning, I had gone through security at the Dalai Lama's residence—passed the metal detectors manned by rifle-toting Indian soldiers, and beyond the Tibetan men in slacks and button-downs who serve as his personal security detail. As I stepped into a wood-paneled reception hall with drop ceilings and yellow fluorescent lighting, a monk cloaked in crimson directed me to a chair in the second row, about ten feet from the plush beige lounger where the Tibetan leader would be seated.

I began to sweat. I had spent years interviewing powerful figures for newspapers and news websites, from US army generals and foreign politicians to former pop stars, sports heroes, and global visionaries. During this conversation I would be lucky to get a question in. And yet, for the first time in my career, my heart was pounding, and I was at a loss for words.

The next forty-five minutes were a blur. I don't remember anything His Holiness discussed with the other Nobel Peace Prize winners—the American anti–land mine activist Jody Williams, the Iranian lawyer Shirin Ebadi, and the Irish peace leader Mairead Corrigan Maguire. All I remember is that when the Dalai Lama said in English, "Any questions?" my hand shot up instinctively—a lone arm extended in a sea of awestruck admirers. As the microphone came my way, the thumping of my pulse almost drowned out the words that spewed from my mouth. Here's what I asked the world's most famous monk:

"What happens to your people if governments that today support Tibetan refugees, like India and Nepal, eventually cave to Chinese pressure?" The subtext: What becomes of the Tibetan exile community when you aren't around to protect them?

The Dalai Lama's answer wasn't overly detailed, or grammatically correct. And he delivered it with his brow furrowed, as if he was annoyed by the topic. But his swift fifty-two-second reply—to a "political" question posed in the middle of a conversation on religion, he reminded me—would send me around the world to contextualize what he said.

"Totalitarian regimes sort of pressure everywhere, even in the United States," the aged Tibetan leader said with a giggle as he peered over the dark metal rims of his Coke-bottle glasses, past the assembled audience of nodding human rights workers, philosophers, and writers. "I think India and Nepal are receiving some *special blessing* from Peking, that's quite clear," he said. "And the situation in Nepal, it's not very settled, not very stable. There are a lot of problems. So Chinese pressure, Chinese Communist pressure, is more effective."

And with that, he nodded for me to pass the mike.

I've spent years puzzling over what the Dalai Lama was referring to that day. What did a "special blessing from Peking" mean in practice? How were Tibetans being pressured in the United States? How about in India, the world's largest democracy? Were Pala and his family feeling this "pressure"? And what was going on in Nepal? What problems were Tibetans in that slice of Buddhist paradise having that needed to be understood?

In some ways, elements of these questions have surfaced for decades. Ever since the arrival of Mao's Red Army on the Tibetan Plateau, the Dalai Lama and his Tibetan compatriots have been subject to China's gaze. In 1935, during the Long March, Chinese forces stormed the region of Ngaba, in modern day Sichuan Province, destroying monasteries, killing monks, and stealing supplies. Kirti Rinpoche, the exiled chief abbot of Kirti Monastery in Ngaba, told us lawmakers in 2011 that the aftermath of the siege "was the first time that Tibetans in this region survived by eating leaves of trees." As the Tibet scholar Melvyn C. Goldstein has noted, the early years of Chinese occupation were aimed at "liberating" Tibet peacefully by introducing a controversial power-sharing agreement.[1] For much of the decade after 1950—and before the agreement's scuttling in 1959—Mao and the Communist Party sought to win over Tibetan allegiance with promises, pledges, propaganda, and economic coercion. In those early days of occupation, Communist cadres spent vast sums to induce Tibet's poorest to revolt against the "evil" rich. Palden Gyatso, a Tibetan monk who spent thirty-three years in Chinese prisons after the invasion, recalls the flashy films and theatrical performances staged by the Chinese "to incite the poor against the landowners." Films like *The White-Haired Girl*, a Chinese ballet depicting misery among local peasant women, were screened outdoors in Lhasa during the 1950s.

In time, though, China's words were matched with action—a stick of influence extending far beyond its physical borders. That is the context in which the Tibetan leader was answering. China's leaders saw the Beijing Olympics in 2008 as affirmation of their great power status, and by 2009, as I sat a few feet from the object of China's ire, they had begun to deploy that power. As the sinologist Bates Gill put it that year, 2008 was China's "coming out party" to the world.[2] For Tibetans, though, there was little to celebrate.

The Dalai Lama mentioned countries only to illustrate how Beijing was bestowing its blessings. But it wasn't long before he would point to specific people.

In May 2012, three years after our meeting, the Dalai Lama publicly accused China of sending Tibetan agents to his doorstep not only to snoop, but to poison. "We received some sort of information from Tibet," he told the UK *Sunday Telegraph*. "Some Chinese agents training some Tibetans, especially women . . . using poison—the hair poisoned, and the scarf poisoned—they were supposed to seek blessing from me, and my hand touch."[3]

The allegation brought a swift Chinese denial. "If the central government wanted to 'eliminate' the Dalai Lama," an editorial in the *Global Times* said, "why has it waited for such a long time?"[4] But the episode did prompt the inevitable question: Just what was China capable of?

The possibilities seemed endless. The following month, a group of eight Chinese men were arrested by police in Himachal Pradesh after a raid at a monastery uncovered thousands of dollars in cash and dozens of Chinese SIM cards. Police later told the *Times of India* that the Chinese nationals, who were in North India on expired tourist visas, were being investigated for possible connections to a plot to harm the Dalai Lama.[5] Indian police never confirmed the links, but a Chinese embassy spokesperson in Delhi acknowledged the arrests and said they were "seeking details" from the Indian government.[6]

With the Dalai Lama's warning still fresh in my mind, and amid news reports indicating just how serious Beijing's "blessings" could be, I paid a visit to the top Tibetan official in charge of keeping the Buddhist leader safe.

The Tibetan Department of Security sits in nondescript building a few miles from the center of McLeod Ganj. The door was ajar on the afternoon that I visited, and pulling back a fraying green curtain, I popped my head inside. Seated behind a sun-soaked wooden desk was a middle-aged monk, working away. I didn't have an appointment, but with a smile the monk motioned for me to take a seat. On a wall to the right hung a framed photograph of the Tibetan capital, with handwritten labels pasted over the glass marking Chinese army headquarters, police barracks, and known prisons. We chatted casually at first—about the poster and the prisons, about life in exile—but conversation quickly turned to China's presence in this tiny town.

"We think there are lots of spies in India," the security officer said matter-of-factly, agreeing to speak only on the condition that I not record him or publish his name. "It's very difficult to recognize them, but lots of people share information with us." For example, if the Tibetan government or a religious office organizes a gathering, mass prayer vigil, or a ceremony, he said, "immediately China knows what happens. People are passing information on. Most of the people we can trust. But a few, maybe they are working for money."

Among the key pieces of information China was looking to gather, the officer said, were details on the Dalai Lama's health. Tibetan pilgrims had been encouraged to collect hair from the Tibetan leader when they receive his blessing, material the monk said could then be used by China to test for evidence of DNA-related illnesses.

The allegations jibed with other claims of skulduggery making the rounds among Tibetans. In December 2009, a Delhi-based surgeon had walked me through the intricate subterfuge needed to plan the medical operation on the Dalai Lama's gallbladder the year before. Because of China's ability to listen in on digital communications, there were no phone calls and no e-mails to discuss plans, only coded messages and face-to-face briefings. The steps were necessary, he said, to ensure that the Chinese weren't able to sabotage the operation, obtain information about the leader's health, or even prematurely kill off their crimson-cloaked nemesis.

Allegations of Chinese-linked murder plots are impossible to verify, but

China's ability to intimidate Tibetans in other ways is not. Perhaps the most common form of harassment that Beijing deploys is a near-ubiquitous ability to listen to what Tibetans are saying.

According to cyber researchers at the University of Toronto, who have documented the electronic warfare being waged against Tibetan refugees, the Chinese "are relentless in their attempts to compromise networks and harvest sensitive information."[7] In March 2009, the Citizen Lab at the Munk School of Global Affairs in Toronto uncovered a sweeping cyber spying ring that compromised the computer networks of the Tibetan government in exile, infecting servers from India to New York, including one that housed the Dalai Lama's own e-mail account.[8]

Tibetan exile officials say they assume China is monitoring everything about them, from their overseas travel planning to His Holiness's lifestyle habits. "I have myself been a victim of many of these surveillance tactics and interferences, both when I was in Dharamsala, from 2011 to 2015, as well as in my current position," Kaydor Aukatsang, then the Dalai Lama's representative to North America, told me in early 2016. "It's very clear that everything we do, at least in terms of our internal communications, is being monitored and intercepted by the Chinese."

\---

China's dominion over Tibetans wasn't always so one-sided. As far back as the seventh century, when the Tibetan king Songtsen Gampo unified the mountainous plateau and pushed Tibet's borders to the edges of those of China's Tang dynasty, the relationship was more even-footed. Tibet's king wielded significant political influence to the east, and took tribute and foreign wives from beyond his borders. One of them, a Chinese princess named Wencheng, was a Tang royal family member whom scholars credit with helping introduce Buddhism to the Tibetan people.

During these early years of the China-Tibet linkage, Tibet operated much like any independent state. In the ninth century, treaties between the two kingdoms even demarcated their respective borders. One treaty from that era was literally etched in stone, a rock tablet erected outside the Jokhang Temple in Lhasa, the Tibetan capital, which served as a bilingual recording of the ties.

"Having consulted to consolidate still further the measure of neighborly contentment they have made a great treaty," a translation of the document from the year 821 reads in part. "Both Tibet and China shall keep the country and frontiers of which they are now in possession. The whole region to the east of that being the country of Great China and the whole region to the west being assuredly the country of Great Tibet, from either side of that frontier there shall be no warfare, no hostile invasions, and no seizure of territory." On the day the treaty went into force, a ceremony with "both Buddhist and non-Buddhist rites" was performed, and included animal sacrifices and leaders' oaths sealed with the dead animals' blood.[9]

From the twelfth century, as China was conquered by successive Mongol rulers, Tibetans deepened their connections with the imperial dynastic orders to the east. By the middle of the thirteenth century, a "priest-patron" relationship had been cemented between one of Tibetan Buddhism's highest lamas, the Sakya Phagpa, and the Mongol ruler Kublai Khan, linking Tibet's star to China's Yuan dynasty through religion.

The patronage relationship did not continue after the Yuan ended in the mid-fourteenth century. But when the Manchus threw out the Ming dynasty in 1644 and established the Qing (China's last dynasty, which would endure until 1911), the Tibetan-Mongol alliance again benefited the Tibetans. When the Great Fifth Dalai Lama visited Beijing in 1656, the Qing emperor reportedly treated him "with great courtesy and respect." The Dalai Lama, who commanded a "broad following among other Mongol tribes, some of whom were a threat to the Qing themselves . . . was not someone to be trifled with."[10] Like a three-legged stool, the Tibetan-Mongol-Qing relationship was mutually supportive. For the Tibetans, with no army of their own, it was also critical.

The Tibetan-Mongol alliance would not protect Tibet forever, however. Following a series of Mongol invasions at the beginning of the eighteenth century, it was the Qing emperor who, in October 1720, marched his soldiers into Tibet to rid the Qings' western flank of Mongol forces. Once free of Mongol rule, the Qing set up an administrative protectorate inside Tibet, the goal of which was "to control the actions of Tibet's fractious leaders, and particularly to prevent its lamas from using their religious sway over the Mongols to harm Qing interests."[11] The Qings' intent was not to absorb Tibet into China, but rather to protect it from external (Mongol) influence and internal (Buddhist) conflict.

For much of the remaining imperial period, a relationship similar to the priest-patron ties of the thirteenth century solidified between the Tibetans and the Chinese. Tibetans governed most of their own affairs but called on the Qing armies to intervene when assistance was needed (something they did with frequency during the eighteenth century—five times, according to Goldstein's count).

Eventually, though, the Qing would face their own challenges to power, and revolts inside China limited the emperor's ability to focus attention on the faraway borderlands. Without a strong China to come to Tibet's aid, the Buddhist leaders in Lhasa were pushed to rely on their own army, and increasingly managed their own affairs. "By the turn of the twentieth century . . . the Qing hegemony over Tibet was more symbolic than real," says Goldstein.

For a brief period after the Qing it was the British who sought control of Tibet. Eager to establish trade links between Tibet and British-controlled India, British envoys mounted a series of trade missions and diplomatic offensives that, for the most part, were rebuffed by Lhasa. Not to be deterred, British expeditionary forces pushed into Tibet in 1903 to force trade negotiations, and by late 1904 became the first Western army to conquer the Tibetan Plateau. British troops eventually withdrew, but not before Tibet was pressured into signing an agreement that opened Tibet's border towns to British trade.

The period between the collapse of the Qing in 1911 and the birth of the People's Republic of China gave way to a more autonomous Tibet. With the British out and the new republic under Sun Yat-sen fighting for stability, Tibet managed de facto independence with a deal signed in Shimla, India, in 1914. Known as the Shimla Convention, the document did not grant Tibet full independence from China, but it did secure Tibetan control over security, currency, and religious and political affairs. That lasted until October 1, 1949, when events far to the east changed the trajectory of China forever.

When Mao Zedong declared the creation of the PRC after the defeat of Chiang Kai-shek and the Kuomintang Nationalist forces, the Communist Party saw Tibet in much the same way that its imperial predecessors had: as a buffer, and a source of resources. But like the Mongols, Mao also viewed Tibetan religion and culture as unique. The first few years of Communist Party control were meant to ingratiate the elite while bringing Tibet's poorest to socialism slowly (waiting to introduce ideas of class struggle, for example). But not even the deliberate pace of reform was acceptable to the Tibetans, and by the late 1950s, Tibetans in Eastern Tibet were resisting. In 1959, unrest erupted into a full-blown revolt, and in March, as the Dalai Lama fled south to India, the Chinese noose on Tibetan autonomy was irreversibly tightened.

Over the next few years, with Tibet's top leader in exile, China exerted a crushing blow to Tibetan independence and autonomy. Political institutions were disbanded, monasteries gutted, and remnants of the traditional elite chased from their perch. Anyone who had supported or participated in the failed March 1959 revolt was sentenced to prison and hard labor. By the mid-1960s, as the Cultural Revolution engulfed Tibet, the region's traditional ways had been erased in the Communists' rush to "create the new by smashing the old."

Mao Zedong's death in 1976 cleared the way for Communist Party reformers, who brought Tibetans some hope of greater political and religious freedoms. During the tenure of party chairman Hu Yaobang, who saw errors in Mao's Tibet policies, Tibetans were given more control over their internal affairs, as Chinese soldiers withdrew from many Tibetan areas inside the Tibet Autonomous Region. Monasteries destroyed during the Cultural Revolution were allowed to be rebuilt, talks on Tibetan sovereignty restarted, and the ethnic Chinese who stayed on the Tibetan Plateau were encouraged to learn the local language. It was the most liberal and inclusive period for Tibetans since Beijing's military takeover in 1950.

Party officials at the time still accused the Tibetan spiritual leader of attempting to "split the motherland," but they also extended an invitation for the Dalai Lama to end his exile, as long as he lived in Beijing, a caveat the Dalai Lama has always refused. In March 1988, Li Xiannian, then the outgoing president of the People's Republic, went so far as to say China had "respect for the Dalai Lama." The problem, President Li said, was that the Dalai Lama "does not respect China, his motherland."

But the events of 1989 put an end to the diplomatic hair-splitting. In Beijing, the rise of pro-democracy advocates refocused the Communist Party's hard-liners, and by the early 1990s China had resumed a more strident rhetoric on the topic of Tibet. In 1992, a Chinese white paper spelled out in detail what Beijing said was historic evidence that the Tibetan Plateau had been under Chinese sovereignty for over seven hundred years. The white paper also did something else: it declared that the Dalai Lama was, in no uncertain terms, an enemy of the state. "The Dalai's words and deeds have showed that he is no longer only a religious leader as he claims. On the contrary, he has become the political leader engaged in long-term divisive activities abroad."[12]

When I arrived on the Tibetan refugees' doorstep in 1997, international support for the Tibetan cause was galvanized against the Chinese position. China's targeting of Tibetan exiles was less obvious, and India's support for the estimated one hundred thousand Tibetan men, women, and children who lived as refugees within its borders was steadfast. But after a brief return to the negotiating table in the early 2000s, China had once more shut the door on a peaceful resolution. With the Olympic torch bound for Beijing in the summer of 2008, China was feeling stronger than ever.

Not long after my meeting with the Dalai Lama, a friend working in the Tibetan home ministry of the government in exile invited me on a tour of the meditation caves that dot the tree-lined ridge overlooking McLeod Ganj. In these austere dwellings connected to local monasteries, monks and mystics spend months, even years, in solitary confinement meditating on the meaning of Buddhist scriptures and the central tenets of compassion, wisdom, and nonviolence. The Ministry of Home looks after this Tibetan population, extending its definition of "home" to include an invisible, cave-dwelling subset. I accepted the invitation, with some reservation, as I wasn't sure how talkative a robed mystic suddenly roused from a meditative state would be.

But I also wanted to ask a Tibetan—especially one who spent hours every day silently pondering patience and peace—what he thought about China's "blessings." So I tagged along.

The climb to the caves high above the Kangra Valley is, quite literally, breathtaking. Eagles soar in the cool, dry air, and sheep graze on tufts of grass clinging to the snowy Himalayan foothills at six thousand feet above sea level. We climbed on a warm, sunny fall day, and my guide, Dorje, bounced knowingly from rock to rock, slowed only by my winded pace and the few extra pounds of rice and barley flour he carried as gifts to those seated cross-legged farther up the mountain.

We stopped at three dwellings that day, eating noodles and sipping tea with monks and old men. Each meditator welcomed us quickly with warm smiles and attentive eyes. My earlier concern about self-imposed silence was swiftly dispelled. It turns out that when individuals abruptly suspend contemplative solitude, they are sharper and more mindful than most of us on our best days.

But it was the conversation on our last stop that was most revealing.

After about an hour up on the climb, Dorje stopped beneath a boulder at the top of a long scree slope. At the base of the rock, invisible from the foot-path below, was a low opening covered by a thick blanket. Pulling the curtain back, he ducked inside and motioned for me to follow. In the dim light it took a few seconds for my eyes to adjust and make out the silhouette of a man, seated crossed-legged against the far wall. Rays of sun from a single window illuminated his saffron robes, and long black hair fell neatly on his shoulders. Passang Tsering introduced himself in broken English.

For over an hour we sat on the dirt floor of Passang's meditation retreat, sipping tea and discussing anger, forgiveness, and Passang's continual frustration with his people's fate. He thumbed prayer beads as he spoke in slow, hushed tones. Smoke from a small incense burner hung in front of his face as he explained what brought him to a rocky outcrop high above the Dalai Lama's residence. He, not I, brought up the subject of China.

As a boy, Passang was patriotic but directionless, spending his days idle in his mother's convenience store in South India. When he turned sixteen, he followed in the footsteps of his father and volunteered to fight for the all-Tibetan military units within the Indian army, the Special Frontier Force. The need for a full-time job drove him to enlist, but anger secretly fueled him: he hoped the military would give him the chance to cross the Indian border into China, and turn his patriotism into flying lead—"to fight the Chinese and take my country back," he said.

But after five years of training, and not a single shot fired from his rifle, he traded in his gun for prayer beads, believing that the mind was a more powerful weapon in this war.

Institutional monastic life didn't suit Passang either, however, and his anger and vitriol remained untamed. After three years he left his small monastery in southern India to come here, a cool cave in the Himalayan foothills, to be near a man who had dampened the fires of his own frustration. The Dalai Lama, whose well-lit and tastefully appointed sitting room was just a few thousand feet below Passang's sparsely decorated rock hole, was an inspiration for a man with a wandering heart and an angry mind.

By the time I met Passang, he had been in his cave on and off for nine years. Alone. Committed Buddhists believe that mastering the mind is the best way to bring peace to their own hearts, and to the world. The Tibetan leader is considered an authority in this practice; many people—not just Tibetans—pore over his teachings for clues on how to emulate him.

That, at least, was the goal for Passang, to emulate His Holiness. But the more Passang and I spoke, the more I got the sense that this would be his final attempt to find peace within, before abandoning his practice again, or even resorting to more desperate measures. Part of what made him angry, he explained, was how obstinate China was despite Tibetans' repeated offers of compromise and discussion (a ninth round of talks between the two sides took place in January 2010, but yielded nothing). Beijing's "blessings," he said, were a source of great consternation.

Passang's soul-searching was not going well on the day we met. Tibetans are angry, he said—furious, in fact. His mind was racing with rage.

"It's natural [to be bitter] when somebody forcefully takes your country, and occupies it, and even does harm to the people," he said. "It's natural that everybody will feel angry."

Tossing his long locks of black hair over his shoulder, he went on: "I'm not totally devoted to Buddhism. War? I [am] ready to [go to] war. Not totally decided Buddha disciple. This freedom . . . I really want freedom.

"Younger generation of Tibetan people," Passang went on, pausing to ponder what he was about to suggest—younger people like me—they "all want to war."

After nine years on a cushion in the corner of a cramped cave, Passang was fixated on a single-syllable solution. And it wasn't "love."

———

When I first visited the Tibetan diaspora, I found that people shared a common vision for Tibet's future: trust the Dalai Lama, and one day Tibet will be free, or at least sovereign. In many ways, what China did or didn't do was of little consequence to these refugees. But after five decades of waiting, talking, compromising, and waiting some more, Tibetans are restless. The pressure that China is applying to Tibetan refugees and their hosts—"blessings," in the Dalai Lama's telling phase—has affected these refugees in different ways. Some, like Pala, seem to take the offensive in stride. Others are growing restless.

But others still, men like Passang, are defiant, possibly dangerous, and ready to take matters into their own hands.

Tibetans, perhaps not surprisingly, are not universally pacifist. In the 1960s, fierce Tibetan warriors from the eastern region of historic Tibet, known as Kham, waged a guerrilla war on Chinese forces. A program funded by the US Central Intelligence Agency, spearheaded by the Dalai Lama's brother and personally approved by President Dwight D. Eisenhower, trained, armed, and supported Tibetan Khampas to fight the Chinese army on Tibetan soil.[13] The Eisenhower administration feared a global communist takeover and worried that unless Mao Zedong's advance was stopped he would march his brand of anti-Western rhetoric all the way to Moscow, creating a band of red power from the Yellow Sea to the Baltic. Supporting Tibetan resistance fighters was one way for Washington to challenge this possibility.[14]

More recently, violence between Tibetans and Muslims in Gansu, Sichuan, and Qinghai Provinces, as well as the Tibet Autonomous Region, has renewed questions about how committed Tibetans are to following their spiritual leaders' Gandhi-like example. Following one particularly violent clash in 2008 during which Tibetans trashed a Muslim restaurant in Qinghai, Tibet scholar Andrew M. Fischer told the *Los Angeles Times* that such violence "is the dark side of Tibetan nationalism. It is almost as though the Tibetans are diverting their anger over their own situation towards another vulnerable minority."[15]

Outside Tibet, Tibetans have spent more time predicting violence by their brethren than practicing it (though isolated melees between Tibetans and Indians have been reported over the years). And nearly every argument among Tibetan refugees begins with a heated discussion of how to get China back to the bargaining table. These ripples of refugee disagreement are yet another way China's strategic silence bears fruit.

In 1988, the Dalai Lama unveiled a plan at the European Parliament in Strasbourg, France, that called on China to allow Tibetans genuine autonomy. The idea, which would come to be known as His Holiness's "middle way" approach, called on China to maintain control of Tibet's foreign affairs and security while allowing Tibetans control "in the field of commerce, education, culture, religion, tourism, science, sports, and other non-political activities."

The proposal has never been accepted by Beijing, and likely won't be under the current government. But its bold admission—that Tibet should remain under de facto Chinese rule—has split the exile Tibetan community, between those who see their role as advocating for freedom (*rangzen* in Tibetan) and those who concede that only a compromise will do. Warren W. Smith Jr., author of *Tibetan Nation: A History of Tibetan Nationalism and Sino-Tibetan Relations*, says the division "has only widened as the policy has failed to produce any resolution with China."[16] And it remains the source of much refugee friction to this day.

Tibetan frustrations with the political direction of their plight hit a new high in late 2010, when the Dalai Lama announced he was giving up his political position in a bid to pave the way for a more democratic transition of the Tibetan government in exile. In a March 2011 speech marking his official departure from politics, he called on his brethren to accept that it was time for him to make way for younger leaders. "I trust that gradually people will come to understand my intention, will support my decision, and accordingly let it take effect."[17]

It did take effect—a Harvard-educated lawyer, Lobsang Sangay, was elected prime minister in August 2011—but it was not, and perhaps never will be, universally accepted by the Tibetan community. Jamyang Norbu, a prominent writer, activist, and critic of the government in exile (he was once a member of it), has been particularly damning of the Dalai Lama's decision. "The Tibetan government-in-exile has, to all intents and purposes, gone ahead and pulled the plug on itself," he wrote in July 2012.[18]

It is against this backdrop that young, anxious, and often fiery Tibetans search for a way forward, a way to navigate the "blessings" that His Holiness has warned about. And it is against this backdrop that Passang, and others like him, consider violent solutions. As another refugee noted in a July 2012 newspaper article, the Tibetan government in exile has been so outmaneuvered by the Chinese that "the only way out" for the masses "is resistance—passive or active, non-violent or armed."[19]

One group that has drawn particular attention for its more assertive tactics is the Tibetan Youth Congress, founded in 1970 to advocate for a Tibet free from Chinese rule. With a long history of advocacy, and former membership that includes some of the exile communities' most important political thinkers, TYC has been one of the most influential organizations in the Tibetan conversation.

In recent years, though, the split between the Dalai Lama's "middle way" and full independence has pushed TYC to the margins. In 2008, the group launched a series of high-profile protests and sit-ins that frustrated not only officials in Beijing, but also in Dharamsala. After the TYC launched hunger strikes and demonstrations outside China's diplomatic missions around the world, the Dalai Lama waded into the morass, and suggested that the group's tactics would only antagonize China.[20]

Chinese vilification of TYC went even further. During the 2008 events, official Chinese media called TYC a terrorist group and compared its organization to Bin Laden's.[21] A 2015 white paper even claimed, without evidence, that TYC has "schemed and incited ill-informed people to engage in violence" inside Tibet, and has "set up military training bases in Dharamsala." TYC has also "had a hand in many incidents of violence and terror in Tibet and other places in China,"[22] the Chinese claims suggested.

Leaders of the youth congress deny China's allegations, and there is no hard evidence that they or other Tibetan exiles have turned to strategic violence to secure their future. Although Tibetans have immolated themselves by the dozens inside Tibet, and in 2003 a top TYC official did say in an interview that violence could help achieve their goals,[23] neither is comparable to a terrorist looking to instill mass casualties. As long as the Dalai Lama is alive, few Tibetans will openly follow those calling for an end to his pacifist policies.

But once his voice of reason is gone, the sparks could fly in the direction that Passang and others like him have suggested. "Tibetans are unlikely to stand indefinitely on the sidelines watching Beijing transform their homeland with impunity," Goldstein once predicted. Writing in his 1997 survey of Tibetan-Chinese relations, *The Snow Lion and the Dragon*, Goldstein surmised that "emotions coupled with desperation and anger make a powerful brew, and there are Tibetans inside and outside of Tibet who are intoxicated with the idea of beginning such a campaign of focused violence—in their view a 'war of conscience,' a Tibetan-style intifada."

Today, the prospect of organized resistance seems unlikely.[24] But as the

Chinese writer and activist Wang Lixiong wrote in 1999, echoing Goldstein, the absence of the Dalai Lama "will leave the Tibetan exiles leaderless, which will likely land them in internal disorder and low morale." Groups like TYC could "dominate the exiled Tibetans" in the aftermath, which would "sharply increase the violence and destruction, [and] put Tibet in danger of becoming a Palestine or even a Chechnya."

In that scenario, China's cross-border "blessings" would become even more assertive than they are today.

TWO CRUSHING LITTLE LHASA

McLeod Ganj, the source of China's ire, sits perched on a ridgeline of pine and rhododendron three hundred miles northwest of New Delhi in the snowcapped state of Himachal Pradesh. Jagged Himalayan peaks frame the corrugated tin homes and crimson-crested monasteries that first sprang up in the early 1960s, when Tibetans fled the Chinese Communist takeover of their homeland. Today, despite the global brand that its most famous resident commands, McLeod Ganj, a suburb of neighboring Dharamsala, remains a dingy, diesel-choked village, where unemployment runs high, only half the homes have refrigerators, and just one in five inhabitants owns a computer.[1] Like the set of a Hollywood movie never torn down, McLeod Ganj's exterior is fraying, a once-temporary refuge showing its age.

By bus or taxi it takes twelve hours from the Indian capital to reach the rocky outpost, a grueling journey over rutted, one-lane roads that cars share with sheep, cows, and the occasional wedding parade. The train is only slightly faster, and cash-strapped airlines like Air India and SpiceJet operate only a few flights a week from Indira Gandhi International (frequently canceled because of pilot strikes or fog). On one February morning when I opted to fly the now-defunct Kingfisher Air, I arrived at the Delhi airport to find a mob of angry travelers who had been stranded in the terminal for two days. They grew heated when told there was a "ninety-nine percent chance" that this morning's ninety-minute hop to the mountains would be canceled, too—for the third day in a row. Given the access options, it's no wonder that proprietors at Tibetan guesthouses in McLeod Ganj offer ivory white prayer scarves for good luck to all their guests when they leave.

"You're not going to do this to me again," howled one man, who said he was a Christian missionary from Mississippi on his way to meditate with Tibetan monks. "I'm not staying in Delhi for another night!" Buddhist calm and endless patience may be hallmarks of Tibetans in exile, but the traits aren't necessarily infectious.

Despite its isolation, McLeod Ganj is firmly planted on the tourist and international hippies' bucket list—a backpacker's must-visit. Since 1989, when His Holiness was awarded the Nobel Peace Prize—besting the former Czech president Václav Havel, among others—the flood of visitors has been nonstop. Indian honeymooners and cricket fans, drawn to a national stadium that opened down the hill in 2003, followed Western hipsters and dharma bums, and today an entire second village has sprung up a few miles away, populated almost exclusively by Israeli college kids killing time after completing mandatory military service (most hotel signs are in Hebrew).

Even Chinese tourists are trekking to this out-of-the-way encampment of meditation and Buddhist kitsch—initially Taiwanese Buddhists, but now mainland practitioners are booking hotel stays in growing numbers. Tenzin Losel, a Tibetan human rights campaigner and a budding entrepreneur in the village, says there are now enough Chinese mainland tourists that businessmen like him are looking to capitalize: he has opened a restaurant with a Taiwanese business partner, called Common Ground. On its menu are Chinese and Tibetan dishes meant to "create dialogue" between cultures.

Navigating the warrens of Tibetan dumpling stands and shops cluttered with bronze Buddha statues and old pirated copies of *Seven Years in Tibet*, it's hard not to marvel at the way a small collection of refugees has managed to captivate the world with their brand of Buddhism and message of tolerance. The global popularity of the Dalai Lama and Tibetan culture has spawned a tourism empire that now extends dozens of miles from the tiny Temple Road complex where His Holiness lives, up the hill and across the valley toward the snowcapped ridge of Triund. Today tens of thousands of tourists visit annually, an impressive showing for a village with spotty electricity and unreliable water pressure.

McLeod Ganj hasn't always been bustling. During the mid- to late nineteenth century, the desolate hill station was an important posting for colonial British soldiers, and through their presence the area emerged as an important trade center and summertime retreat from the oppressive heat of the

North Indian plains. But in 1905 the village was leveled in a 7.8 magnitude earthquake, and some twenty thousand people were crushed amid the jostling bricks and stone. For the next half decade, McLeod Ganj was effectively frozen in time.

For India, which somewhat reluctantly welcomed the Dalai Lama in 1959,[2] handing over forgotten land to what was then an obscure group of refugees was not without political risk. Prime Minister Jawaharlal Nehru granted the Dalai Lama and his entourage entry, but with significant hesitation. Calls for succor from Western democracies, and an Indian public that supported their Buddhist brethren, were heeded over China's objections and threats of war (which were made good on just two years later).[3]

As India grappled with the politics of hosting the exiled Tibetan leader, it also had to accommodate the eighty thousand Tibetans who crossed the border in the years immediately after him. Not long after the Dalai Lama's arrival, Prime Minister Nehru sent messages to India's state governments requesting land be made available for the establishment of self-contained refugee "settlements." The idea, pushed forward by His Holiness—and supported by Nehru, who sought both to uphold India's "humanitarian obligation" but also potentially to increase India's agricultural productivity with Tibetan labor[4]—was to keep Tibetans together in homogeneous camps built around an agrarian economy.

The South Indian state of Karnataka (then called Mysore) was the first to welcome Nehru's request. In 1960, officials there offered to lease up to fifteen hundred hectares (5.8 square miles) of uninhabited jungle to accommodate three thousand Tibetans in the town of Bylakuppe, about 135 miles southwest of Bangalore. Tibetans arrived in the Indian monsoon belt to land that was far hotter and more treacherous than the snow-swept steppes they had left behind in Tibet (some even suggested staying in Chinese-controlled Tibet might have been easier). But with foreign support they eventually built homes, schools, and granaries for their crops, and settled in. Tibetans "were initially paid a daily wage for their labor, and villages were established with groups of five persons allocated a 5-acre plot and a one-room tenement."[5]

Additional states soon followed Karnataka's lead, and during the 1960s, Tibetans who crossed the border were sent to Tibetan-only camps throughout the subcontinent.

On April 29, 1959, the Dalai Lama officially established the Tibetan government in exile, with a goal of pushing freedom in Tibet while advocating education and democracy for the Tibetan refugees. By 1970, an estimated thirty thousand of his bretheren had resettled in Tibetan colonies in India, Nepal, and Bhutan. These communities ranged from agricultural enclaves to smaller settlements that turned out handmade crafts like carpets, paintings, and Buddhist statues. In the last full refugee census in 2009, there were 128,000 Tibetans living outside their ancestral homeland, and roughly 83 percent of them were resident in self-contained settlements and Tibetan-majority communities in South Asia.[6] The rest resided in cities across North America, Europe, and Australia. To put those numbers into perspective, exiled Tibetans account for just 3 percent of the total ethnic Tibetan population of China.

According to Oxford University's Fiona McConnell, Tibetan communities in India today have evolved significantly from their earliest days of hardship and despair. "At first glance Tibetan settlements in India fail to fit conventional definitions of refugee camps," she notes. "They are not—or at least are no longer—spaces of major international humanitarian relief operations. Nor are they spaces of insecurity, violence and incubators of insurgency." Rather, in the twenty-first century, they are self-contained and relatively prosperous communities. They are also often sites of huge monastic colleges and centers of Buddhist learning that rival the great monasteries of Tibet—and beyond the scope of anything found in the West.

Despite Tibetans' current geographic reach and relative wealth, the Indian gift of McLeod Ganj remains—for now at least—the political beating heart of Tibetan exile. From a rocky overlook some sixty-eight hundred feet above sea level, this hardscrabble village has enabled a battered collection of refugees to reestablish their culture, practice their faith, and harden their resolve.

— — —

China's war on Little Lhasa is not easy to see—there are no soldiers advancing in columns down Temple Road, no fleets of warships steaming toward an unguarded coast. Old-timers struggle to come up with examples of how China affects their daily life. But turn on the television or pick up an Indian newspaper, and the war is ever-present, manifesting itself politically, economically, and everywhere in between.

Not long after I stepped onto the tarmac at the tiny Dharamsala-Kangra

Airport (our flight eventually took off, beating the odds) I paid a visit to Dhondup Dorjee, a Tibetan journalist for Radio Free Asia. He invited me to his house to show me how ubiquitous Chinese propaganda was in this Tibetan village. Switching on his television set, he cycled through Lhasa TV, Sichuan TV, and Chengdu TV, piped into the Tibetan exile capital free of charge—the only free stations he could access on his old rabbit-ear set. On each channel were images of singing nomads, "emancipated serfs," and fuzzy yaks on snow-covered mountains glistening in perfect sunshine. It was like *The Sound of Music* set to a Chinese soundtrack. "Every Tibetan watches these channels, but no one believes the messages," Dhondup told me as his boy zoomed around on the floor pushing a toy truck. "Even my son, my eight-year-old, says it is a lie."

Yet truth doesn't stop China's propaganda network from delivering more and more of it. Anne-Marie Brady, a professor of political science at the University of Canterbury, in New Zealand, who studies China's ethnic propaganda efforts, says that the promotion of ethnic harmony to foreign audiences is a key component of the Communist Party's policy of self-legitimacy. The goal, she argues, is to counter the West's perception of China as a weak, fractious state. Through globally placed state-controlled media, policy papers, and hundreds of cultural and educational organizations like Confucius Institutes, China seeks to use its vast network of propaganda tools—valued in the billions of dollars[7]—to promote its views on power and culture. And while most of this propaganda on Tibet is consumed with suspicion by foreign audiences—like the "emancipated serfs" dancing under snowy peaks on Dhondup's analog television set—it is China's negative propaganda, deployed "to isolate dissident forces and their foreign supporters," that is more dangerous and arguably more effective.[8]

I was in Little Lhasa that winter on a quest: to understand as intimately as possible how China was squeezing Little Lhasa socially, culturally, and politically, and whether these efforts were having an effect. Gangchen Kyishong, a small complex of yellowed two-story buildings that houses the Central Tibetan Administration (CTA), the refugees' government in exile, held many of the answers.[9] Formed soon after the Dalai Lama's flight to exile, the CTA today handles all aspects of Tibetan refugee affairs, and purports to speak for Tibetan refugees in India and around the world—as well as the six million Tibetans inside Tibet (a claim China obviously takes issue with).[10]

From the center of McLeod Ganj it's a thirty-minute amble downhill to the government headquarters. A crimson-and-gold gate stands at the entrance to the complex, built in 1967 to house the ministries of home, religion and culture, finance, education, security, and health. Nearby, monkeys bound from boulders and cows pick at heaps of trash that steam in the mid-morning sun. Aside from the wildlife and a small white shrine in the middle of a parking area, the collection of offices looks more like a village hall in upstate New York than the seat of an exiled people made famous by a Nobel laureate. But inside, monks and nuns work alongside Tibetan bureaucrats in suits and ties, conducting business with a sense of urgency and purpose.

My first stop was to the Department of Information and International Relations (DIIR), the Tibetan government's own source of propaganda and information. China is often singled out as the sole actor spewing jingoistic venom at foreign audiences, but Tibetans produce their own content, including reams of colorful brochures that seem to litter just about every coffee table in McLeod Ganj. Housed in a dark, wood-paneled office building set back from the main complex, the DIIR has a wide remit—from producing content for Tibetan-run publications and programming, to managing the CTA's overseas missions in eleven countries. On the November afternoon that I visited, the building was buzzing. Thupten Samphel, then the chief spokesman for the Dalai Lama's government, was monitoring a bank of television screens on the top floor. Chinese programming beamed into McLeod Ganj from China was airing on each set.[11] Like my journalist friend from Radio Free Asia, Samphel was dismissive of the content.

"This is television broadcast from the Tibet Autonomous Region, based in Lhasa," Samphel said, giving me a tour of what he was watching and recording. "And this show, in Chinese, comes from Amdo, what the Chinese call Qinghai Province, and probably from the provincial capital, Xining." On screen, young Tibetan-looking women pranced around in sync to stringed tunes beneath a glorious blue sky, snowcapped mountains, and verdant fields of grain, in a joyful operatic image of China's most infamous minority—true ethnic harmony.

He cycled through the programming. "Life in Tibet, they portray it as happy, with singing, dancing minorities who are blessed by this Chinese Communist rule," said Samphel, a wry grin turning into a knowing chuckle.

"There's no negative news at all," he added, incredulous. "Even the weather seems sunny, and no wind."

The blatant tone of China's propaganda—material that Harvard political scientist Joseph Nye might call a piece of Beijing's "soft-power" playbook—can leave educated Tibetans scratching their heads. Ham-handed, clumsy, and amateurish, videos of Tibetans twirling wistfully under Lhasa's Potala Palace in a loving embrace of the "motherland" are so at odds with actual life inside Tibet that it's impossible not to snicker at the absurdity. In the past, production values have been low, the cheese factor high, making it hard to understand why Chinese broadcasters would bother sending this material into the world—where trusted international news sources offer a ready counternarrative.

Yet while bad Chinese television is not likely to sway Tibetans' longtime supporters, its prominence amid Tibetan exile is symptomatic of broader Chinese goals. As scholars like Brady note, China isn't looking to grow Nielsen ratings for its programming. Rather, it is simply seeking to sow seeds of doubt among Chinese and foreign audiences by challenging ethnic minority claims of mistreatment. And when these seeds germinate, they can be nurtured to Beijing's advantage.

The sophistication of these activities has evolved since my earliest visits to McLeod Ganj. In a 2017 paper published by the *American Political Science Review*, researchers at Harvard University revealed how China employs millions of cyber commentators to feed social media with deceptive content. The Harvard researchers estimated that each year, Chinese-funded cyber efforts produce some 448 million fabricated social media posts—a massive amount of content that far exceeds any analog programming. But rather than to serve as fodder for debate on sensitive matters, "the goal of this massive secretive operation," the researchers concluded, "is instead to regularly distract the public and change the subject, as most of the these posts involve cheerleading for China, the revolutionary history of the Communist Party, or other symbols of the regime."[12]

The propaganda responses to protests in Tibet in 2008 offer a telling example of this approach. On March 10 of that year, a few hundred Tibetan monks in Lhasa staged a small demonstration against China's occupation. Within days, the wave of unrest had mushroomed into the largest mass mobilization of Tibetans in decades, reaching all three of the historical provinces of Tibet. Hundreds reportedly died. As the International Center on Nonviolent Conflict noted in a 2015 summary, the apparent spontaneity of the uprising took many Tibet watchers by surprise. A Chinese document obtained by the Tibetan Centre for Human Rights and Democracy, for example, notes that "machine guns" with live ammunition were used on the crowds.

In the Chinese news media, however, a very different picture was presented. As Western news coverage used the protests to question China's pre-Olympic commitment to human rights, outlets in China were drumming up nationalistic support. One outlet, MSN China, "launched an avatar-based pro-Beijing campaign ('I "Heart" China') in response to Western criticisms of China's ethnic policies."[13] This effort was amplified by official Chinese media, and online by Chinese activists.

"Within China and abroad, Chinese netizens used online forums, public rallies outside China—and even a few within China—to express their support for Beijing's ethnic policies and its handling of the situation in Tibet," the University of Canterbury's Brady concluded. "Ultimately, the outcome of the crackdown on the protests in Tibetan areas could be regarded as a success for China's ongoing efforts to unite the Chinese population and many of the overseas Chinese through nationalism."[14]

Around the same time that China's post-2008 propaganda efforts were gaining steam, international support for Tibetan refugees was heading in the other direction. According to a 2012 Pew Research Center survey of Americans' attitudes toward Tibet, only one-third of respondents saw Tibetan freedoms as "very important" to the West's relationship with China.[15] World leaders themselves were starting to snub the Tibetan leader during his travels. In 2001 the Dalai Lama met eleven heads of state; by 2013, traveling more than ever, he sat down with only two.[16] China's efforts to pressure foreign governments to abandon the Dalai Lama were gaining ground.

By late 2010, discrediting the Dalai Lama and the CTA were full-time, global obsessions for China, and no Tibet-related issue was too trivial to draw the attention of China's diplomats. China was challenging governments, intimidating whistleblowers,[17] and withholding development or infrastructure aid from nations that most staunchly supported Tibetan refugees. Not even an independent film festival halfway around the world was far enough down the geopolitical food chain to hide from China's wrath.

The events leading to the opening of the Palm Springs International Film Festival, in Southern California, in January of that year were indicative of China's approach. The inclusion of a pro-Tibet film, *The Sun behind the Clouds: Tibet's Struggle for Freedom,* brought frantic phone calls, tense meetings, and not-so-veiled threats from Chinese officials in the consulate in Los Angeles.[18] If the film was screened, Chinese diplomats warned festival organizers, California could say goodbye to cross-cultural cooperation. Darryl Macdonald, director of the annual Palm Springs event, said it was, to his knowledge, the first time any festival in the United States had been approached by the Chinese about not showing a film on Tibet.

"Less than a week before the festival I got two calls. The first in the morning was from somebody who left a message saying she was the cultural representative from the Chinese consulate in Los Angeles. I thought nothing of it at the time. Then, at about two o'clock in the afternoon, I got another call, this time from somebody identifying himself as the vice-consul. He asked for a meeting."

A few days later, Macdonald said three diplomats from LA arrived at his offices in downtown Palm Springs—the Chinese vice-consul, the cultural attaché, and the vice–cultural attaché. "We sat down around that table, and the vice-consul started the conversation by opening a book with pages with handwritten notes; it was a speech, about why he thought it was inappropriate for us to run the Tibetan film."

The lecture continued for nearly an hour, Macdonald remembers. "They didn't want Tibet to be looked upon as a once-independent country that has been invaded by China," he said. But it was wasted breath; after the visit Macdonald and his team were even more convinced they needed to show *The Sun behind the Clouds.* "Our mandate is to present as many perspectives and points of view [as possible]," he said. So the festival refused to pull the Tibet documentary, and China retaliated by yanking a pair of Chinese movies that had been on the program for months.

Tibet activists hailed Macdonald's ethics,[19] but when the stakes are higher, it's easy to see why others are less willing to follow his lead.[20]

There are many more examples of institutional acquiescence to China's Tibet-related pressure; universities relying on students from the Chinese mainland have been pressured especially hard. In 2008, for example, London Metropolitan University awarded the Dalai Lama an honorary degree for "his demonstration, through all his words and deeds, that peaceful means of resolution always remain possible."[21] In the days that followed, university administrators faced a flood of condemnation from Chinese students, who went online to call for a boycott of the school. Concerned that the publicity might prompt mainland students to stay away, university officials sat down with Chinese diplomats. Those talks were interpreted as an apology.[22]

In a statement a few days later, the university clarified that it "has not and will not be apologizing," nor would it be rescinding the award. But the vice-chancellor nonetheless "expressed regret at any unhappiness that had been caused to Chinese people by the recent award" and that "it was not the university's intention to cause any such unhappiness."[23] The carefully chosen words were a reminder that upsetting China—or its students—can carry the real threat of fiscal consequences, especially from tuition-paying pupils. As the journalist Tim Johnson has noted, there were some fifty thousand Chinese students studying in Britain at the time of the incident.[24] Money, no doubt, was a factor in the school's rhetorical backpedaling.

The reaction in London—accepting a dressing down by Chinese officials, and to produce a statement of "regret"—had ripple effects in higher education far beyond the United Kingdom. The following year, at the University of Tasmania in Australia, similar Chinese pressure was more effective, when university officials there acceded to Chinese objections and canceled a planned conferral of an honorary degree to the Tibetan leader. Anna Alomes, who resigned her post as director for the school's Centre for Applied Philosophy and Ethics following the reversal (and later briefly joined the faculty at the London School of Economics, where I was a student in 2016–2017), told a school newspaper that the cancellation was a direct result of Chinese threats. "Only eight weeks out from the event taking place, and after a visit from representatives of the Chinese government during which direct threats were made to impact the financial bottom line of the university, fear replaced enthusiasm."[25]

At the time, an Australian politician speculated that the $30 million in Chinese tuition fees was the motivating factor for the withdrawal. "Was there an element of blackmail involved?" Australian Greens leader Bob Brown pondered publicly. "We all have a right to know."[26]

If university presidents have been loath to challenge China, they are in good company: heads of states have been no stronger. Presidents and prime ministers, pontiffs and politicians have all buckled to Beijing's belligerence. In October 2009, President Barack Obama gave in to Chinese demands not to meet the Dalai Lama when he visited Washington, DC, becoming the first American president in nearly two decades to snub the Tibetan leader. (The two eventually met four times during Obama's presidency, but always with muted ceremony, away from media cameras.) In South Africa two years later, the postapartheid government turned down a visa request for the Dalai Lama to attend birthday celebrations for Archbishop Desmond Tutu, a personal friend of His Holiness. An African National Congress delegation was in Beijing a week before, sealing Chinese investment deals valued at $2.5 billion.

Even Pope Francis has shunned the Tibetan leader, refusing to meet him in December 2014, "for obvious reasons concerning the delicate situation" with China, a Vatican spokesman conceded.[27] The church was at the time in discussions with China to solidify its presence in the Middle Kingdom.

Low-level diplomatic meddling continues apace, but is also increasingly matched with even more assertive means of interference that extend far beyond China's physical borders. In early 2016, Beijing was reportedly going after Chinese journalists, pro-democracy advocates, and other "dissidents" who had fled to Hong Kong or Thailand after criticizing Chinese government policies. Under the noses of Thai and Hong Kong authorities, dissidents were being snatched off the streets and returned to China to stand trial.[28] China watchers said the snatch-and-grabs were unprecedented, and indicative of China's growing global clout.

But it was in October 2015 that Reuters offered one of the most striking examples to date of how bold Beijing has become in defending its core interests, in particular its stance on Tibet. Not even the inner chamber of the United Nations Human Rights Council—where the aggrieved turn for succor—was free of Chinese interference. According to Tibetan and Chinese dissidents who have traveled to Geneva to tell their tales of abuse to the UN, it's common to be photographed and harassed by Chinese officials in the very moments before taking the microphone. The practice is even well known to UN officials, who seem powerless to stop it. As one Western diplomat who has witnessed the Chinese pressure told Reuters: "This gave China a new level of confidence about what they can do [at the rights council] if their core interests are at risk."[29]

China is now the world's second-largest economy by GDP, and in its insatiable thirst for raw materials—iron ore, uranium, oil, natural gas—it pours cash into infrastructure and development projects around the world, both as a means to secure those materials, and also to curry political favor. China's outbound direct investment into the global economy jumped more than 800 percent between 2007 and 2009, from $26.51 billion to $245.75 billion.[30] The expenditures, which coincided with the "Great Recession," underscored the world's reliance on China's economic engine.

But they also illustrated what international relations scholars refer to as Beijing's "economic statecraft"—its ability to use purchasing power to buy political allegiance. But they also illustrated what international relations scholars refer to as Beijing's "economic statecraft"—its ability to use purchasing power to buy political allegiance.

China's stance on Taiwan is a key example of this ability. In late 2016, China restored diplomatic ties with the tiny African nation of São Tomé and Príncipe, after that island state cut ties with Taiwan. Previously, São Tomé and Príncipe had been one of a handful of countries that recognized the government in Taipei. At the time of the reversal, a Taiwanese official accused the island state of dumping Taiwan for "an astronomical amount of financial help" from China, a claim Chinese officials denied.[31]

But in fact, big money was on the table. According to numbers compiled by China Aid Data, which monitors Chinese development pledges in Africa, Beijing had been promising development funds to the African nation as early as 2013. The pledges included funds to upgrade sewer facilities; build roads, an airport, and a hydropower dam; and pay for construction of a deepwater port, worth $800 million, to facilitate oil exports and seaborne commerce.[32]

Amid such economic opportunity, few countries have been willing to go against China by supporting Tibetans' calls for self-determination. While President Obama's successor, Donald J. Trump, sounded a more strident tone early in his tenure—speaking by phone, after his election, to Taiwan's president, for instance—it remains to be seen whether his combative stance toward Beijing will last or, as has happened to nearly every American president since Nixon, he too moderates his position and seeks to adapt to China's worldview.[33]

Despite their meager budget and modest numbers, Tibetan exiles are considered by China to be one of five entities capable of threatening the Communist Party (the others include Falun Gong members, Uighur separatists, Taiwan pro-independence activists, and pro-democracy activists).[34] A Chinese dissident, who said he once worked as a spy for the People's Republic of China, told us lawmakers in March 2009 that Beijing "uses huge expenditure of funds to suppress ordinary citizens and even extend their dark hands overseas."[35] Peter Navarro, an adviser to President Trump on trade policy, estimates that China has some one hundred thousand documented agents or informants around the world,[36] forming a virtual "beehive" of global spies.

How China conducts its campaign against Tibetans may best be viewed through leaked documents and testimony from those who have spent years marginalizing another vilified "separatist" entity: the quasi-religious sect known as Falun Gong.

Chen Yonglin, a former Chinese first secretary and consul for political affairs in Sydney, Australia, detailed Beijing's anti–Falun Gong blueprint in testimony to Congress. Chen said Falun Gong, which formed in the 1990s, was tolerated at first but, as it grew in size and influence, banned by Beijing. In July 1999, China's leadership feared that the group's membership—its leaders claimed tens of millions of adherents—could threaten the Communist Party's hold on power. While the officially atheist Communist Party was at the time loosening restrictions on popular religions such as Christianity, Taoism, and even Buddhism, the mass mobilization capabilities of Falun Gong were seen as a threat to one-party rule. As the Chinese religious scholar Adam Chau notes, ever since the Communist Party faced down pro-democracy protesters in 1989 in Beijing's largest public square, Chinese leaders have treated mass mobilization—for any purpose—with skepticism.

"The state's paranoid reactions to these challenges speak volumes about how much ideological significance it still invests in these spaces (e.g., urban spaces, public parks, squares), which were originally created and continue to be maintained by the state,"[37] Chau says.

China's "paranoid" reaction to Falun Gong was manifested in the arrest, harassment, and imprisonment of its practitioners. Many members abandoned the practice following the crackdown, and others went underground. But Falun Gong was not snuffed out completely. Adherents who could leave China fled overseas—to India, the United States, Australia, and elsewhere.

And then China did something more associated with a superpower—it gave chase. In 2000, China's embassies and foreign offices created a special task force called the Central 610 office, later dubbed the Department of External Security Affairs—to coordinate efforts to control, influence, splinter, and marginalize Falun Gong adherents who had left China. In Sydney, according to Chen, this office was especially active in its undertaking, and took its work seriously. In 2005 there were an estimated three thousand Falun Gong supporters in Australia, but Chen told Congress that Beijing employed "over 1,000 Chinese secret agents and informants" to keep tabs on them. Chen said a similar campaign—with similar ratios—was under way inside the United States at the time.

Chen offered details of Beijing's anti–Falun Gong campaign. He described a massive intelligence gathering and diplomatic offensive with orders "to fight intensely and give no ground, to attack at will, and aggressively." A diplomatic memo from Sydney, drafted during Chen's four-year tenure, said officials' job was "to actively respond, take the initiative to strike, work to create the inner dispute, to convert some soft elements and 'disinfect' the existing bad influence."[38] They did this by manipulating local media, pressuring policy makers, investigating and threatening Chinese nationals sympathetic to the movement, and by applying economic pressure whenever possible. Similar efforts were also under way across Europe. One particular "big victory" during those days, Chen said, occurred when an unnamed European communications company caved to Chinese pressure and agreed "not renew its contract with the New Tang Dynasty Television," a pro–Falun Gong television channel.

China's anti-Tibetan activities overseas follow a similar, if less publicly detailed, script. For instance, at a meeting in Beijing in 2000, party leaders hosted a conference on how to improve the country's Tibet-related propaganda efforts, with a focus on producing scholarly works more sympathetic to the party's point of view. Zhao Qizheng, then the minister in charge of the Information Office of the State Council, told academics on June 12, 2000, that using "pin-pointed research" to challenge the West's views on Tibet was of critical importance to maintaining China's stability.

"Western countries, including the United States, want to topple our country and further the cause of their own social and value systems and national interests," Zhao said in remarks that were leaked and translated from Chinese by the International Campaign for Tibet.[39] "In order to achieve this, they will never stop using the Tibet issue to westernize and split our country and weaken our power."

What China needed, Zhao concluded, was "an effective army" of research-ers from across the disciplines—religion, philosophy, political science, law, history, and archaeology—to produce "scholastic arguments, handy mate-rials, and consummate intellectuals for external propaganda. Tibetologists should develop confrontation strategies and approaches. They should pro-duce effective articles, ideas, and materials for external propaganda."

These propaganda efforts—part of an "urgent war for our basic national interests and international prestige," he said—have been ongoing ever since.

The last stop on my tour of the Tibetan government in exile was at the offices of Dicki Chhoyang, the refugees' de facto foreign minister, one Tibetan exile with arguably a tougher job than the Dalai Lama. I wanted to hear her strat-egy for out-communicating China, and to learn what she thought about the uptick in China's propaganda efforts.

Chhoyang is a modern Tibetan bureaucrat and one of the fresh new faces to join the Central Tibetan Administration after the Dalai Lama announced his political retirement in 2011. She is smart, holding degrees in business from McGill University in Montreal and in Central Eurasian studies from Indiana University. She is accomplished, having left a solid job in Canada as a community liaison officer for a large hospital project. And she is stylish. Her shimmering black hair was cropped in a tight bob on the morning that we met, and on the streets of New York City or London, Chhoyang, who accents her traditional dress with purple highlights and pearl earrings, could easily be mistaken for the chairwoman of a global bank or a Fortune 500 company. Instead, at the time she was running an underfunded arm of the Tibetan government, earning just a few hundred dollars a month.[40]

We spoke for about an hour, discussing Tibetans' approach to politics, and the Dalai Lama's insistence that his people are not asking China for a sovereign Tibet but one that enjoys a degree of religious and cultural au-tonomy. "We've steadfastly held on to our values and the middle way com-promise," Chhoyang explained. As if speaking directly to concerns raised by some Western government officials—that the Tibetan exile movement risked fracturing among those who favor more violent tactics—she added: "We are not going to deviate from that. Our struggle transcends generations, transcends individuals."

Our conversation meandered through the entire canon of the Tibetan issue, everything from self-determination to self-immolations. "The international community needs to speak in one voice, and to demand China allow access to the region, for both international press and foreign representatives," she pleaded at one point. "We don't have any power to change what's happening on the ground. We are calling on the Chinese government to respond in a way that is constructive."

On the wave of Tibetan self-burnings that was beginning to ripple through Tibet at the time, she said: "It's important to understand that the people's resolve is there. From our point of view it's clearly a political act. The message we read into those is it's an emphatic rejection of China's repressive policies in Tibet."

With our time just about up and Chhoyang hurrying off to another meeting, I had time to ask her one last question, something that had been on my mind since my encounter with the Tibetan leader in late 2009. "What does China fear most about the exile community?" I asked.

She replied without hesitation: "The flow of information. You control people's minds as long as you control information." And at the time, no place on earth was more important to the movement of information into and out of Tibet than the small collection of offices in which we sat.

My own journey to the front lines of this soft-power war began on the floor of a philosophy professor's classroom in upstate New York. Every Tuesday morning in late 1996, as gamblers placed their bets on the ponies at the nearby harness track, I settled into a cushion on the floor of Ladd Hall and meditated on the illogic of materialism. Dr. Joel Smith guided us through the Bodhisattva's way of life, the complexities of the Mahayana tradition, and Buddhist views on living and dying, causality and action, wisdom and compassion, and attachment and impermanence.

One notable Buddhist thinker who featured prominently in our classes was a second-century Indian philosopher named Nāgārjuna. As classmates and I sat with our backs arched, eyes closed, hands folded neatly in our laps, Dr. Smith would elaborate on Nāgārjuna's two truths, a tenet of Buddhist philosophy. "There are two types of truth in Buddhism," Smith explained, his tone soft to match our state of mindfulness. "There's conventional or relative truth, and ultimate truth, which describes reality as empty of concrete characteristics." Nāgārjuna, he continued, taught that it is impossible to achieve true peace—nirvana—without mastering these concepts.

For reasons I could not articulate, Buddhism tugged at me in ways that the institutional Catholicism of my childhood never did. Mystics like Nāgārjuna promised the keys to understanding reality itself—complex and esoteric, but tangible. I was transfixed by the possibility that "ultimate truth" and "faith" weren't mutually exclusive.

In the winter of 1997, a month after earning a B in Dr. Smith's Buddhist philosophy course, I was on a plane bound for India, where I would spend the next six months with the School for International Training, tracing the contours of Tibet's philosophical and religious roots. I sought teachings from Tibetan mystics and oracles, climbed mountains to perch on rocks and meditate (a framed photo from one of these meditative hikes still hangs in my parent's house in Vermont), and sipped tea with monks and nuns who, like me, sought only to understand the nature of being. From my cushion in the courtyard of the Dalai Lama's monastery in McLeod Ganj to the retreat caves of great yogis like Guru Rinpoche and Milarepa in southern Tibet, I heard stories of Buddhist masters that made impossible ideas less textbook, and more real.

But I heard other stories, too, which began to compete with my quest for religious clarity. Tales of Tibetan persecution, torture, arrest, and exodus were ubiquitous everywhere I traveled. It was these retellings of great personal triumph that eventually captured my imagination and overshadowed my initial drive for mystical meaning. Politics, not faith, would become my bond to Tibetan refugees. And my first window to these allegories of suffering was as a houseguest of a cherubic Tibetan shopkeeper and former farmer I knew for decades only as Pala.

Few of McLeod Ganj's homes in the 1990s had good heating, beyond a small bucket filled with coal that was fired up at night after dinner. To stay warm when the embers died down, Pala's family slept under thick wool blankets on platforms of wood fitted with handwoven carpets. I had my own bed, a relative luxury, but the chill of the Himalayan winter still found its way into my 20° sleeping bag, and the best way to shake off the bitter cold and dampness was to rise early with the sun.

Most mornings these wake-ups took me on a circular walk, trailing just a few paces behind the old man of the house I called Pala. We'd wake around 6 a.m., share a thermos of *pur cha* (a watery, caramel-hued tincture of tea leaves, butter, water, and salt that tastes more like chicken soup than Indian *chai*), and then set out for the kora, the circular pilgrimage of prayer wheels and vibrantly colored *mani* stones that rings the Dalai Lama's residence. Pala always went first, nodding frequently to neighbors or acquaintances he recognized as we ambled through town to the narrow, rocky footpath. In his right hand he sometimes spun a mobile prayer wheel made of hammered brass and wood that encased a cylinder of Buddhist scriptures. He clutched oak-colored prayer beads in his left hand, and one by one with his thumb slid the small wooden beads along the string, muttering a prayer with each flick of the finger. I followed closely behind, emulating him with my own wooden prayer beads that I had bought in the market.

This was my daily routine during the winter of 1997. Pala prayed the entire ninety minutes that we walked, never talking as he endlessly recited the *om mani padme hum* blessings to invoke the attention of the bodhisattva of compassion (conversation would have broken the spell). But no words were needed to capture the mosaic of personal narratives that formed the backbone of the Tibetan diaspora. At that hour the trail of homage and devotion around their spiritual leader's house was packed with people just like Pala—men and women in their sixties and seventies who, like the man they venerated, had endured bone-chilling cold to walk over the Himalayas and escape China's grasp some four decades earlier. The morning meander was originally my way to bond with an old man whose devotion I admired and whose faith I little understood. But the more I returned to the kora over the years, the more I viewed it as a window into the Tibetan diaspora itself: displaced for decades, unyielding in its devotion.

— — —

The next time I saw Pala was in late 2014, a full five years into my "blessings" research. I had been back to McLeod Ganj a few times before then, but on each visit failed to track down the stout, wry, whiskered old man who had made such an impression with his unfailing commitment to Nāgārjuna's ethos. The home goods store he ran in the center of town—Shop No. 5, number *nga*—had always been dark and shuttered.

But in November 2014, my luck changed. As I instinctively strolled past his store just as I had in the late 1990s (and subsequent visits afterward), the metal curtain was rolled open, and a young Tibetan man I recognized as Pala's youngest son, Kalden, was manning the till. Stepping inside, I introduced myself with a smile. "What happened to your father?" I began. Assuming that Pala, who would have been in his eighties by then, had left this life long ago, I added solemnly: "When did he die?"

Pulling a notepad and pen from my bag, I stood poised to scribble his reply. But Kalden, hardly looking up from the television that flickered Hindi soaps on the floor in front of him, just snorted. "Why don't you ask him yourself?" he said. Pala, he added, was very much alive.

With contact made, I arranged to return the next day with a translator. Pala and I met at the storefront just before noon, shook hands knowingly, and headed for his house for tea and conversation. As we set off, I trailed behind and studied his gait, processing the years of memories that had shifted slightly over time: he was shorter than I remembered, and sported thick reading glasses (had he always worn them?). He also balanced a gray woolen cap atop his head about an inch above his ears, a style statement I didn't remember, either. I did remember his thumb; the opposable digit on his right hand was partially missing, cut off in what I imagined was some dramatic hunting accident on the wild Tibetan Plateau. The thumb stuck with me because he had used it so frequently to help count Tibetan numbers when we dined. (I later learned that the injury was far more mundane, and dated to when he was a child in Tibet. "We were playing with a stone and someone smashed it accidentally on my thumb," he told me, chuckling slightly. Just like that, half a thumb gone.)

But it was his general appearance that I remembered with the fewest errors of time: with tiny hairs protruding from a square chin, he had the appearance of a Tibetan garden gnome—minus the blue jacket and gray beard.

As I pushed open the gate to Pala's courtyard, more memories flooded back—the pastel pink walls of the first-floor dining room where we had eaten and counted together; the narrow concrete stairs that lead to the top floor where I had slept; the laundry hanging from drainage pipes; the dark and windowless kitchen where Pala's wife spent hours over a small two-burner propane stove to feed the family. So much had changed in my life but, it seemed at that moment, so little had changed for Pala.

He offered me a chair, and a piece of information I had longed to hear. "My name," he began, "is Dorjee."

"Everyone here knows me because I talk to everyone," he added.

And so he began to speak with me:

When the People's Republic of China was officially born in the fall of 1949, Purang Dorjee was a teenage farmer living in the shadows of Tibet's holiest peak. The snowcapped triangular slice of Mount Kailash, a twenty-two-thousand-foot pyramid-shaped summit that serves as a beacon for devout Buddhists and Hindus, had framed his family's worldview for centuries. And for Dorjee of the valley Purang, the grasslands and other jagged peaks surrounding the picturesque mountain had long supplied a home.

Tibetan Buddhists believe that Mount Kailash is the source of great tantric masters, inspired gurus, and meditational deities that are embodiments of supreme bliss and universal harmony. In the Tibetan language the mountain is called Kang Rinpoche, or "precious snow mountain." Locals refer to it as the "water peak," owing to its significance as a source of snowmelt for some of Asia's most important rivers—including the Brahmaputra, the Sutlej, the Indus, and the Ganges.

The first few months of Mao Zedong's China had little direct impact on Dorjee's family, or on the relative bliss in the villages and towns beneath their holy mountain, including Takla Khar, the valley's largest commercial center. As Mao's soldiers marched on Tibet's eastern flank in late 1950, life in Purang continued as usual.

But by February 1951, plans were laid to conquer Tibet's western frontier. In a telegram sent to Chinese military officers stationed in Xinjiang, the Chinese Central Military Commission in Beijing detailed what the army's task for Western Tibet entailed. "All of Tibet must be liberated this year," the instructions read. "No delay is allowed."[1] Soon some four thousand Chinese soldiers, their families, and relevant Chinese and Tibetan officials had begun to march into Ali Prefecture, the area around Mount Kailash, their weapons and rations transported on the backs of twice as many horses and mules.

From afar the operation was deemed a success. In a memo sent to the Northwest Bureau of the newly formed Communist Party of China the following year, Mao wrote that when this military mobilization unfolded, China's soldiers "focused all their efforts on practicing meticulous and careful budgeting, and on self-reliance and self-sufficiency in production." In the process, the Communist Party chairman declared, they had "a firm foothold and gained the enthusiastic support of minority nationalities."[2]

Dorjee remembers things differently. He was around fifteen when Tibet fell in 1950, and he recalls China's arrival in broad strokes, more a sense of unease and dread than specific details like armed convoys or drab Mao suits. "When China was arriving, when more Chinese army soldiers came into the Tibetan areas, and when Tibetan people were moving out one by one, the situation was tense; everything was crazy," he told me as we sat under the warm afternoon sun of his McLeod Ganj foyer. "There was danger, threats to our life as the Chinese came into our area."

Over the next half decade tensions would flare, rebellions rise, and the treachery of occupation would materialize under the shadows of Dorjee's holy mountain.

Tibetans throughout the barley-growing region of Purang were leaving Tibet in droves, but his family's decision to flee was not an easy one, Dorjee remembers. As a boy, he and his seminomadic brethren survived as they had for centuries, breathing the thin mountain air under a searing sun as they grazed their horses, donkeys, and yaks on the high-altitude pasturelands. During warmer months they would sow the black and loamy soil with barley—a staple of Tibetans' diet—and other crops like wheat and lentils. Hardy root vegetables, like carrots and radishes, would occasionally sprout from the hills that Dorjee and his family tilled. Western explorers and travel writers have marveled at the region's "wind-scorched tableland" and treeless hills that "roll caramel brown to the horizon."[3] Flight meant leaving the mountains and the nomadic sense of freedom for an uncertain, more restricted, future.

But when the day came with news that the Dalai Lama had left for India following a violent uprising against the Chinese occupation of the capital city, Lhasa, on March 10, 1959, Dorjee's family dusted off their plans and prepared to follow. Fear, he remembers, was the driving factor, not faith or fealty. If the Dalai Lama wasn't strong enough to stay in Tibet under China's rule, no Tibetan was, they reasoned.

Perhaps it was his family's profession as free-moving herders that made it possible to pick up and go. The villages and towns of the Purang region were not under immediate occupation at the time, and yet, following the Dalai Lama into the unknown was preferable to remaining leaderless in Tibet. (As I would later learn, the opposite is true for Pala's children. Grounded in McLeod Ganj by their father's store—fixed to its moorings like a rooted plant—his offspring have had a harder time moving on from their own, Chinese-squeezed surroundings.)

Physically, the journey was straightforward. "If you go one night, you reach the Nepal border, and then one night, you reach India," Dorjee said. Nestled in a teat-shaped appendage of Tibet that protrudes into the Indian subcontinent, Purang had long been a center of trade and regional commerce. During Dorjee's childhood, the border along the Himalayas was loosely guarded, and in many stretches travel in both directions was unrestricted. Hindu pilgrims arrived in the valley on foot on their way to circle Mount Kailash in veneration of Lord Shiva. Nepali merchants from Humla and Darchula labored over the mountains with bags of rice and spices strapped to snaking goat trains. And Tibetan farmers journeyed in both directions, trekking out their barley and salt to return with Indian spices and Nepali fabric. Many Tibetan refugees endured far greater hardship when they ran.

Far more complicated, Dorjee said, was slipping eleven children, cousins, aunts, and grandparents into India's urban fabric. In the late 1950s and early 1960s, newly circumspect Indian police patrolled the Tibetan frontier with greater scrutiny, as the border-sharing agreement between New Delhi and Beijing had vanished when China began annexing portions of the Tibetan Plateau. Along well-established trade routes like the trails from Purang, money, papers, or a compelling story were now needed to make the journey safely.

"We had to lie," Dorjee said of his family's conversations with the security they encountered during their exodus. "We said we were going to India for pilgrimage." They weren't; they were escaping. But the Indian soldiers accepted their religious reasoning, and less than a week after trekking over the mountains of Tibet, they were in the lowlands of the world's largest liberal democracy, everything they owned on their backs or carried by the train of donkeys that made the journey with them.

"And then," he said with finality, "we never went back."

The family's first extended stay on the other side of the Tibetan border was in Dehradun, the state capital of Uttarakhand, which rests in the rainsoaked foothills of the Himalayas, a few hundred miles to the northeast of the Indian capital, New Delhi. There, Dorjee found work, utilizing the flock of four-legged porters he had smuggled across the border to carry goods for his new hosts. With his livestock he became something of a transport consultant, using his background as a herder and nomad in Tibet to move Indian military supplies deep into the mountains.

"I worked for the Indian army for one year, in 1959, for soldiers with the Indo-Tibetan border force," he said. "But I wasn't fighting; I was helping with transportation. I worked with them, with the army, in Tartu-la Pass."

Popular culture suggests Tibetans are fierce fighters; many are. Dorjee, stooped and standing just five foot two inches, is the cartoonish exception.

Piercing eyes, furrowed brows, and a downturned smile punctuated with a small dimple on his right cheek betray a serious tone, yet even as a young man in his prime it was clear that his stocky frame and thick thighs were built for transport, not warfare.

"There were many different items that I had to transport—such as clothing, cooking pots and pans, weapons, bullets—many different kinds of things. The Indian army was not preparing for the 1962 war [with China] exactly, but was just doing border security."

That lasted for about a year. Then, in 1960, Dorjee—who had earned the nickname Dorka Singh, a surname adopted by a certain warrior caste in northern India that hinted at his powerful build and tireless work ethic—traveled to the birthplace of the Buddha, at Bodh Gaya in northern India, to hear the Dalai Lama speak. "After seeing him," Dorjee recalls, "I decided to come to Dharamsala," where the Tibetan leader was living. Dorjee sold all his horses and donkeys, and for the second time in two years, uprooted his life. He has been living in His Holiness's shadow ever since.

Roughly the same age as the man he venerates, Dorjee arrived at His Holiness's temple empty-handed. In the 1960s, McLeod Ganj and Dharamsala served as the key intake points for the scores of Tibetans who were fleeing over the Himalayas. In those days, Indian and Western generosity provided housing, clothing, and in many cases, a job. Dorjee needed all three.

"At first I was supposed to go to Mundgod, Camp No. 9, in the South of India [one of the largest Tibetan settlements, with roughly ten thousand residents], but somehow I was delayed and there was no room for the new family to come. I had no choice but to stay in Dharamsala. In Mundgod there wasn't enough room, and registration was full, so we had to stay here."

By the late 1960s, many of the eleven cousins, aunts, and siblings who had made the trek to freedom with him had died, moved away, or returned to Chinese-controlled Tibet (contrary to popular belief, the door between China and India is a revolving one, even today). But in India, Dorjee was just getting settled. With bricks and bags of sand, he and his brother began building homes on Bhagsu Road in McLeod Ganj, about a mile up the road from His Holiness's residence. And he found a way to make money again—by taking out a loan to open a small roadside stand offering housewares and trinkets in a town with few amenities.

During the ensuing decades this stall would sprout walls from the dirt and gain a proper name. In time it would burn to the ground, rise again, and become a symbolic anchor of a community in perpetual motion. But more than anything, it would become the narrative glue of one family's struggle to navigate an insidious war that China is waging on a group of people eager to do nothing more than move on.

To register as a refugee and see their living god in India, Tibetans must first navigate some of the most imposing terrain on the planet. Each year since the Dalai Lama fled in 1959, thousands have followed on foot, as Purang Dorjee did through the mountain passes of western Nepal. Today, though, the Himalayan footpaths are teeming with paid informants, and if refugees come by land they often aim for muddy strips of potholes and snarled traffic in ramshackle border towns on the southern edge of the Tibetan Plateau. For decades, one of the busiest crossings was a tiny backwater called Kodari.[1]

Despite its location on the Nepal side of the Friendship Bridge international border, Kodari is more a Chinese village than a Nepali one. At the bars on the dusty main street, the beer is Tsingtao, and restaurants serve rice and noodles with Sichuan spice. Shopkeepers speak Mandarin, and Beijing opera pours from radios in guesthouse lobbies. From an economic standpoint, the traffic in both directions has been mutually beneficial. But in Kodari, "friendship" is more than a bridge name: it's also been an unwritten anti-immigration strategy.

In 2008, as Beijing tightened security in Tibetan areas following a wave of Olympic-timed protests, security along China's southern border was ratcheted up. Overland routes between China and Nepal become more liabilities than economic arteries. And as Beijing pushed officials in Kathmandu to stem the flow of Tibetans seeking a new life abroad, Kodari came under new scrutiny. Almost overnight this high-altitude border post became ground zero for the "blessings" that the Dalai Lama had told me about. By late 2009, the number of Tibetan refugees crossing from Chinese-controlled Tibet into the democratic sliver of Nepal had dipped to 838, from a high of 3,500 just a few years earlier.[2]

In February 2010, after reading about frequent arrests and the occasional shooting[3] of Tibetan asylum seekers along one of the world's most imposing borders, I cajoled my wife, Judita, to join me for a working holiday. I wanted to see this immigration freeze firsthand, to glimpse a Tibetan paradise lost. After a few days in Kathmandu poking around Newari temples and white-washed Buddhist stupas, we hired a driver to take us three hours north, to an eco-adventure camp in a tight canyon near the Tibet border. With its raging rivers and jagged peaks, Nepal is paradise for adrenaline junkies, and most of the guests holed up in the canvas tents and thatched dining hall at the Borderlands Resort were headed south for bungee jumps and river rafting. We were headed in the other direction, ten miles north.

Judita and I arrived in Kodari in the late morning. As we walked uphill past green-shuttered shops and monkeys bounding from tin roofs (including one that somewhat menacingly threw a rock in our direction), the first cargo trucks of the day were waiting to motor north to markets in Nyalam, Tingri, Shigatse, and other Tibetan towns between Nepal and Lhasa. To the east was Dram (Zhāngmù in Chinese), and across the torrent of water that forms a natural border, rays of sun were glittering off the windows of the Chinese customs building.

Kodari is something of a tourist attraction in its own right: human rights groups, journalists, and anyone curious to see how life unfolds on the margins between a communist megastate and a struggling, impoverished slice of democracy come to peer across the physical, ideological, and geopolitical divide. Instinctively, I reached for my camera, but before I could fix the view-finder, a young Chinese man in civilian clothes approached from behind an idling truck, waving his index finger. Pointing to the camera he shouted, in Mandarin: "*Bù kě yǐ*"—"No you can't." When I asked why, or what authority he had to prohibit the taking of photographs from Nepali soil, he replied with "*jiàn dié.*" The words mean "spy," and I couldn't tell if he was bragging about his profession, or accusing me of being one, too. Either way, I lowered the lens.

A few seconds later, after I relented, a Nepali army officer who had wit-nessed the exchange came to repair any hurt feelings. "Follow me," he said in English, leading us behind a truck and out of view of the actual *jiàn dié*. "Here is good, for photo," he said, pointing to the northern side of the span. After I snapped a few—admittedly bland, washed-out—photos of the bridge and thanked him, he reached for his wallet, pulled out a ten-ruble note, and asked for rupees in exchange for the Russian currency. It was a clever means of extracting a photo bribe, and yet one more way China and Nepal coexist on the margins.

This would not be the last time a journalist would feel Chinese law on the Nepali side of the border. In February 2012, Chinese police operating in Kodari physically assaulted a CNN film crew doing a story on Tibetan refugees. Footage that aired around the world showed that as Chinese men moved in, grabbing the crew's cameras, Nepali officials stood by and watched (not dissimilar to how they handled my run-in with a Chinese agent). As justified as the photo ban might have been for reasons of national security, the tactics were rare confirmation that on Nepali soil in Kodari, at least, China's writ rules.

We returned to Kathmandu the next day, and I was more motivated than ever to understand China's hold on Tibetans in this tiny sliver of democracy. I set to work interviewing Nepali government officials, Western aid workers, humanitarian groups, and Tibetan refugees to learn just how deep China's claws had sunk into Nepal on the issue of Tibet (requests to interview Chinese embassy officials in Nepal were never answered). Many of these interviews were conducted in secret, in the dark corners of cafés, in hushed tones and low whispers, and not before looking around to see who might be listening.

One conversation during that period captured well the ominous mood. On March 9, a day before the annual commemoration of the failed 1959 uprising in Tibet, a young Tibetan who was active in the pro-independence movement offered his views on the Dalai Lama's description of life in Nepal. He agreed to meet me only if we did so covertly, on the top floor of a nondescript hotel in a heavily populated part of Kathmandu. He said that he worried Chinese spies might be watching and recording his every move (and having just met one in Kodari, I understood his concern).

"Nepal government is like this," he said, putting his hand to his face: "One eye closed, one eye open. Tibetan issue is big bargain for them."

Speaking only on the condition that I not publish his name, he added:

"During the last two years, Chinese officials have come here often, paying visits, promising so many things like [construction of] hydropower [dams], roads. These all are due to the Tibetan issue, the bargain they have." In the big picture, he reasoned, Tibetans like him were expendable.

A key reason I had traveled to Nepal in the spring of 2010 was to be in the country for the Tibetans' March 10 anniversary celebration, the day Tibetan exiles around the world mark the 1959 uprising in Lhasa that resulted in the flight of their spiritual leader to India. The Dalai Lama had told me that Nepal is ground zero for the discharge of Beijing's "blessings," and with Chinese interference growing, I was certain there would be no free pass to demonstrate against the Nepal-supported one-China policy. Crossing this line would bring consequences.

Weeks before the day's events, Nepal's security forces were already telegraphing their intentions to curb Tibetan protests. Each morning brought fresh reports of Tibetan refugees being arrested and detained. Some were beaten; all were forced to pay huge sums to get out of jail. Trinlay Gyatso, the Tibetan exiles' unofficial government representative to Nepal at the time (unofficial because although his office operates under the radar, it was technically shut by Nepal's former king in 2005, another ode to Chinese demands), said the shakedowns were aimed at presenting an unambiguous warning: that any Tibetan caught demonstrating against China would be punished.

"Young Tibetans, they will try to demonstrate," Trinlay said. "They will try to go in front of the Chinese embassy. And they will get arrested."

On the morning of March 10, the Boudhanath neighborhood, the heart of the Tibetan community in the Kathmandu Valley, awoke early. Anticipating a clash, keyed-in visitors, human right workers, and journalists took up positions high above the prayer wheels. For hours as I hunched low against a whitewashed wall, peering through the viewfinder of my Nikon D5000, legions of truncheon-wielding Nepali police in riot gear pushed and dragged dozens of Tibetan refugees off to jail. In one baton charge, the cracking *thwak* of the policemen's bamboo sticks mixed with the screams of young monks and texting teenagers. Tibetans shielded their faces from the assaults, and many wailed as they were dragged off to prison. The young man who had spoken in secret the day before was among those carried away.

After that harrowing afternoon, every conversation offered another layer of insight into the Chinese blanket of security that was draped over Tibetans.

One UN human rights official said that China was footing the bill to turn Nepal's army into an immigration force to corral fleeing Tibetans—or to stand by idly as Chinese officers did the work for them. A Western diplomat confirmed that millions of Chinese yuan were being spent annually to upgrade Nepali riot police with gas masks, truncheons, and protective gear—possibly even the very equipment worn by officers rounding up Tibetans at the Boudhanath stupa in Kathmandu that year. The aim, he said, was to devise strategies to shut down the trade routes that had long served as open lines of communication for Tibetan pilgrims and the outside world.

By early 2010, China's overtures were paying off: Tibetans inside Tibet were virtually cut off from fleeing to Nepal and on to India, their historic route to freedom. This shuttering continued throughout the decade. Wealthy Tibetans still left Tibet, fleeing to Western Europe or North America with forged documents and by air. But for those without means or method, traffic slowed considerably following China's border squeeze, and most Tibetans inside Tibet who wanted to leave were stuck.

On February 26, 2010, Nepali media reported on just how successful Beijing's operation had become. In one of the largest immigration operations against would-be Tibetan refugees in Nepal's history at the time, the Nepali army arrested seventeen fleeing Tibetans—men, women, and children—on the Tibet-Nepal border. Newspapers said the seventeen could face "deportation to Tibet,"[4] where they would face the brutality of Chinese justice. Deepak Chand, an investigation officer with Nepal's immigration ministry, explained that the arrests were meant to send a message to other potential asylum seekers.

"The Chinese want Nepal to be like quicksand for Tibetans who try to escape Tibet; they don't want them to go anywhere," Deepak said, using uncharacteristically blunt language to describe an issue of bilateral importance for his country. Through politics, coercion, and brute force, Deepak added, China is "trying to kill the goose by cutting off its head."

For centuries, ties between Nepal and Tibet were cordial, even familial. During the seventh century, the Nepalese princess Bhrikuti Devi was wed to the first Tibetan emperor, Songtsen Gampo, and is widely credited with helping to introduce Buddhism as the official religion of Tibet. The Nepali princess and her husband oversaw construction of the Potala Palace and the Jokhang Temple in Llasa; both are among Tibet's most important buildings (and the Jokhang, adorned with images and statues that the princess bestowed as gifts, remains its most sacred).

But if Nepal's relationship with and commitment to the Tibetan people were once guided by shared cultural and religious principles, that era ended with the creation of the modern Nepali state. Indeed, the two nations' more recent history is littered with border wars and territorial skirmishes, including a brief one from 1855 to 1856.

Still, the rise of Communist China pushed Kathmandu to choose sides, and early on, the Nepali government sided with the Tibetans. Between 1959 and 1989, the Nepali government even recognized and registered Tibetans crossing its northern border as "refugees," something India did only for the first few years after 1959. But in 1989, the same year that the Dalai Lama won the Nobel Peace Prize, Kathmandu changed course. As Human Rights Watch later concluded, "The King of Nepal stopped allowing Tibetan refugees to settle permanently in Nepal" that year after reaching "a diplomatic rapprochement with China."[5] Since then, a nonbinding "gentleman's agreement" was inked between Nepal and the United Nations High Commissioner for Refugees, a deal that pledged "safe passage" for refugees from Tibet to continue on to India. But officially, starting in 1989, Tibetan refugees were no longer allowed to put down roots in Nepal.

And by February 2010, the seventeen Tibetan men, women, and children arrested in a small Nepali border village called Lamabagar were among the first to find out how ungentlemanly this agreement had become.

Twenty miles to the east of the crossing at Kodari, the picturesque valley where Lamabagar sits boasts hewn-stone homes, cascading rivers of green, and granite peaks guarded by a gauntlet of paid informants and Chinese watchmen. From the steppe perched at seven thousand feet it's only half a day's walk to the Chinese border, a well-worn route that Tibetan and Nepali traders have navigated for centuries. In early 2010, it was also the front lines of China's bid to keep Tibetans from slipping away.

My interaction with the Chinese agent in Kodari a few days earlier had whetted my appetite for physical evidence of China's soft-power war on Tibetan refugees. So after I read news of the arrest of the seventeen in the local papers, I set out to test how dangerous the Nepal-Tibet border actually was for the men and women trying to cross it. (Judita, recovering from a particularly nasty bout of dysentery caused by an undercooked meat momo, waited it out in the capital.) A Chinese defense attaché, General Chen Chong, had made the trip to Lamabagar a day earlier, and sources told one Nepali journalist that the general was interested in preventing any further crossings of Tibetans into Nepali territory.[6] Nepali immigration officials told me the same thing.

It was late afternoon by the time I reached the village—after a full day's drive from Kathmandu, followed by a day of walking once the road ended at the tiny village of Bodle. At the time, the Chinese were starting to build a hydroelectric plant that would eventually bring a road to the border post, but in early 2010, the only way in or out of the valley was over grinding switchbacks and donkey paths high above the Tamakoshi River.

As we ambled exhausted past dirt-floored shacks fashioned from rounded boulders and pine beams, our Nepali guide, Nima, tracked down a former village chief who had lived in Lamabagar his entire life. In the late 1990s, when Chinese bureaucrats were crafting policy papers condemning the "Dalai clique" for trying to split the motherland, Pemba Norbu Sherpa, a Nepali farmer, was trading butter and yak meat with Tibetan herders on the other side of the mountains. For about a decade, Pemba, now forty-four, was Lamabagar's top elected official.

Pemba's house was dark from a lack of electricity, and the afternoon sun cast long shadows across the cramped living space. A small, wood-fired stove burned in the corner. His wife welcomed us in, and one of the children ran off toward the terraced barley fields to fetch his father. A few minutes later a short, portly man dressed in plaid walked in, shot me a bewildered smile, and sat down.

Through a translator we chatted about life in the valley, and his village's ties to Tibetans on the other side of the border. I sat on a low couch covered by a blue-and-white Tibetan-style carpet handcrafted from hand-dyed wool. He sat on a chair with a similar covering. We sipped *pur cha*—butter-and-salt tea—a Tibetan favorite.

In 1966, an agreement inked between Nepal and China allowed inhabitants of the border districts to cross without a visa or passport, and to travel up to thirty kilometers, or about eighteen miles, in either direction "to carry on petty trade, to visit friends or relatives, or for seasonal change of residence."[7] The agreement held that they didn't need passports or visas "but shall register at the border check post or the first encountered duty [*sic*] authorized government agency of the other country." The ten-year agreement was renewed twice, but even after its expiration, Tibetans cited it as justification to travel farther.

Evidence of these cultural and political ties is everywhere in Lamabagar: Tibetan prayer flags flap in the wind, and red, yellow, and blue prayer stones carved in Tibetan script rest neatly along the main footpaths. In 2010, merchants on both sides of the border still organized monthly chamber of commerce meetings with their counterparts; Pemba had attended one just a few days earlier, he said. In the late 1980s, a Nepali researcher counted ninety-five families in Lamabagar; about a quarter were ethic Tibetans and practiced Tibetan Buddhism.[8]

But as Pemba spoke, it became clear that he viewed his northern neighbors as business partners only, and not as cultural or religious equals. Some Tibetans were traders and therefore valuable. Others were troublemakers: Kampas, Pemba said—Tibetans from the eastern province of Kham who are known for their fighting prowess.

Pemba was repeating a common point China often brings up, too, especially when countering the suggestion that Tibetans are universally peaceful and nonviolent: that Tibetans were once rifle-toting pawns of the American intelligence service. The CIA's covert campaign fizzled in the late 1960s, a few years before President Nixon traveled to China in 1972, but China continues to draw on this history to chastise the Dalai Lama (who, historians note, never personally approved the CIA-led program) and vilify Washington as a hegemonic global meddler. Former fighters with the program, now well into their seventh decade, still live in refugee camps near Nepal's second-largest city, Pokhara. Their continued presence is one reason why, as Asia security expert Jonathan Holslag notes, China believes that the "concentration of Tibetans in neighboring countries represents a potential bastion of resistance."[9]

For Pemba, the seventeen men, women, and children arrested a few days earlier were no different from those former freedom fighters. "Definitely, we have to arrest the Kampas and other Tibetans trying to flee," he said. "Kampa people support the Dalai Lama. China doesn't like that."

Pemba said he hadn't seen the large group as they walked by his living room a few days earlier, nor did he know where they were from (they weren't from the historic region of Kham, which is farther to the east; they were actually from Tibetan towns just over the border, I learned later). Perhaps they slipped through at night and were arrested farther down the valley? Or maybe, he hinted knowingly, they were nabbed closer to Lamabagar and then handed over to police for cash. "Nepali police get some money for handing over Tibetans to China," Pemba said, not elaborating on how he knew such details of interstate bribery. A confidential US State Department cable, published online by WikiLeaks, made a similar claim: China frequently rewards Nepalis with "financial incentives" for returning Tibetans attempting to cross the border. How much money the cable didn't say.[10]

I stared at the former village official sitting across from me, whose living room was physically closer to Tibet than to his own capital, and whose taste in tea and interior design was decidedly Tibetan, and fixated on the idea that Nepal's border towns were overrun with informants. Nepalis (perhaps even Pemba—there was no way of knowing) were on the receiving end of kickbacks costing Tibetans their freedom and livelihoods, and helping China wage war on the world's most recognizable refugees.

As I stood to leave I shot one last glance around Pemba's living room. In the far corner above a small bookshelf, a red-and-gold bag adorned with Chinese script was strung on a hook. It was a type of gift sack Chinese businessmen and politicians use to present liquor or cigarettes—nods to future favors. I had been given similar gift bags during my yearlong stint teaching English in China a decade earlier.

Then, as I turned toward the front door, a tattered three-foot-tall Chinese propaganda poster taped to the wall above the couch held my gaze. Peering from the browning paper was an image of then–Chinese premier Hu Jintao, the former regional committee secretary of the Tibet Autonomous Region in the late 1980s. Hu was staring stoically into Pemba's living room, beneath deep blue skies and the shadow of Lhasa's Potala Palace, the Dalai Lama's winter home for centuries. A trio of smiling Tibetan women flanked him, their arms extending goblets of tea. And Hu, bespectacled and grinning, was himself wrapped in a Tibetan prayer scarf. Chinese and Tibetan characters at the bottom read: "Celebrating forty years of the Tibet Autonomous Region." It's an administrative delineation on the Chinese map—the TAR—that Tibetans only grudgingly recognize.

Like the seventeen Tibetans arrested just a few days earlier, I began to wonder on which side of the border I was actually standing.

———

In the 1990s and early 2000s, Nepal's leaders didn't outwardly worry much about China's prickliness on Tibet. The rectangular-shaped melting pot of 102 ethnicities and castes has long been more politically and culturally aligned toward India, with its people preferring curries and Bollywood to stir fries and tai chi. Even during Nepal's decade-long civil war, when Maoist guerrillas controlled much of the mountainous state starting in 1996, political winds in the capital, Kathmandu, blew decidedly toward New Delhi, and away from Beijing.

But by 2010, Pemba—like his nation—was an easy mark. Nepal is one of the poorest countries in Asia, and Nepalis are desperately dependent on international aid and assistance. Nepal's federal budget was just $4.15 billion in 2010, less than the annual state budget of Vermont (which has roughly thirty million fewer people). Per capita income in Nepal is less than $600 a year; Nepal's financial troubles grew even more pronounced after a major earthquake in 2015 led to a slump in tourism. With poverty like this, the slightest hint of a quid pro quo, at the governmental or personal level, can be enticing in a country ranked by the international corruption monitoring group, Transparency International, as one of the world's most given to graft.

Yet corruption—and payment for information leading to the arrest of undocumented Tibetans in Nepal—is not the only way Beijing has managed to push its Tibet agenda with its Himalayan neighbor, to "bless" Kathmandu. Buoyed by the global economic crisis of 2008, and with it, increasing fiscal clout, Beijing found new ways to induce once-unsupportive governments to cast aspersions on the Tibetan cause. In a statement in September 2007, the Chinese embassy in Nepal even admitted its gifts come with strings.

"The Nepalese Government and people [have] shown friendly sentiments to China and delivered its valuable support to Chinese people," the embassy said. That support, including on "the questions of Taiwan and Tibet and other major issues related to China's sovereign rights and interests," came "in return" for China's funding of key infrastructure projects—including a stadium, a convention center, and the capital's main highway.[11]

In time, Chinese tourists began following their country's development aid. By 2012, the number of Chinese visiting the Nepali holy site of Lumbini, the birthplace of the Buddha, quintupled from the year earlier, the site's marketing director said. When a massive airport upgrade is completed in 2018—work undertaken by a Chinese contractor—Gautam Buddha Regional International Airport will bring even more tourists from China, linking one of Buddhism's holiest sites with nonstop service to the communist heartland.

Today in Kathmandu, Chinese-language signs for hotels and restaurants nearly outnumber those in Newari, Tibetan, or Hindi script, a dramatic switch from a decade ago. There seem to be more Chinese food stalls and discos than Tibetan trinket shops or dumpling stands. Busloads of Chinese tourists descend on the Buddhist stupas and holy sites, where once the only pilgrims were Tibetans or Indians. Even the propaganda is in Chinese: China's Tibet Bookstore, originally managed by a Chinese businessman, Zhang Jun, turned on the lights in the Nepalese capital in December 2009. Its grand opening ceremony in the tourist area of Thamel was covered by China's state news agency, Xinhua.

Nothing was for sale when I visited soon after its ribbon cutting; but there were free pamphlets disparaging the "wolf in monk's clothing," as the Dalai Lama is often referred to by Beijing. "Just take it," a young Chinese shopkeeper told me as I attempted to pay for the stacks of paper and books tucked under my arm, all unabashedly critical of the Tibetan government in exile and its leaders. "We're trying to spread a message." One message, delivered in a seventy-five-page brochure titled *The 14th Dalai Lama*, includes chapters such as "Promoting Buddhism or Making a Mess of It," "Benefiting Tibetans or Doing Them Harm," and "Driving Tibet to Paradise or Hell."

A passage from the concluding chapter says that the Dalai Lama, since leaving Tibet, has been on a nonstop campaign to "split the motherland" by spewing lies and engaging in "numerous criminal activities." Published by the state-run China Intercontinental Press in 1997, the biting rhetoric and baseless charges read like crib notes to a party member's dinner toast.

To be sure, tourism dollars and cheap brochures are not the only means of influence peddling, or even the most important. Beijing is even more overt in how it pushes, cajoles, and incentivizes Nepal to toe the Communist Party line on the topic of Tibetan exiles. "Beijing has asked Kathmandu to step up patrols of Nepali border forces and make it more difficult for Tibetans to enter Nepal," Penpa Tsering, the parliamentarian of the Tibetan government in exile, told US government officials in 2010.[12] In March 2012, during another reporting trip that took me to Nepal, government officials confirmed Penpa's observations, and went beyond them.

As Tibetans in Nepal that year marked the anniversary of their failed 1959 uprising in Tibet, the second such anniversary I was to witness in three years, I snacked and sipped tea at the Saturday Café, a rooftop restaurant over-looking one of the holiest Buddhist sites in city, and heard firsthand how Nepal had acquiesced with Chinese efforts. My lunch guest that afternoon was again Deepak Chand, the investigation officer from the immigration department I had met a few years earlier. He was assigned to the Boudhanath Stupa and the surrounding Tibetan areas that day, and his task was to ensure that Tibetan refugees in this part of Kathmandu didn't get out of hand.

He wasn't worried. Days earlier, a group of thirteen Tibetan students had been arrested for protesting illegally outside the UN building. Their bail was set at 27,000 Nepali rupees—roughly the equivalent of six months' salary for a Tibetan lucky enough to have a job (few do). The steep fine, Deepak said, was intended as a warning. "We needed to send a message not to demon-strate."

These are strong incentives for Tibetans, young and old, to stay quiet. For those who can't resist, security officials operate with impunity at sites of Ti-betan pilgrimage or potential protest. Arrests are common, and informants are compensated well—with cash, prostitutes, and even lavish parties. Just a few days before my tea with Deepak, a Chinese diplomat had paid him a visit at his office, he said, to see about security preparations for the March 10 anniversary. The Chinese official wanted to make sure he was "getting value for his investment," Deepak chuckled. (The diplomat also wondered if Deepak needed night-vision goggles for the operation. "Night-vision gog-gles?" Deepak recalled laughing at the idea of using such gear for a daytime protest.)

Of the numerous March 10 gatherings I had witnessed, that of 2012 was by far the most restrictive. The government was in the midst of major infra-structure talks with China, and the Maoist-led government in Kathmandu was inching ever closer to Beijing. Two years earlier, hundreds of Tibetans, mostly young and idealistic, had swarmed the gate of the Chinese embassy with chants of "Free Tibet" and anti-Chinese slogans. Now, Tibetans caught with images of the Dalai Lama or unfurling flags were being detained proactively. It seemed as though they were being arrested even before they opened their mouths or raised their fists.

I asked Deepak why Nepal was unable or unwilling to stand up to Chinese pressure and allow a few hundred unarmed refugees to blow off a little steam. Tibetans had lived in Nepal for decades—though their numbers were diminishing rapidly, as most young Tibetans were headed for India or abroad—and had maintained strong trade and cultural relations for centuries. Why crack down now?

"China," he said. "They are very strong and exert a lot of pressure." Nepal, like it or not, had to come to terms with the fact that China's first priority for its southern neighbor was to silence Tibetan critics. Nepal's own corruption, and woefully backward infrastructure, made China's goals in Nepal easy to achieve, Deepak said. As one of Asia's poorest countries, Nepal needed friends, but it needed money more.

— — —

The seventeen arrested near Lamabagar in February 2010 were lucky; all were eventually let go, following pressure from Western aid officials and a Nepali group called HURON (the Human Rights Organization of Nepal, which provides legal assistance to Tibetans and other refugees). Three of the seventeen met me at a small monastery in central Kathmandu a few days after their release. The youngest was in his twenties, the oldest, about fifty. Officials from HURON helped translate.

Each of the men had been in and out of custody for days, shuttled between dank, unlit holding cells before arriving at the refugee center on the outskirts of the capital.[13] Nepali border guards had confiscated their bags filled with butter and yak meat, gifts for family in the valley, they said, and they were clothed in garments donated by a local charity.

Each man told me a variation of the same story: how the group of seventeen had crossed the Nepal border at Lamabagar after walking for days from their home village of Rongshar, just inside Tibet; how they had come to buy rice, corn, and other essentials for their families back home—something they had done countless times before; how they intended to continue down the valley to visit family and holy sites in Kathmandu (admittedly in violation of the 1966 agreement permitting travel for border residents up to thirty kilometers); and how Nepali police swarmed them in the early morning as they ambled along the banks of the Tamakoshi River.

"When they were caught, they were really afraid," the translator said after a few minutes of conversation in Tibetan. "It's never happened before, and they don't understand why it happened this time. They are thinking that the Nepalese policeman caught them to take their money, maybe to beat them. They had heard these things."

That the men who had been arrested were speaking to a journalist was evidence that even amid increased Chinese pressure, Tibetans in Nepal still had powerful friends, the United States and the United Nations among them. The remaining fourteen were also out of custody, individually plotting how to return home. All were anxious, the three said, because if they didn't leave Nepal soon, their wheat crops and yak herds inside Tibet would suffer. The distance between a healthy harvest and hunger in the unforgiving climate of the Tibetan Plateau is a few weeks of neglected fields.

The young Tibetan in his twenties leaned forward. "Three years ago," he said, flipping back his long beaded hair, "we could come and go as we pleased. All the time we come [to Nepal] and we can go back. There has never been a problem for us."

But now, he said, pausing—"something changed."

FIVE

THE WALMART OF LITTLE LHASA

The frenzied streets surrounding Purang Dorjee's shop attract all kinds of seekers. Lost souls who reek of hash and patchouli come to McLeod Ganj looking for guidance navigating life's quandaries. Dedicated practitioners of mysticism and meditation, their shoulder bags stuffed with cushions for long hours of sitting, arrive looking for answers from within. Politicians make the journey from New Delhi to pledge support for India's most famous refugees. And journalists like me travel to this Indian-Tibetan village to ask questions that only lifelong members of the diaspora can answer.

When Dorjee first arrived in Tibetan exile's "Little Lhasa," in 1965, the sparsely populated mountain town was without schools, crippled by intermittent electrical outages, and guarded by peaks of nearly impassable rock. So cut off from the rest of India was the Dalai Lama's new home that even he speculated that his hosts were sending a message by "trying to hide us somewhere without good communications in the hope that we Tibetans would disappear from the sight of the outside world."[1]

Among the few jobs available to the freshly minted Tibetan exiles was work connecting their isolated haven to the rest of the country. Indian highways and roads in the isolated North were dangerous and precarious, and the young country needed men to carve passages through thick jungles and twisting limestone. His Holiness personally saw to it that Tibetans were considered for this lucrative if dangerous work.[2]

But Dorjee wanted to be a trader; business, not brawn, was his gift. And for a man from a commercial crossroads on the other side of the world's tallest peaks, his new home—with few stores, poor transport, and little by the way of services—presented a clean slate. Leaving the roadwork to younger men, Dorjee claimed a patch of land not far from McLeod Ganj's only other retailer at the time—Nowrojee & Son General Merchants—and sold his wares on a tarp laid out in the dirt. For fifteen years the ground in the center of town was his domain. Notebooks, pens, lightbulbs, umbrellas, shoes, slippers, envelopes, underwear, biscuits, and bags were his trade. "I always tried to have everything," Dorjee told me. "If someone asked for something, I always said 'Yes!' even if I didn't have it. Then I'd go out to stock it."

Northern India's isolation played to Dorjee's strengths. As a former herder and nomad in Tibet, and later a transport consultant for the Indian army, he was acclimated to the dangers of the road, skills he put to work traveling even farther into the Indian heartland in search of items to stock at his makeshift trinket stand. Needles and thread formed his initial niche, but eventually his tarp of household trappings expanded to include toilet paper, rubber bands, rope, and even Chinese-made padlocks.

It was "business every day," he said. As other traders died, moved away, or took to different occupations, Dorjee's tarp and trinket stand remained.

Eventually his sales outpaced what could be delivered from a temporary sheet of plastic. So he searched for a physical space to expand into, finding one on nearby Temple Road in a building occupied by members of the Chushi Gangdruk Committee, the Tibetan warriors who had fought the advancing Communists in Tibet in the 1950s and '60s. On the top floor of the building these warriors-turned-landlords operated the Tibetan equivalent of a VFW hall. But at ground level they maintained a few retail spaces and a grain-storage shed. Kunga la, a personal bodyguard of the Dalai Lama at the time, agreed to lease Dorjee the unused feed room at a reasonable price.

By the fall of 1980, Dorjee had traded his tarp for a small room a few feet across with a roof and a proper name. His offerings expanded accordingly, and shelves were stocked with socks, electrical switches, soap, and just about anything else a Tibetan refugee might need in the mountainous expanses of India's far North. In the early years he even hung a mailbox, a stand-in for the less-than-reliable Union mail system that couldn't keep track of Tibetan homes in the chaotic warren of impromptu refugee construction.

Shop No. 5—so named because it was the fifth Tibetan-run store from the bus station at the time—has been good to Purang Dorjee. He met his wife, a refugee from the Tibetan town of Gyantse and a frequent customer, at the store; his oldest son, Tenzin Choephal, met his wife the same way. And the tiny storefront that supported his family for decades propelled them into an income bracket few Tibetans in India can claim. Travel, schooling, and modest needs were taken care of. "Because my shop lies on the Dalai Lama Temple Road, the main road in McLeod, I am very lucky," Dorjee said. "This is the main road that people walk on; I can sell things more easily. Even selling needle and thread we get an income; that has clearly been very helpful to us."

Every time I return to the once-forgotten village of eleven thousand, it seems that a new hotel, restaurant, or towering apartment building competes for sunlight with the conifers. One photo I have of Dorjee's youngest son, from 1997, shows him standing on a concrete staircase overlooking a green, verdant valley. Smiling into the camera, Kalden is framed by a background of sloping hills and lush green trees; only a few houses dot the hillside. When I returned to the same spot during a visit in late 2015, the view was unrecognizable. A stepped sea of drab-gray concrete, glass, brick, and splashy neon had replaced the green foliage. With buildings literally perched on top of each other, the entire area looks poised to slide down the mountain with one torrential rainstorm or earthquake. A replay of the 7.8 magnitude temblor of 1905 would surely do more damage now.

The congested view is evidence of the town's popularity, among both Western visitors (who have been coming for decades) and Indian tourists (who seem to just be discovering it). Since January 2013, when the first international cricket match was played at the twenty-three-thousand-seat Himachal Pradesh Cricket Association Stadium, Dharamsala has emerged as an Indian tourist mecca (indeed, in Indian travel literature, such as in-flight magazines, it is not Tibetans' whitewashed monasteries but the cricket stadium that serves as the photographic backdrop for Dharamsala's isolated magic). McLeod Ganj—a twisting and bumpy fifteen-minute taxi ride up the hill—has been pulled into this orbit.

"Because of that, McLeod Ganj has been nationalized in all parts of India," a local Tibetan official once proclaimed. And because of that, Shop No. 5 is a beneficiary of more foot traffic than Purang Dorjee ever thought possible when his plastic sheet first spread out on the ground.

When the Dalai Lama requested political asylum in India in March 1959, Prime Minister Jawaharlal Nehru granted it, but with caveats. The prime minister's decision to open India's door was partly motivated by religious obligation.[3] For centuries Tibet's rulers had been keepers of a Buddhist tradition that, though born in India, came to maturity outside of it. The Indian public, cognizant of Tibet's role in nurturing this historic faith, was strongly supportive of putting out the welcome mat for Tibetans fleeing Chinese control.

But Nehru's decision to welcome the Dalai Lama was also guided by political pragmatism. Isolated with his pro-China policy at home, and struggling to explain away the turbulence unfolding on India's northern flank, Nehru faced growing pressure to get tough on the "Reds."[4] By offering the Dalai Lama a safe haven, Nehru found an opportunity to do just that.[5]

Still, the prime minister moved carefully. In the first few years after India's independence in 1947, Nehru echoed the British policy of recognizing suzerainty for Tibet—de facto independence within the Chinese state. But by April 1954, with the signing of the Panchsheel trade agreements with China, Nehru signaled that New Delhi would no longer question China on its reading of the Tibet issue.[6]

On April 5, 1959, during a news conference in New Delhi, Nehru was asked about his decision. As one journalist put it: "There has been a lot of speculation that because of expression of sympathy with the Tibetans and the offer of asylum to the Dalai Lama the relations between India and China may deteriorate. Is this true?"[7]

Nehru, sounding defensive, said India's policy on the Tibetan issue was formed of three key considerations. The first two, he added, were not related to Tibet at all.

"Naturally, conditions are such that difficult, delicate, and embarrassing situations are created and may continue in various shapes and forms, and we have to keep the various factors in view, the major factor being, of course, our own security. After all, every government's first duty is to protect its country in every way. The second factor, our desire to have and continue to have friendly relations with China. The third factor: our strong feeling about developments in Tibet.

"Now, sometimes there is certain contradiction in these. That is inevitable. One has, therefore, in so far as one can, to balance, adjust, and sometimes to make difficult choices."[8]

China chafed at Nehru's decision to provide shelter to the Dalai Lama, and Nehru, despite his tepid welcome to the Tibetan spiritual leader, did not allow the refugees free rein. When another journalist suggested that the Dalai Lama would now be "free to operate politically" in India, Nehru was curt: "I don't think that is the general assumption at all." Nor has it been; to this day the Dalai Lama must seek approval from the Indian government to travel.

Tibetans' ability to maneuver in India grew even more constricted in subsequent years. By 1962, the year India and China clashed in a brief border war, Tibetans arriving on India's doorstep were no longer automatically granted "refugee" status upon entry[9] (those arriving between 1959 and 1962, including the Dalai Lama, were[10]). Instead, most were registered under the Foreigners Act of 1946, which carries significantly fewer rights and opportunities than a refugee label.[11] Foreigners in India must register their movements, are barred from government employment, and are generally not eligible to receive government subsidies. These restrictions continue, even for Tibetans born in India. They are houseguests who won't (or can't) leave. There are signs that this legal ambiguity is changing. In March 2017, the Indian Ministry of External Affairs ordered government passport facilities to process applications from Tibetans born in India between January 26, 1950, and July 1, 1987. Then, in November 2017, the Delhi High Court ruled that passports couldn't be denied to Tibetans living in designated Tibetan refugee settlements.

Still, legal hurdles remain; entire generations of Tibetans have been raised under this nonpermanent rubric, a fraction of noncitizens who give birth to children with the same label. Of the estimated one hundred thousand Tibetans who live in India today, only a handful have managed to secure an Indian passport. The rest are technically stateless, unable to return to Tibet or legally call the place that adopted them home.

——

For Tibetans like Purang Dorjee, that ambiguity has had practical implications—for his life, and for his business. As a noncitizen guest he can't legally own a store. So he leases the property from the Tibetan government in exile (an entity called the Central Tibetan Relief Committee), which in turn rents it from the state of Himachal Pradesh. What this arrangement has meant on paper is that Dorjee has very little control over the roots of trade and commerce that sustain his family. Every fifteen years, when his lease comes up for renewal, it is the state and the relief committee—not Dorjee—that decide whether the store will go on.

And yet, despite the uncertainty, Dorjee has been luckier than most. Tibetan business owners or aspirants, especially new arrivals from Tibet, rely on more dubious means of securing space for their ventures. According to the Tibet Justice Center (TJC), a United States–based legal association that tracks issues Tibetans face, "it is far more common and practicable" for a Tibetan in India who wants to purchase land for a home or business "to pay an Indian citizen who, in turn, buys the property in his own name with the informal understanding that the Tibetan will use it."

These arrangements have a name: *benami* transactions, which in Hindu law are deals done by someone else. They are a common feature of land deals throughout India and are used by many (Tibetans or otherwise) who can't legally lease land in the state in which they live. But benami deals have a hidden cost, too. Because they are illegal, anyone who enters into one knowingly is at the mercy of an Indian government intent on ending the practice.

Like most things in politics, money drives the call for change. Surjit Bhalla, an India-based economic adviser for the Observatory Group in New York, estimates that for every $100 paid in taxes in India, some $200 more is never collected.[12] In the United States, only $20 for every $100 goes unpaid. The loss of tax revenue in land deals like benami transactions significantly lightens India's coffers; one estimate suggests that the Indian economy loses 1.3 percent of annual growth because of poor controls on property transfers. Contested land deals also clog the courts—upward of 70 percent of all legal disputes that Indian judges adjudicate are over land issues.[13] India has spent decades trying to end the practice, with additional measures planned.

And yet the benami issue continues to plague India's Tibetans. Some of Dharamsala's most important buildings and centers of learning are built on property to which Tibetans hold no title.[14] These include several important monasteries; the main Tibetan elementary school in McLeod Ganj, the Tibetan Children's Village; and the massive Norbulingka Institute, a sprawling complex of crimson-and-gold pagodas dedicated to preserving Tibetan culture and arts. Unfortunately, old benami doesn't mean legal benami. As long as Tibetans remain outside the law, their future in India remains tenuous.

"There are many institutions, monasteries, facing problems in the courts," the Dharamsala settlement officer, Sonam Dorgee, told me in 2015. Only a few lawsuits have been filed, "but one day, the problem will come out for Tibetan institutions, which will face huge problems."

According to the TJC, "huge problems" have already come; at least four Tibetan communities in India have received eviction notices tied to the practice. One case involved the houses along Bhagsu Road, including Purang Dorjee's. These homes were eventually spared the wrecking ball, but only after the national government intervened to protect India's "honored guests." But three other cases linger. One aimed at Tibetan families near Shimla, the capital of Himachal Pradesh, dates to August 19, 2010, when eviction notices were delivered to 125 Tibetan families to make way for a municipal parking lot. Plans to relocate the Tibetan families there are pending.

Two other cases involving Tibetan institutions are also ongoing—one on benami land in Dharamsala, and another on farmland in eastern Orissa state. Although neither of those cases is expected to result in evictions (at least not according to Tibetan officials), they have kicked up lingering uncertainty about residents' long-term future. "Even a favorable resolution" in both cases "fails to strengthen the legal protection of these communities and address their underlying vulnerability," the TJC concedes.

———

None of this, of course, has China's hand directly on it; the legal uncertainty Tibetans face in India has grown domestically. But as with many issues related to the Tibetan diaspora, Beijing is always in the background. As Nehru himself conceded in 1959, the welcome that the Indian government extended to Tibetans was determined first through the lens of India's relations with China. That policy continues to affect decisions that India takes to this day.

One contemporary example involves the government-run Nalanda University in Bihar, which opened to students in 2014 and is modeled after the ancient center of learning of the same name. Tibetans consider the old Nalanda University—which was destroyed in the twelfth century—to be a holy pilgrimage site, as it educated some of the original founders of their brand of Buddhism. At its peak, some ten thousand students from throughout Asia studied at what would be the oldest university in the world were it still in operation. But when Indian officials announced plans to open a new Nalanda for the modern era, inviting governments from across Asia to collaborate in the planning of the new school, Tibetans were intentionally excluded. China, which also has ties to the ancient school, contributed $1 million to the project. In early 2017 a senior official at the school told me that Tibetans, and specifically the Dalai Lama, could not participate in the new school's planning, for that would "upset China."

The long shadow of China also affects how the Tibetans' own government, the Central Tibetan Administration, shapes its policies. The ongoing struggle with Beijing is one reason Tibetan leaders don't officially support Indian citizenship for members of the Tibetan diaspora—even though doing so would lessen the threat of lawsuits and court challenges for men like Dorjee. As Dorsh Marie de Voe, a University of California anthropologist, once observed, "Keeping refugee status is viewed as an action, an act of integrity in defense of faith. Taking citizenship, on the other hand, while giving functional benefits, renders the Tibetan unrecognizable, in both a profound and practical sense."[15]

Dorjee never spoke to me about the legal or political challenges he has faced as a noncitizen businesses owner in India, or whether a passport would change his views. He instead focused on the positive aspects of raising a family so close to the Dalai Lama, and on the generosity of the Indian government in making it possible. "I am fortunate to be here," Dorjee said during one conversation. "Because of His Holiness, I always think about mutual benefits. Everyone wants happiness; being a peaceful society and world is best and suitable for everybody. With His Holiness here, there are more people coming [to Dharamsala], more international people, and more Chinese people."

Eventually, though, Dorjee hinted at his longing for more certainty within the Indian legal system. "We don't own the shop, but since 1980 we run it. It's almost like ours. It used to be that you'd go to the West and stay five years and you became a citizen. In India, you can stay for fifty years, and not.

"Yes, I've built a house here, a business, but . . ." He trailed off, stopping short of unintentionally criticizing his hosts, or appearing to doubt the wisdom of the Tibetan leadership.

"I don't want to express whether this place, India, feels like home," he said, changing the subject. "It's for the Tibetan exile government, the CTA [to decide]. Whatever they say, I want to listen."

Little Lhasa, so outwardly Tibetan in presentation and appearance, "belongs" to Tibetan refugees in name only.

Dorjee says he is content with his legal standing in McLeod Ganj, and confident that Shop No. 5 will survive long after he is gone. His current lease expires in 2020. If he lives to see its renewal, he will be eighty-five. "There is no question the business will continue," he said. "As long as the municipal committee renews the lease, it will continue." But there was a time, not that long ago, that even the perpetually positive Dorjee had his doubts about his business's future.

In the predawn hours of December 20, 2004, a thick wall of flame swept through the residential and commercial block that Shop No. 5 occupies. Local media estimated damage to the dozen buildings—apartments, shops, and a hotel—at $228,000, a massive sum for the community at the time. "The shops numbered 1–10, and Kailash Hotel on the second floor and residential apartments on the ground floor, got burned down," a member of a McLeod Ganj retailers' association told Radio Free Asia.[16] The hotel proprietor Lodoe Sangpo said those affected by the blaze "have again become refugees. Everything has been destroyed. Even the clothes I'm wearing have been given by friends."[17]

Word of the blaze spread quickly, far beyond the tiny town's border. An online obituary of the market appeared on a popular Tibetan online news site, Phayul, lamenting Shop No. 5's apparent demise most poetically.[18] "A prominent part of Mcleod Gunj [sic], Dharamsala, was gutted by a fire two days ago. Luckily, no lives were lost.

"But the blaze that was subdued all too late left forever scarred and altered a small town, which spawns a history and identity almost parallel to the story of Tibetan exile. The death of a place and with it, a physical reference for nostalgia and memory, the end of a life as it was."

The obituary of Shop No. 5 was, of course, written prematurely. Within days of the fire the Tibetan and Himachal governments began clearing the land, issuing insurance payments, and planning for reconstruction. Skeptical that his livelihood would be restored so easily, Dorjee quickly moved to hold the space by building a small metal shack among the embers, with metal-sheeted walls and a bed. He stayed in his shack for six months, rarely leaving and sleeping on the ground to guard the real estate from potential takeover (reminiscent of the tarp from which he originally operated). He said he didn't trust the law to protect him. Dorjee's status as a noncitizen refugee meant his word and reputation were his only sources of certainty. Handshakes wouldn't do it this time.

Eventually the market was rebuilt, and his store returned to him with the help of savings and a few hundred dollars in government assistance.[19] Today, the tight row of shops, tea stalls, and restaurants lining the southern side of Temple Road looks very much as it did in the late 1990s; commerce continues apace, and infrequent visitors would be hard pressed to know anything had ever happened to the store that locals refer to as the Walmart of Little Lhasa.

I've often wondered how many more times I might step off the overnight bus from Delhi, instinctively wander over to the green-and-white storefront on Temple Road, and find the metal shutters drawn wide for business, wool sweaters and hand-knit socks swinging at the entrance. How much more needle and thread could a family sell in a town that seems to be bursting at the seams?

During one of my last visits to Dorjee's home on Bhagsu Road, in January 2016, I pressed him on his plans for the brick-and-mortar roots he had planted in a place he never thought he would settle in, let alone likely die in. What's next for Shop No. 5?

"I have a son, so the business will continue," he said matter-of-factly, sipping at a warm mug of tea. "Here, if you have a son, the business will continue forever, in a way. There is no question the business will continue. As long as the municipal committee will decide to renew the lease, it will continue."

That seemed a bit optimistic, given what I would soon learn about his family—that his oldest son had sworn off a merchant's life in favor of government service, an opening the fire paradoxically enabled; that his youngest son was equally uninterested in the family business; and that all his daughters were either busy with their own families or living overseas.

"Perhaps it is time . . . to sell?" I started to say, but stopped sort. I didn't have the heart to suggest that after so many decades in operation, Shop No. 5 might one day succumb to the realities of life in semipermanent exile, killed off not by fire or corruption, shady land deals or expired leases, but by time itself.

It seemed an apt metaphor for the changes consuming Tibetan exile these days. Not even the perpetually patient Dorjee could alter that calculus.

SIX BEADY EYES AND A DEAD LAMA

While many of India's Tibetan settlements are struggling to find their footing, not all of them are. At the Tibetan refugee camps of Bylakuppe, in South India, crimson-clad monks traipse through acres of corn and sugarcane, and gold-gilded temples sprout over rolling pastures that provide income for the thirteen thousand Tibetans living nearby.[1] In the summer, temperatures soar to over 100° Fahrenheit; monks born in the shadows of the Himalayas cover their heads with robes and cotton umbrellas to block out the searing sun. Even in cooler months, Indian Ocean winds spread a suffocating blanket of humidity.

The weather and geography may be wrong, but Bylakuppe's sprawling settlements, in India's Karnataka State, feel like a lost Shangri-La. They are among the most vibrant Tibetan communities outside Tibet today. There are none of the diversions of more northern Tibetan tourist traps—no over-eager turquoise touts, no cinemas screening Martin Scorsese's *Kundun* on repeat. Few foreigners ever venture to the sprawling agricultural enclaves of Dickyi Larsoe and Lugsum Samdupling, six hours southwest of Bangalore. The Indian tourists who do come stay for little more than a few photos and a bagged lunch. A sign near the entrance warns non-Indians they risk five years in prison if they visit without a "Protected Area Permit." It can take up to four months to obtain one.

But for all its idyllic isolation, Bylakuppe has a sinister side, too—one smeared with China's fingerprints. Tucked among the cultivated rows of solitude, down a dusty drive lined with wood-carvers and auto mechanics, is a moderate-size monastery where His Holiness is shunned with wrathful disdain. Here, at a temple known as Serpom, monks who venerate Lord Buddha also pray for the day the Dalai Lama dies.

When Tibet's spiritual leader told me about the "blessings" Beijing bestows from afar, I focused first on the external to explain the effects: namely, how China's soft and hard power were changing what it meant to be a Tibetan refugee. But some of the deepest fissures that divide Tibetans originated as self-made ones. Although China benefits from Tibetans' political and religious infighting (and in many cases actively encourages it), there are some fights that China didn't start. One of the most destructive—the centuries-old veneration of an esoteric, wrathful deity known for pushing peaceful monks to do bloody deeds—counts Bylakuppe as an epicenter.

The roots of this split trace back centuries to when Tibetans identified more with the brand of Buddhism they practiced than the country they shared. Most Tibetan Buddhists subscribe to one of four main schools—the Gelug (known as the Yellow Hats, to which the Dalai Lamas belong), the Nyingma, the Kagyu, and the Sakya. And while the differences are difficult for the layman to determine, Tibetan adherents have gone to great lengths to protect their traditions, including all-out war with other sects.[2] During the seventeenth century, the Fifth Dalai Lama, Ngawang Lobsang Gyatso, defeated competing sects, putting an end to one long-running dispute. But his victory, which gave rise to a pan-Tibetan state under a Gelug banner, also produced fissures among Yellow Hat believers that reverberate to this day.

The ever-evolving mythology underpinning these rifts claims that a contemporary of the Fifth, Drakpa Gyaltsen, himself an important reincarnation who had been considered a candidate for the Fifth's position, saw the unification strategy as a threat to the purity of the Yellow Hats' doctrine. Some believe Drakpa's opposition to the Great Fifth's policies caused considerable discord within the school and between the two men. But evidence is thin; as is often the case when there is more than one candidate for an important lama's position, there were some who argued that Drakpa was "the true reincarnation of the Fourth Dalai Lama"[3] and thus, despite his lesser title, was religiously superior to the Dalai Lama himself.[4] Without hard historical evidence to support these assertions, however, much remains unclear.

What is clear, says Gary Beesley, a contemporary scholar of the Shugden rift whose work is among the most detailed on the subject, is that tensions between the men's advisers was palpable. Drakpa's wealthy, influential, and politically ambitious mother was at odds with the equally Machiavellian regent to the Fifth, Desi Sonam Chopel, who had repeatedly expressed outright contempt for Drakpa. Even the late Trijang Rinpoche, a leading figure in the modern Shugden movement until his death in 1981, suggested Drakpa was murdered on the instruction of the Desi by a relative of the regent.

But no matter how relations played out between the two sides during their lifetimes, it was after Drakpa died that his impact was most telling.

Following the passing of Drakpa, a subset of Gelug practitioners began to propitiate a deity that they viewed as a protector of the Yellow Hats' doctrine. That deity was called Dorje Shugden, and today he is depicted as an unforgiving character with bared fangs, bloodshot eyes, and a cloak of orange flames. Whether Shugden was a reincarnation of Drakpa or a protector spirit of some other origin matters little (to nonbelievers, at least). What is most important—to supporters and opponents alike—is the belief that Shugden brings rewards to those who venerate him, and death to those who oppose him.

To this day the Yellow Hats remain divided over the role Shugden plays in their faith: he is either a protector of tradition and lineage, or a deliverer of destruction and carnage. During the revolt and uprising against the Chinese army in the late 1950s, warriors from Eastern Tibet invoked Shugden as their earthly protector and military guide.[5] Tibetan scholars and quiet practitioners have all turned to the deity for succor; the current Dalai Lama himself once worshiped him. But in 1996, after "long and careful investigations," the Fourteenth Dalai Lama sided with those skeptical of Shugden's intentions, and announced that he "strongly discourages Tibetan Buddhists from propitiating the fierce spirit."[6] Those who refused were asked not to attend any more teachings by His Holiness. "This is not a matter of what is in the Dalai Lama's interest," he said, "but what is in the interest of the Tibetan nation and its religion."

The Dalai Lama's directive called on Tibetans to choose: venerate the Dalai Lama, or worship Shugden, but not both. It was an easy decision for most, but not all: in 2008, some three hundred monks from the great monastic college of Sera Mey in Bylakuppe packed up their prayer mats and moved out. But they didn't go far, and built a new temple on a fenced-in property just a few hundred feet to the northeast. Today, all that separates their home from the one they left behind is pastureland, a low row of trees—and a red-and-yellow concrete wall topped with fittings for razor wire.

————

Serpom Thoesam Norling Monastery was only a few years old when I visited in May 2012, but it already looked settled. A bronze bust of Bhimrao Ramji Ambedkar, a member of the drafting committee of India's constitution and a fierce supporter of India's Dalit ("untouchables") caste, guards the opening of a vast landscaped courtyard, just a few hundred yards from the monastery of Sera that its inhabitants vacated. A sign at the base of the welcome statue proclaims that Serpom is a testament to the magnanimity of the people of India, and "the people of the world who love truth and justice." Judging from the upkeep and grandeur of the temple in front of me I figured there must be many people—from within India and far beyond it—with deep pockets that do.

A few young monks were sweeping the walk at the front gate when I arrived, and a group of older monks were working in an outdoor kitchen sculpting huge blocks of butter that would be painted and used as offerings or in rituals. Other than that, the place was quiet. A dog crouching on a stairwell overlooking the kitchen sauntered off when I approached. He didn't bother barking.

I headed to the second floor, following signs for the administrative office. A monk, probably in his twenties, barely glanced up from his cell phone as he waved me through to a wide staircase. In the corridor upstairs, long tables covered with floral place settings were laid out for lunch.

The main temple was closed, but a few Indian tourists were milling about and peering through the glass at the statues and paintings in the main prayer hall below. "On top of the eastern door, the main doorway, is a painting of the 21 Taras and the Taras protecting us from the eight fears," a plaque nearby read. "And underneath them are paintings of Dharmapala Dorje Shugden"— the wrathful dharma protector. One of the Indian tourists seemed impressed. "Nice, right?" he said, extending a hand for a quick shake as he walked by. "Lord Buddha," he muttered before walking off.

I ducked into the kitchen looking for someone to chat with. "English?" I asked hopefully. Many months of Tibetan language instruction over the years had still left me with only the limited ability to count to ten (*chu*), or comment on how delicious a particular dish was (*shimpo*). Neither seemed appropriate.

A monk washing dishes just shook his head, but another put down the plate he was drying and motioned for me to follow. He pulled back a curtain to the monastery's administrative offices and waved me in. Across the room, standing near a desk soaked in sunlight and papered with files, log books, and documents, was the monastery's secretary, Samdup Wangmo.

Samdup introduced himself. His beady eyes and patches of splotchy skin made him look as if he had just gotten over the chicken pox or a nasty bout of the flu. A jaw of blackened teeth and a thin mustache added a touch of menace to his crooked grin. There was something calculating about the way he cocked his neck when he said "hello," as if he was asking a question rather than offering a greeting. He did not offer me tea or invite me to sit, as is customary in most Tibetan offices or homes.

Aware that Serpom was a by-product of the Dalai Lama's directive, I trod carefully, worried that prying too much might set Samdup off. "Your monastery," I said in a feeble bid to break the ice. "It's . . . beautiful."

There were about six hundred monks at Serpom in May 2012, up from three hundred when the monastery formed in 2008, he told me. That made it a small monastic college in a field crowded with many larger ones. Next door, Sera Mey boasted some three thousand in its ranks at the time, while Namdroling Monastery, the largest teaching center of the Nyingma sect in exile, and located just a few miles east of Serpom, counts over five thousand. The Dalai Lama has reportedly looked into making Namdroling a seasonal residence.[7]

From the looks of the monks I passed sweeping the courtyard when I entered, the majority of Serpom's flock were no older than twelve. Samdup didn't say where the young conscripts were from, but I had heard from officials in McLeod Ganj that many new monasteries in South India recruit from non-Tibetan communities across Asia, especially in the Himalayan region of Nepal. Recruiting efforts, Samdup added, were picking up after years of stagnation.

I sensed that Samdup wasn't in the mood for a long conversation; English, he said, wasn't his strong suit. Mindful of the claims made just a few days earlier by the Tibetan government in exile—that some Shugden adherents were so at odds with the Dalai Lama's brand of Buddhism that they might want him dead[8]—I cut the small talk. "How are things today?" I asked. "There was lots of tension between Serpom and Sera not that long ago. How are your relations with the community?" You know, I added, there are many rumors about Shugden supporters.

"It's getting better," he said. "Slowly, it's better." (I found this somewhat surprising. Near the lobby of the guesthouse I was staying in, just a few miles away from Samdup's monastery, a sign welcoming visitors doesn't mince words: "Your attention please. Anyone—monks, nuns, and lay people—whoever have relationship with Dhoegyal [Shugden] or its clique are not allowed to come here for we forbid our service for them." Poor syntax notwithstanding, the message was clear.)

But then Samdup added an aside that still gives me chills. Things were better, he said, but from a religious standpoint they weren't great. They wouldn't be great until the Dalai Lama was out of the picture. "It won't be totally perfect until the Dalai Lama is dead," he said, stone-faced. "As long as the Dalai Lama is alive, not perfect."

And with that, Samdup bid me a good day and good-bye.

— — —

Samdup wasn't the first Shugden adherent to wish harm on nonbelievers. Supporters had been implicated in murders and violence before, including an especially vicious stabbing of three pro–Dalai Lama monks in 1997 not far from the Tibetan leader's bedroom. On the evening of February 4, around the time I left McLeod Ganj for the first time, armed men took turns stabbing a confidant of the Dalai Lama, a well-known Gelug educator who supported the Tibetan leader's de facto ban on Shugden worship. Lobsang Gyatso, seventy, was murdered along with two of his students from the Buddhist Dialectic School in a small room just two hundred yards from the Dalai Lama's residence.

The crime has never been solved, but Gyatso's room remains a memorial to that night. The walls are covered with photos of the slain monks, their lifeless bodies covered in blood from multiple stab wounds and punctured skulls. In one corner, the single bed on which the elderly monk slept remains draped with his favorite linens. To this day the room remains a memorial to the prevailing sentiment: that the killers—possibly Tibetans themselves—were operating with explicit orders from China. (Some Tibetans have more recently suggested, albeit without evidence, that Zhu Weiqun, an influential Chinese politician and critic of the Dalai Lama who served as deputy head of China's United Front Work Department, ordered the killing.)

What is clear is that the assailants arrived in India from China days before the killings, and then apparently returned to China afterward. In 2007, Interpol issued a Red Notice calling on China to extradite two of the men thought to have fled. Beijing has never responded to Interpol's request.[9]

Opponents of Shugden have played dirty, too, if less violently. Shugden devotees have had their faces plastered on "wanted" posters as far west as New York City, and once-respected Tibetan businessmen have watched their livelihoods wither under crippling boycotts. In one particularly heated exchange in 2000, at another refugee settlement in South India, thousands of anti-Shugden monks and laypeople tossed rocks and shouted invective at a pro-Shugden temple. Police were called in to disperse the crowd.[10]

For the most part, though, the two-decade-long rift has been measured not in the number of deaths or attacks on opposing sides, but in the number of places to pray. And by this measure, Shugden has the upper hand by a long shot.

Close to home, in Asia, most Tibetans have sided with the Dalai Lama; there are just three Shugden-affiliated temples in India, three more in neighboring Nepal, and only a smattering elsewhere in places like Hong Kong, Taiwan, and Malaysia.[11] Two decades after His Holiness called on Tibetans to abandon the practice, the vast majority of those in exile have listened. But the few who haven't play an outsize role is perpetuating this split, especially in the West, where the institutionalized, daily propitiation of Shugden is booming.

Globally, there are hundreds of Shugden-affiliated monasteries and temples, and in New York alone there are some twenty-seven centers catering to more casual, less-committed Western students who often do not know of the Shugden links their Buddhism and weekend meditation teachers maintain. The Fourteenth Dalai Lama's decision to strongly discourage the practice—and follow in the footsteps of his predecessor, the Great Fifth, by championing a narrative of pan-Tibetan unity tied to nationality rather than a single Buddhist school—may have made it more popular than ever. It also gave China an opening.

The majority of those operating these centers are former students of Trijang Rinpoche, a onetime junior tutor of the Dalai Lama who helped raise Shugden's prominence among the diaspora's Gelug practitioners before his death in 1981. Forced from the refugee fold by the Dalai Lama's edict, these former-students-turned-teachers went on to establish dharma centers worldwide. For instance, Serpom's chief abbot, Yongyal Rinpoche, who was not in residence when I visited Bylakuppe, spends most of his time in Los Angeles, where he teaches at another center he founded, the Lamrim International Dharma Center.

One of the most visible disciples of Trijang, and most active promoters of Shugden in the West, is a frail, freckled, bespectacled monk named Geshe Kelsang Gyatso. In 1991, a few years before the Dalai Lama's directive, Kelsang Gyatso incorporated the New Kadampa Tradition (known as NKT; the name refers to an ancient line of teachers revered for their strict adherence to Buddhist fundamentals—a play on the Shugden rift). When the Dalai Lama made his de facto ban public, Kelsang organized demonstrations against the Tibetan leader in the British capital, and he told an interviewer that while he had nothing against the Dalai Lama personally, the Tibetan leader's views on Shugden were destructive. "Demonstrating should have been a teacher for him," he said. "But he never changed."[12] Until the group shifted tactics in 2016, the Dalai Lama was met with pro-Shugden protests whenever he visited Europe or the United States.

Kelsang Gyatso rarely appears in public now (he popped up on Facebook in April 2017, the first sighting since 2013, ending years of speculation that he was dead), but even from the shadows his work continues to challenge the Dalai Lama. NKT aims to build "a Kadampa Buddhist Temple in every major city in the world" and is well on its way to that goal. Today there are some twelve hundred Kadampa centers in forty countries. NKT's holdings include temples, retreat centers, cafés, art studios, and hotels from Australia to Brazil. With reported income of $4.2 million in 2011, NKT had receipts roughly equivalent to a quarter of what the entire Tibetan government in exile budgeted for its programs that same year.[13]

Tibetans and activists who support the Dalai Lama see plenty of conspiracy in NKT's work. In 2007, around the time when China was putting the squeeze on Tibetan exiles in earnest, donations to Kelsang Gyatso's UK-based charity topped $2.8 million. In 2008, the year Beijing turned up the heat on

Tibetan refugees, anonymous donations poured in to the NKT, reaching over $4 million. One Kadampa meditation center in upstate New York reported additional earnings of $1.18 million in 2008.[14] It's not clear from US or UK tax filings who donated or where the funds originated, but Tibetans and Tibetan scholars see China as a likely source.[15] At the very least, according to a 2015 investigation by the Reuters news agency, NKT supporters are "unwitting agents of Beijing," if not outright recipients of Chinese assistance.[16]

Paradoxically, it's easier to trace China's Shugden ties inside Chinese-controlled Tibet. Ben Hillman, a political scientist at Australian National University who studies monastic politics in China, has written that the central government immediately sought to take advantage of the Dalai Lama's de facto ban by allocating a "disproportionate amount of funds" for renovations to pro-Shugden monasteries in Eastern Tibet, which today includes parts of Sichuan and Yunnan. In 2003, local governments followed suit; at one Tibetan monastery that Hillman visited, monks from Shugden-affiliated administrative units (called *khangtsens*) noted a surge in travel approvals for documents needed to study in India. "Similarly, in 2004, one of the monastery's smallest and (previously) poorest khangtsens began to build an elaborate new prayer room and residence for its handful of members. Financial support had been obtained from Beijing through a network of pro-Shugden lamas with access to officials at the highest level."[17]

Official favoritism has only become more explicit in the years since. In early 2014, Communist Party officials in the Tibet Autonomous Region published directives detailing how Tibetans should "correctly" view the issue: by supporting Shugden.[18] Siding with the Dalai Lama on this matter, rather than the Communist Party of China (CPC), would result in criminal charges or imprisonment.

By December, China was making good on its promise. On December 15, Radio Free Asia reported that Jamyang Tsering, a seventy-seven-year-old Tibetan man from Chamdo, in Eastern Tibet, was sentenced to eighteen months in prison for advising a group of students to heed the Dalai Lama's advice and not worship the divisive deity.[19] Three days later the radio reported on a similar case, with a very different outcome: Uyak Tulku Lobsang Tenzin, sixty, received a decade.[20]

— — —

Among the first Tibetans that China's then ambassador to Nepal, Yang Hou-lan, visited upon arrival to his post in Kathmandu in 2011 was a cherubic, balding lama named Gangchen Rinpoche. Jovial and stout, with an uncanny resemblance to a Chinese laughing Buddha statue, Gangchen also happens to be one of the monks most visibly defiant of the Dalai Lama's boycott of the Shugden deity—and another disciple of the tutor, Trijang Rinpoche.

The meeting between Ambassador Houlan and Gangchen, at the lama's Kathmandu center, took place on August 21, 2011. It lasted just a few minutes. A photograph released by the Chinese Ministry of Foreign Affairs shows the ambassador bowing slightly as he and his wife receive blessings from Gangchen, his signature shiny bald dome and bushy beard offering a visual counterpoint to the stoic Chinese couple.[21] Long white prayer scarves are draped around the diplomats' necks, and ivory-colored prayer beads rest loosely on their wrists. Gangchen, apparently in midsentence, has his right index figure raised as if punctuating a key point of Buddhist doctrine.

An accompanying photo caption declares that Ambassador Houlan "went to the Tibetan community in Kathmandu" and "familiarized himself with the life of local Tibetans." He also held "a cordial talk with the Living Buddha," a term Beijing uses to refer to reincarnated Tibetan lamas. (Since the 1990s, the Communist Party has mandated that Tibetan Buddhist teachers identified as reincarnations be approved by the Chinese state; the use of the term "Living Buddha" indicates Beijing's approval of Gangchen's status.)

Over the last decade and a half that I've traveled to Nepal, first as a student, then a tourist, and later a journalist, I've had more conversations with members of the "Tibetan community" in Nepal than I can count. I've met student activists and scholars, former guerrilla fighters and carpet weavers, shopkeepers and housewives. Not once during all those years has anyone ever mentioned Gangchen's name. Most Tibetans I know would prefer to change the topic of conversation than openly admit having ties to or affinity for Shugden. Even among close friends the topic is rarely discussed, and it is not uncommon for adherents of this deity to keep their practice secret, even from their own family.

In his open defiance of the Dalai Lama's directive, Gangchen Rinpoche has not only caused rifts within the Gelug school of Tibetan Buddhism, but has earned himself general condemnation among Tibetan refugees throughout Nepal, India, and beyond. In promoting Shugden so forcefully, Gangchen and teachers like him are essentially pushing Buddhists to abandon the Dalai Lama. Among Tibetan exiles, these efforts have fallen flat, and Gangchen's main support comes from non-Tibetan Buddhist associations in Indonesia, Thailand, Brazil, and across Europe. He is currently running a one-euro-a-day fund-raising campaign on his website. Nonetheless, China sees him as a pillar of Nepal's Tibetan community.

Lama Gangchen has deep ties to China. From his base in Milan, Italy, Gangchen, who is well into his seventies, operates dozens of meditation and tantric self-healing centers around the world. But he is also a frequent visitor to the Chinese capital, and an honored guest in public with Chinese leaders at party-sanctioned Buddhist forums. He has rubbed shoulders with some of the Communist Party's most important politicians, from leading Tibet policy maker Zhu Weiqun to former Chinese leaders Wen Jiabao and Hu Jintao.[22] Largely ignored by Tibetans in exile, Gangchen, and other Tibetan gurus of the Shugden mold, have become favorites of the Communist Party.

In fact, they may even be employees. A December 2015 investigation by Reuters alleged that China's United Front Work Department pays members of the Shugden movement to organize activities of the sect's followers overseas, including protests against the Dalai Lama. "The Chinese are using them as a tool to make the Dalai Lama look fake, to achieve their own ends, to undermine Tibetan Buddhism, and to fragment Tibetan society," said Lama Tseta, a monk and prominent former member of the Shugden movement. Tseta told the news agency he was paid by China to organize the sect's overseas activities.[23]

Gangchen's own ties to the Communist Party date to at least 1997, when he publicly offered blessings to the Chinese-appointed Panchen Lama, Gyaincain Norbu.[24] The display of veneration for China's Panchen over the Dalai Lama's choice, Gedhun Choekyi Nyima, cemented Gangchen's allegiance to China in the eyes of many Tibetan refugees. The same year that Gangchen endorsed the Chinese appointed Panchen, Gangchen's organization helped construct a new tantric college at the historic Tashilumpo Monastery in Shigatse, Tibet, which is the Panchen Lama's historic seat.[25] Access like that would not have been possible without China's blessing.

Such ties have brought condemnation from mainstream Tibetan refugees, and a fair amount of mythmaking. In one story, recounted to me over dinner by Hubert Decleer, a longtime Tibet scholar based in Nepal, Gangchen allegedly tried to encourage the Karmapa Lama to bow to the Chinese chosen Panchen, as Gangchen had. "The Karmapa," one of Tibetan Buddhism's most important figures and head of the Karma Kagyu sect, "responded by slapping Gangchen across the face," Decleer told me. "And the Karmapa was only twelve at the time."

Intrigued by the Chinese diplomatic embrace of a controversial Tibetan religious figure, in early 2012—a few months before my visit to Serpom—I set out to find this "pillar" of Tibetan exile.

The Gangchen Lama Meditation and Retreat Center, tucked down a narrow alley in the shadows of the giant Boudhanath Stupa, in Kathmandu, is not easy to find. There are no signs affixed to the green iron gates guarding the complex, no neon lights announcing its location. Gangchen Labrang, as it is known locally, seems to hide in plain sight: even with Tibetan prayer flags and large cylindrical victory banners—copper cones that symbolize the Buddha's triumph over spiritual obstacles—flying over the surrounding low-rise apartment blocks and Internet cafés, no taxi driver I had was able to find it. I needed parts of two days, walking long stretches of road, to locate it, and lots of knocking on the wrong doors.

Eventually I did arrive, a few weeks after the Chinese ambassador's visit. Pushing open the gate, I was met with a wide-open courtyard and an unattended guard shack. To the left a small shed, where Nepali employees of Gangchen Himalayan Handicraft churn out Buddhist altars and shrines, was dark and quiet. Human rights researchers in Nepal had told me that Gangchen's primary funding source was through the sale and shipment of Tibetan trinkets. On this day, though, the courtyard was the opposite of buzzing.

An older Tibetan man, who looked to be in his mid-fifties, put aside his cell phone long enough to ask if I was lost. He wore a black down jacket, tattered at the sleeves and dusty from Kathmandu's persistent blanket of grime. "Can I help you?" he asked, politely but firmly.

"Is this the Gangchen Labrang?" I replied. "I'm interested in a Tibetan medical consultation; I was told there is a medical center here?"

It was true—I was interested in a consultation. But I had also been warned that Gangchen might be suspicious of a journalist stumbling into his courtyard unannounced, and that the best way to meet him or his confidants would be to keep the notepad in my bag and seek the center's medical services.

"The lama isn't here," he said curtly. And that seemed to be that—mission failed.

But as I turned to go, feeling for a moment defeated, the cell-phone-toting guard asked me to wait. He disappeared up a small staircase, reemerging a moment later to wave me up to the small balcony overlooking the courtyard below. I followed.

At the top of the stairs I was introduced to a monk seated at a white plastic patio table slowly picking at a bowl of cut papaya. He was a cousin of Lama Gangchen, the cell phone greeter said, and one of only eight monks that lived at the Labrang center full time.

"How did you hear about this place?" the cousin asked, sounding surprised that I was standing in front of him.

I read about it on the Chinese Foreign Ministry's website, I thought to myself. And who hadn't heard of Kathmandu's pillar of the Tibetan community?

"Friends," I answered.

Apparently, China's idea of a Tibetan community center hadn't been relayed to those running it.

A few awkward minutes passed; I assumed they were trying to figure out what to do with me. It turns out I had missed Gangchen Rinpoche by about two weeks. He had been in Kathmandu for the annual Losar festivities—the Tibetan New Year—but had since left for three weeks of teachings in Indonesia. He spends no more than a few weeks in Nepal each year, I was told, and largely splits his time between Italy and Southeast Asia, Thailand in particular.

The small talk continued for a few more minutes, and just as I was about to make my exit, a Western man wearing a felt vest and jeans appeared from inside the center's main dining area. He put down his own bowl of papaya and extended a hand, offering a warm hello. Antonio Bianchi, one of Gangchen's closest aids, was in Kathmandu for the summer.

Bianchi and I talked for an hour—about the center, his boss's connection to Nepal, and their collective ties to China. Bianchi said that he, like many Westerners, was drawn to Gangchen's brand of Buddhism for its focus on philosophy and tantric tradition; Bianchi himself studied how Buddhist teachings have influenced Western sciences.

I saw no photographs or statues of Shugden, the wrathful deity, and no indication that this was a center run by its adherents. The main dining hall where we sat was fitted with colorful wall hangings and bright brocades, standard for any Tibetan monastery. Decleer had told me that Gangchen houses a divination hall for Shugden, a place where an earthly medium enters a trance in which to communicate directly with the deity. This hall, Decleer said, was similar to the one the Dalai Lama frequents for his oracle, the Nechung, but I saw no sign of it (and I didn't ask to see it; perhaps all the mythmaking had put me off on being too pushy).

What I did ask Bianchi was what he thought of Gangchen's frequent visits to China and his teacher's chummy relations with Chinese diplomats. "It's a necessary partnership," he said, and means access to Tibetan areas inside Tibet that few foreign-based Tibetans enjoy. For example, Gangchen's center had recently been granted permission to use donations to upgrade the bathroom facilities at the Yellow Hats' giant Tashilumpo monastery near Shigatse. "They didn't even have showers when we arrived," Bianchi said.

It was just one of many projects Gangchen and his students have helped with, Bianchi continued. Every summer since 2003, Gangchen's Help in Action foundation has traveled to "arid, rocky, and icy cold" Tibetan villages, according to the charity's website, to deliver food, clothing, and school supplies to young monks and children. They post "photo reportage" evidence of their work when they return.

But access comes with a price, Bianchi concluded. "Gangchen Rinpoche isn't well respected within the Tibetan community here," he said matter-of-factly. "We're not connected with the Tibetan exile community, so it makes things easier in Tibet."

My mind returned to the foreign ministry's photograph of Gangchen and Ambassador Houlan, and to the caption: "Ambassador Yang Houlan went to the Tibetan community in Kathmandu. He visited the Tibetan households and familiarized himself with the life of local Tibetans. Ambassador also had a cordial talk with the Living Buddha, Gangyan. Both sides stated that they will make unremitting efforts in the Motherland's prosperity."

And there it was: the price of Gangchen's access was conceding to China's story line.

Bianchi took a final bite of papaya. Our meeting was over. Gathering my bag, I stood, thanked him for his time, and headed for the stairs, past the other monks and cousins who were still seated around the plastic patio table on the second-floor balcony.

Making my way to the first floor, I turned to peer inside the showroom of hand-carved wooden cabinets, bronze statues, and freshly stitched brocades, products headed for the international market. I now understood how some of the proceeds of Gangchen's handicraft business might be used: to pay for shower stalls and sacks of food, all in the name of "the Motherland's prosperity." While the operation was creating much-needed jobs in Nepal, it was also likely helping fund Shugden monasteries beyond what the Chinese government was already supporting. I wondered how many buyers of his products knew the deal that Gangchen was making on their behalf.

Waving to Bianchi, smiling one last time, I pushed open the green gate and stepped out onto the street.

Shugden supporters may pray for the day that the Fourteenth Dalai Lama dies, but what happens the day after is a question not even they can answer. In China's Tibet, reincarnation is more politics than faith.

Religion hasn't always been so contested in China. During much of China's imperial history, "religion," at least in the Western sense, did not even exist. Rituals and rites were rooted in superstition and cosmology—like veneration of "kitchen" gods and door guardians—and also served as the bedrock of an emperor's legitimacy. Only the Son of Heaven had the mandate to communicate directly with the gods.

But this top-down, paternalistic relationship with faith began to change in the sixteenth century, when Jesuit interpretations of religion were introduced through translations of Chinese texts. Over time, China's blend of spirituality shifted from a system of rites underpinning imperial authority, to something more aligned with a Western conception of the transcendent. By the late nineteenth century, Chinese reformers associated Western beliefs with modernity and sought to replace cultish magic with organized faith. The Hundred Days' Reform movement, in 1898, was a period of great upheaval, with the goal of reinvigorating China's educational, economic, military, and cultural systems.

Since the dawn of the People's Republic, in 1949, China's Communist Party has varied in its views on organized religion, oscillating between periods of reluctant acceptance and destructive disdain. The CPC's vilification reached its zenith during the Cultural Revolution; for Mao Zedong, anything but class struggle was a capitalist opiate of the masses. But in the years after Mao's death in 1976, organized faiths—and especially Christianity, Islam, and Buddhism—found space to operate once more.

Over the succeeding decades, temples and churches were built (or rebuilt) at a dizzying pace, and today much of China identifies with the spiritual as well as the national.[1] Christianity is one of China's most popular and fastest-growing religions; by one estimate, China has more than one hundred million Christians within its borders, more than the membership of the entire Communist Party (which counts about eighty-nine million members today).[2] Church numbers might be even higher if it weren't for rules requiring all new and existing party members to remain atheist.[3]

But Beijing's reconciliation with religion in principle has not meant a radical shift for the Tibetan Buddhist experience in practice. Rather, religion remains *the* key point of friction between Tibetans and their occupying foes. As the American anthropologist Melvyn C. Goldstein has observed, for Tibetans, "the value and worth of their culture and way of life and the essence of their national identity" is Tibetan Buddhism. "It is what they felt made their society unique and without equal."[4]

Between 1950 and the Tibetan uprising of 1959, moves by Beijing to "liberate" Tibet did not immediately translate to direct checks on Buddhist practices. But following Tibetans' 1959 revolt, and with the Dalai Lama in India, China engaged in a full-on assault on Tibet's monastic core. According to a secret petition penned in 1962 by the Tenth Panchen Lama, the second-most important Tibetan religious figure after the Dalai Lama, Mao's campaign had reduced Tibetan religion to rubble.

"Before democratic reform, there were more than 2,500 large, medium, and small monasteries in Tibet," the Panchen Lama wrote. "After democratic reform, only 70-odd monasteries were kept in existence by the government. There was great damage and destruction, both by man and otherwise, and they [the monasteries] were reduced to the point of collapse, or beyond."

In return for publishing his observations, the Panchen Lama was labeled an enemy of the party, the people, and of socialism; he spent the next fourteen years in prison and under house arrest.

Monks and lamas imprisoned during the post-1959 upheaval were eventually released during the reforms of Deng Xiaoping. The Panchen Lama was freed in October 1977. Monasteries were rebuilt, and according to the University of Birmingham's Tsering Topgyal, "the CCP abandoned the Cultural Revolution–era policy of violent assimilation and returned to the traditional Chinese belief that the frontier-barbarians would voluntarily adopt the 'superior' and 'advanced' culture of the Chinese."[5] Mao-era restrictions on Buddhism were once again rolled back in Tibetan areas.

A surge in funds and labor led to the reconstruction of many monasteries. The Chinese government paid for some of the rebuilding efforts from its own coffers (including reconstruction of the Jokhang Temple in Lhasa), even though China's overarching goal remained the socioeconomic transformation of the region.[6] But after a series of pro-democracy protests in Lhasa that began in 1987 and culminated in March 1989, Chinese officials began turning the screws once more. Martial law was declared throughout Tibet. In January 1989, the sudden death of the Tenth Panchen Lama kicked off a parallel search for his reincarnation, exacerbating tensions further.

By 1991, Beijing began meddling even more directly in Tibetan religious affairs. A directive that year gave the CPC, and not Tibetans, final say over the selection and enthronement of *tulkus*—reincarnated lamas identified and trained to carry on the religious teachings of their deceased predecessors. A China State Council order concluded that while "reincarnation is allowed" in Tibetan Buddhism, the number of reincarnations would be controlled, and only lamas approved by the Religious Affairs Bureau would be recognized as the real deal.[7] A further order spelled out who is authorized to search for "living Buddha soul children," and how to settle disputes about a reincarnated lama's religious worth.

China first applied its stamp of *tulku* approval on September 27, 1992, when the government recognized Ogyen Trinley Dorje as the Seventeenth Karmapa, the historic head of the Karma Kagyu lineage.[8] It was a curious move for China, given that two months earlier, the Dalai Lama had done the same thing, after he was asked to settle a dispute over the true identity of the Kagyu leader (to this day the second rival claimant continues to challenge this selection).

But China's meddling in Tibetan religious affairs took a different turn in May 1995. That month, after the Dalai Lama announced his choice for the Eleventh Panchen Lama, a six-year-old boy from northwestern Tibet named Gedhun Choekyi Nyima, China declared the selection invalid, arrested the child and his family, and shuffled them off to a secret prison. Six months later, in a ceremony in the Tibetan capital of Lhasa, Chinese officials selected their own "Great Scholar" reincarnate, and even pulled the name of the Chinese-approved Panchen Lama from the "golden urn," a controversial custom for divinations introduced by the Qianlong Emperor in the eighteenth century.

Today the "Chinese Panchen," Gyaincain Norbu, is being groomed to assume the mantle of Tibetan religious leadership under a watchful Chinese eye. And Gedhun Choekyi Nyima, the Dalai Lama's selection for one of Tibetan Buddhism's most important roles, is considered the "world's youngest political prisoner." He has not been seen or heard from in over two decades. The changes in China's approach to *tulku* recognition after the enthronement of the Seventeenth Karmapa have been traced to policies developed during a July 1994 meeting in Beijing, known as the Third National Forum on Work in Tibet. According to Human Rights Watch, policies that resulted from that forum led to increased monitoring of suspected dissidents, control over monasteries, and the introduction of "patriotic education." The forum also set the stage for China's aggressive response to the Dalai Lama's selection of the Eleventh Panchen Lama.

With the Panchen Lama(s) under China's thumb, Beijing might have hoped to be in the driver's seat when those praying for the Dalai Lama's demise get their wish. The Panchen Lama has historically been responsible for finding the Dalai Lama's reincarnation, and vice versa. Though the Fourteenth Dalai Lama has suggested that his successor may be found outside of Tibet or China (Mongolia is one possibility), or that he might not be reincarnated at all, the reality is that the Fifteenth Dalai Lama—or more likely *Lamas*—will be among the most contested "reincarnations" in the history of Tibet.

— — —

Over the last quarter century, China has used its stamp of *tulku* approval 870 times.[9] The Seventeenth Karmapa, Ogyen Trinley Dorje, a baby-faced philosopher-monk considered by many to be the future of Tibetan unity, is one that got away.[10]

On the morning of January 5, 2000, the Karmapa, accompanied by only a few aides, arrived in McLeod Ganj in the back seat of an Ambassador taxi.

Nine days earlier, the young boy had slipped away from his monastery under the cover of darkness, some nine hundred miles on the other side of the Indian border inside Tibet. Traversing the world's tallest peaks on foot and horseback, just as the Dalai Lama had done four decades earlier, the Karmapa risked death and capture to seek asylum in India. It was, for Tibetan refugees, a coup of historic proportions.

The Seventeenth Karmapa represents an unbroken line of succession that dates to the twelfth century, older than the institution of the Dalai Lamas by about four hundred years. As the writer Mick Brown notes in his biography of Ogyen Trinley Dorje, the Karmapas were "spiritual teachers of the khans of Mongolia and the emperors of China," and believed to be miracle workers who "mastered a range of talents, including divination, prophecy, the ability to appear simultaneously in different places, and the power to control weather."[11]

By arriving in India, the Seventeenth Karmapa had essentially performed a modern magic trick: recognized as the legitimate Kagyu head by the captors he fled, he was now simultaneously embraced by the refugees that China hated.

For China, the Karmapa's flight was deeply embarrassing. His escape meant that China's form of religious and patriotic indoctrination—achieved through the direct manipulation of Tibetans' faith—had failed. In the days after the escape, China sought to downplay his departure, suggesting that the young, Chinese-approved Karmapa had only gone abroad temporarily. He had left, Beijing said, to retrieve religious artifacts, musical instruments, and a ritual black hat that had been used by the previous Karmapas for religious ceremonies. Most important, China said, he "did not mean to betray the state, the nation, the monastery, and the leadership."[12]

But the longer Ogyen Trinley Dorje remained in India, the clearer it became that China's plans for him had failed. The Karmapa's escape, according to China scholar Tien-sze Fang, "was damaging to Beijing's assumption that the Tibet issue would naturally be resolved when the present Dalai Lama was out of the picture." His flight not only spelled the end of that strategy; it also meant that a Chinese-groomed Karmapa could "not be used as a tool against the Dalai Lama."[13]

Despite his strategic value, though, the Karmapa's arrival in India was not universally welcomed by New Delhi. Some Indian intelligence officers worried that he might be "a planted Chinese agent."[14] In 2011, the discovery of piles of cash tucked away in his monastery only heightened the intrigue; the monastery said the money had been raised from devotees, but Indian police expressed doubt.

Today, most Tibetans and religious scholars have accepted the backstory, and the controversy has died down. A competing claimant for the Black Crown worn by the Karmapa has also largely been discredited, at least among refugees, although the rift did expose divisions within Tibetans' own religious establishment. In 2016, Ogyen Trinley Dorje visited India's Arunachal Pradesh, which China claims as part of southern Tibet. A loosening of travel restrictions, which had curtailed the Karmapa's movements within India for years, enabled the visit. The move suggested that New Delhi now trusted their Tibetan guest. It also hinted that the Karmapa was becoming an important political figure in his own right.

I first began reaching out to the Karmapa's office to request an interview with His Holiness in the fall of 2016, months before I was to make another trip to India. But that trip came and went, and after a half dozen polite but firm rejections over the subsequent months, I began to lose hope that an interview with the future of Tibetan Buddhism would be possible.

Then, in the spring of 2017, after the Karmapa's office announced his first-ever visit to the United Kingdom—another indication that the young monk's "international profile [was] on a steady, upward trajectory"[15]—a friend at the International Campaign for Tibet who was helping to organize the trip reached out with good news: the stars for a sit-down were finally aligning.

The Karmapa's plane touched down in London on May 17, and within hours I was making plans to attend events to hear him speak. I wasn't alone; during a talk at Battersea Park, an estimated forty-five hundred people packed into a banquet hall on the banks of the River Thames to hear the Karmapa wax on about happiness, karma, and the roots of suffering. At a book talk in Central London a few days later, dozens of invited guests heard the Karmapa answer questions about the nature of mind, morality, interconnectedness, and compassion. No question, it seemed, was off limits; he even counseled a young Chinese woman who wanted to know what she could do to ensure that her late father would be "reborn as a human." His answer was delivered offstage a few minutes later, but the radiant glow on the woman's face after the talk suggested she was satisfied with his reply.

It went like this at each stop: adoring crowds of Tibetan and Western devotees clutched prayer beads and ivory-white prayer scarves, some weeping as they basked in the glow of their (other) "living Buddha." The Karmapa is not the religious rock star that the Dalai Lama is; crowds are smaller, and Chinese protesters nonexistent. But those closest to the Karmapa believe strongly that his time is coming, and that the future of the Tibetan struggle will soon rest squarely on his shoulders. According to one official account of his ten-day UK visit, the "double arch of a luminous rainbow" appeared at one of the stops, mythmaking proportional to his stature.

My interview with the enlightened, rainbow-drenched monk took place on the morning of May 27, on his final day of public events in the United Kingdom, at a retreat center on the banks of a swan-filled lake about an hour from Central London in Surrey. Sandwiched in between morning prayers and an afternoon talk with Tibetan and Nepali Buddhists, a twenty-minute block was placed in His Holiness's schedule.

When I arrived at around ten, on an overcast, blustery morning, thousands were already queued up, waiting to pass through security, which had been tightened after the terrorist attack at a pop concert in Manchester a few days earlier. My escort met me in the parking lot and whisked me past the full-body scanners and gun-toting British agents, into a back room behind the stage where the Karmapa would be speaking later that day.

The scene was a far cry from the fortresslike setting in which I had met the Dalai Lama eight years earlier. In McLeod Ganj, teams of Indian military sentries and Tibetan officers dug through my belongings, scanned me with metal wands, clicked my camera, and seemed to study my very intentions. In Surrey, I more or less walked right in.

The meeting room where we talked was equally surreal. Unlike the ornate reception room that the Dalai Lama occupies, the Karmapa's domain that morning was sparse. On the walls of the lounge at the Lakeside International Hotel were photos of world dart champions—men and women who, since the 1970s, had conquered the arena of professionally tossing pointed missiles at cork. Each January, the Lakeside lodge is the epicenter of the competitive dart world. In a corner of the room, a bar, which I assumed was reserved for the players to imbibe before (and possibly during) their quest for glory, was shuttered with a rolling chain gate.

The Karmapa's handler opted for seats in the far corner, near a window overlooking the lake. Before the Tibetan leader walked into the room, we tried to tidy up as best we could, to make it suitable for the presence of such a prominent religious figure. We swapped out a plush lounge chair burned with cigarette ash, and placed a few bottles of water on the table, angled out of view of the bar. But for the most part, the blemished, imperfect setting fit the stage of a Tibetan superstar in the ascendant. The interview room was, just like the Karmapa's brand, a work in progress.

Time was short, and the Karmapa, like the Dalai Lama, does enough interviews with Indian and Western media that I was keen to avoid repeating questions he had addressed elsewhere. A few weeks earlier, for example, he had offered an interviewer an intriguing summary of life for Tibetans in India: as many as five thousand Tibetans were leaving every year, he said, headed for the West or back to China, pushed out because of a lack of "proper rights" in their host country.[16] Had I had unlimited time, I would have explored these thoughts more deeply, given that most Tibetan leaders shy away from offering even a hint of dissatisfaction with India's refugee policies. But with only twenty minutes, I opted to use my brief window to zero in on a place he knows better than most: China.

I asked him how Tibetans might connect with the Chinese people, if not the government, to facilitate an eventual return to Tibet. Dialogue, I suggested, was the only way to move the Tibet issue forward—but where to start?

"Tibet and China have had a relationship for a very long time," the Karmapa began, stroking his chin as he leaned back in the non-cigarette-burned chair. "From among Tibet's neighbors, the two most influential have been India and China, throughout history. From a spiritual perspective, the most influential has been India. But from a more secular, or temporal, perspective—our food, our clothing, and many of our habits come to us from China. I really have the outlook that Tibetans and Chinese are siblings."

How practical is that, I wondered, to think of the Chinese as Tibetans' brothers and sisters, rather than as enemies? Many Tibetans I had met over the last eight years had a far more vitriolic view.

"There have of course been some difficulties in recent history in the relationship," he continued, bluntly. "And because of these difficulties, there is a little bit, some bad blood, on the level of feeling from Tibetans toward Chinese. A little bit. But there is still a closeness of mind and a closeness of heart that exists between Tibetan people and Chinese people. And that's a very important connection for us to acknowledge, and keep and build upon."

I looked into His Holiness's eyes as he spoke, observing an intensity that I hadn't noticed in the Dalai Lama. Unlike the jovial head of the Gelug sect, who often appears more at ease standing beside late-night comics than heads of state, the Karmapa is more serious, and deeply contemplative. At times, he can even appear uneasy in his role. The protégé doesn't laugh as easily as his teacher, and the seriousness might be off-putting to Western audiences. But he also delivers his views with such gravity that one feels he has been contemplating for years the very question he was just asked.

"In terms of the difficulties," he went on, "you could say it's not really a difficulty between the Tibetans and the Chinese. It's actually more of a difficulty between the Tibetan people and the policies of the Communist Party of China. It's not really personal, when you look at the matter carefully. And so, it's very important for us to have harmonious relations with the Chinese, and promote harmony, to maintain whatever harmony is there, and build on that with further efforts."

He continued: "There are some people who talk about exerting pressure on China from the outside in order to ameliorate the Tibetan issue. But, I think, at the end of the day, the only hope we have is for the change to be coming directly from harmony between Tibetan people and Chinese people. At the end of the day, there's no other method than that to improve the situation. Maintaining this connection of harmony and building upon it, in the direct relationship itself, is our greatest hope."

With that, the Karmapa stood up, signaling that my brief but hopeful conversation with Tibet's future leader had come to an end. As he disappeared through a side door, just beyond the shuttered bar and the framed pictures of dart champions on the wood-paneled walls, I reflected on what he had just said. Blessings, he seemed to be saying, are most effective when bestowed peacefully.

In a humble housing project a few hundred feet below the Dalai Lama's monastery, another Tibetan pursues his own strategy for living without a country. Quiet, cautious, and reserved, Tenzin Choephal, the eldest son of "Pala" Purang Dorjee, is unwilling to challenge his fate with ferocity, or to sell his views for access to his homeland.

Instead, he has chosen a path that, in the long run, might prove more effective: embracing his refugee status. In doing so, the dutiful son, responsible brother, loving father, and dedicated government employee is the type of Tibetan refugee China may never be able to box in.

I hadn't seen Tenzin since we roomed together in McLeod Ganj in the winter of 1997, when I lived with his family off Bhagsu Road. So when I received an informal invitation to join his family over the New Year's holiday in 2016, I quickly accepted. The Dalai Lama was scheduled to return from an extended stint in South India that month, and while his teachings for the year had been canceled because of health concerns (he just needed rest, Tibetan officials insisted), his return would mean a critical mass of Tibetans, expatriates, and scholars with whom to connect. Tenzin's invitation only sweetened the deal.

As with past visits, simply arriving in McLeod Ganj was exhausting. I had hired a car from the guesthouse to meet me at the airport in New Delhi, assuming that traffic over a twelve-hour road trip was more predictable than the flight path and weather over the mountains. But my Tibetan driver, who was in his forties, had spent his entire life in India's northern provinces, much of it as a soldier in India's Tibetan border force, and from the moment we left the terminal we were lost (we couldn't even find the car), and it took two hours to locate the road north once we did start driving. As the car sat idling in Delhi traffic, a thick blanket of diesel exhaust consuming the hood, the driver's bewilderment with his adopted homeland's capital city seemed to underscore his people's presence as perpetual outsiders in India.

For Tenzin, however, being an outsider has its advantages.

We met the next day near his office at the Kashag, a four-story yellow-and-red-trimmed building that serves as the parliament building of the government in exile. Not one for formalities, the wiry thirty-seven-year-old smiled when he saw me, but instead of a handshake or hello he just motioned for me to follow and turned up the hill in silence. By comparison with his father—the man who once said everyone in McLeod Ganj knows him "because I talk to everyone"—Tenzin seemed more timid.

Twenty years had passed, but he looked the same: with a round jaw and face, and a high forehead that peaks at a small tuft of jet-black hair, he looks a bit like Charlie Brown in his later years.

We headed for his apartment, a small one-bedroom flat in a dimly lit concrete building that houses employees of the Central Tibetan Administration. In the front foyer—an exposed, windblown patio framing the sweeping Kangra Valley—motorcycles, scooters, and bicycles leaned against the wall. Despite having small windows, lacking heat, and sitting in shadow at midday, the building had a homey, safe feel, the kind of place where children are looked after by whichever adult happens to be in the vicinity. One of the neighbors' kids, a five-year-old named Gyalpo, chased a ball near the parked cycles as Tenzin walked in.

Tenzin's home was furnished in typical Tibetan fashion: in one corner a small television flickered on, mute, and against the adjacent walls beds that double as couches were covered in handwoven Tibetan-style carpets. Above the door, paintings of Buddhist deities—Chenrezig and Palden Lhamo—peered knowingly into the living room. Photos from past family holidays smiled back. On normal days there was plenty of room for his wife and seven-year-old daughter to spread out, but during holidays, the room and adjoining kitchen can feel sticky and cramped. When I visited, a niece and the couple's eldest daughter (who is normally at school in a town twelve hours away) were both staying, bringing the house total to five in a space that most New Yorkers would have to themselves.

Eventually the small talk turned to silence, and Tenzin filled it by suggesting a walk along the kora, the same path I had once frequented with his father. His chosen predinner activity made Tenzin something of an anomaly in McLeod Ganj, as many young Tibetan refugees have since abandoned the ritualistic aspects of Buddhism.[1] I eagerly accepted, laced up my shoes, and followed his lead out the door and up the hill. Tenzin came alive within a few minutes of pushing through the crisp evening air, firing off what seemed like more questions than he had asked during the entire winter that we roomed together. At the time I was living in the United Arab Emirates, and he wondered deeply about my life across the Indian Ocean.

"Abu Dhabi, that's in the Middle East, right? And it's Muslim? What kind of government? So it's not democratic? That means you can't say what you want to say, or question the government? And the president, he's like a king, has full power, full control?"

I replied quickly with one- and two-syllable answers, partly to keep pace with the rapidity of his inquiry, but mostly because the town's elevation of sixty-eight hundred feet had sucked the wind out of me: "Yes," "Yes," "Tribal," "No," "Right," "Kind of," I said in between gasps of air as we plodded uphill.

We kept walking and talking, dodging cars and motorbikes as the sun dipped below the horizon and the dim, blinding headlights of oncoming traffic sent us balancing on sidewalks that tumble off steep cliffs into darkness. I asked him about his kids, their education, and his own educational ambitions. He never went to college, but he regretted it. Back then, in high school, college "was useless, just wasting time," he said. His sense of duty as his father's eldest son pushed him toward the family business and the running of Shop No. 5, following his father's retirement in 2000.

"How big of a problem is ISIS?" in the Middle East, he wondered as we passed the security gate along the back of His Holiness's residence. Two Indian soldiers shouldering assault rifles looked up from their conversation as we walked by. "It's ever-present, but a strong security presence has so far kept the threat out of the UAE," I said. The idea that strong security might mean trading some freedoms for others seemed to satisfy his curiosity for the time being. "Modi is a confident leader; I like that quality," he said of the Indian prime minister, nodding, in somewhat of a non sequitur.

We continued to plod uphill, and we continued to query the contours of each other's lives. In 2000 he graduated from a local Tibetan high school and started assuming shop responsibilities full time. By 2002 he was married (he met his bride while working behind the counter of Shop No. 5, just as his father had), and before he knew it he "never really pursued college." By the time he was twenty-three, his life as a permanent refugee shopkeeper appeared set in stone.

I was surprised by Tenzin's chosen path, given my memories of him during our time as roommates, and the stacks of geography, math, and English text-books piled high on his nightstand. He once described school as his job; "My only job is to study. In this I've done my duty," he said. But by 2002, he was content.

Then, one evening during the winter of 2004, an electrical short-circuit in a restaurant above the family store—ironically called the "Kailash" eatery, named after the mountain in Western Tibet where his father, Purang Dorjee, was raised—erupted into a five-alarm blaze, engulfing a dozen buildings in the center of McLeod Ganj. "It was in the middle of the night, around eleven or twelve. Somebody came to our house and shouted that fire had broken out, so we rushed there," Tenzin said. "When we got there, fire was raging across all of the shops. All were damaged. We could not do anything."

It would take over a year to rebuild. During that period of limbo, Tenzin, out of work and in need of a paycheck, found a job with the Tibetan government in exile. He was clever and a quick study; despite no formal training, he was offered a job as a plumber to ensure that the water supply to Tibetan offices in Dharamsala flowed smoothly. The posting offered more stability—better pay, shorter hours, a pension, and an apartment—than he had ever known, so he readily accepted, hanging up his shopkeeper's apron, he hopes, forever. When the store reopened a year later, it was his younger brother, Kalden, standing behind the glass counter.

As we meandered past the main market, not far from the store that Tenzin had said goodbye to, it struck me that his hometown appeared less Tibetan than it ever had; Indians were discovering it in droves. A few days earlier, as I was sipping tea inside the Moonpeak Thali Restaurant on Temple Road, an Indian teenager on holiday with her parents said that when she looked up Dharamsala and McLeod Ganj online, "the only thing I thought was here was a cricket stadium. I had no idea *this* was here," she said, motioning out the window to throngs of tourists, backpackers, and Tibetan families among a sea of jewelry stands, stacked carpets, Kashmiri brocades, and wool hats. A five-story parking garage opened in 2015 to accommodate the expected tourist surge, and plans were in the works to convert parts of the village into a Disney-style pedestrian-only Buddhist resort, complete with a cable car from lower Dharamsala—capable of moving over one thousand people an hour.[2] Even the vendors hawking "Special Tibetan Momos"—the venerable Tibetan dumplings—in McLeod Ganj these days are Indian.

I asked Tenzin if his place of birth felt like his home, now or ever.

"No, it's not mine, but that's okay; I feel happy that this place is famous," he said. "When I travel, people ask me where I've come from. When I say 'Dharamsala' they are really surprised; everybody knows about my hometown. When people come from other [Tibetan] settlements, they don't know those names. But . . . everybody knows Dharamsala. This is a small place, but a famous place," thanks to the Dalai Lama.

After we completed our lap around the Tibetan leader's home, we turned back down the hill to Tenzin's for dinner. Careful not to tumble off the slope in what was by then total darkness, I asked him if he had ever considered becoming an Indian citizen. Tibetans born in India are entitled to citizenship, but for a number of reasons, few Tibetans are ever able to exercise this right. (The opposite is true in the United States, Canada, and many other Western destinations, where Tibetans who are lucky enough to migrate have had an easier time securing a foreign passport.) If he was so content with Dharamsala, I prodded, maybe it was time to secure his legal right to reside in India, and trade in his life of uncertainty for something more permanent.

Tenzin bristled at the suggestion. "The Dalai Lama has said that something is coming," Tenzin replied. And that "something," he said, is that all Tibetans will return to Tibet before the Dalai Lama dies. "Why would I want Indian citizenship? Our identity is Tibetan."

"Can't you have both?" I asked. "Can't you retain your identity and still have a passport from a country not of your birth?"

"Why would we need it?" he wondered, incredulous. "I have faith that I don't."

And with that, he pushed open the door to his house and sat down for dinner.

———

Tenzin's reaction to the question of legal status in India is not uncommon among Tibetan exiles. The government of India does not recognize Tibetans in India as "refugees," but as "foreigners." This legal definition allows for the national government to regulate Tibetans' movements and requires them to regularly register with the Indian authorities.

Given this legal rubric, Tibetans in India have long relied on separate documents issued by the Indian government—"Indian Registration Certificates for Tibetans," or RCS. A valid RC, which proves a Tibetan's identity and right to reside in India, is needed for another Indian-issued document that is akin to a passport, called an Identity Certificate (which is required for travel purposes). But as Oxford University's Fiona McConnell notes, "RCS and ICS are issued only to Tibetans with de facto 'refugee status,' meaning that those Tibetans who arrived in India after 1979 are denied this document and the rights and entitlements that go with it."[3] Indeed, many Tibetans in India live in a state of constant flux, fearful that they will be arrested, fined, and even deported because they don't possess the proper documents (deportations, though rare, are not unheard of).

"The police, they came to my area and knocked on doors wanting to see RCS," one refugee told McConnell. "But I don't have RC yet, so every time I have argument and every time I must pay bribes. For this I am scared."

Technically, Tibetans who have lived their entire lives in India should have more stability. According to the Indian Citizenship Act of 1955, anyone born on Indian lands between January 26, 1950, and July 1, 1987, "shall be a citizen of India by birth." Tenzin, who was born in 1978, could, on paper at least, secure an Indian passport if he wanted one. But law in India is rarely black and white, and the de facto policy has been to deny most Tibetans who apply. Tibetans who have tried to push back say they have been met with shrugs, stalling, and bureaucratic delays. Despite signs in late 2017 of a thaw, change remained slow. Hiring a lawyer to upend this reality can cost upward of 100,000 Indian rupees,[4] simply out of the question for Tibetans with an average annual household income of around 80,000 rupees (about $1,300).[5]

Even with the cash and the desire, though, Tenzin would face steep odds against overturning his guest status. Only a handful of Indian-born Tibetans have publicized their success in wresting a passport from the Indian courts. One, a flamboyant artist and entertainer named Lobsang Wangyal (he organizes, among other ventures, the annual Miss Tibet pageant), earned his legal victory in the Delhi High Court in September 2016.[6]

But most Indian-born Tibetans share Tenzin's hesitancy and are unwilling to brave the spotlight that a publicized court battle would entail, or that the law may allow. Despite their pacifist reputation, Tibetans can be ruthlessly judgmental. One of the first Tibetans to win her case in the courts was an ambitious, petite young woman named Namgyal Dolkar. In 2011, at just twenty-five years old, she took on the legal establishment in New Delhi, and won. Today she works for an organization in McLeod Ganj that assists former Tibetan political prisoners. While she insists she doesn't regret her decision, taking it has made her something of a pariah in her community.

"It's easy for the exile community to just come out and judge," she told me a few years after her court victory. "But if people find it wrong, with all due respect they can . . . " she said, stopping herself.

"It's never possible to erase you roots, your blood, your bone—you can never do that," she continued. Even with an Indian passport, "I still remain a Tibetan, and say it with pride."

Nonetheless, when other Tibetans quietly seek her advice on doing the same thing—and plenty do, she said—she always asks if they are certain they want to move forward. "It's not an easy road. It involves filing a case against the government of India. It's not very comfortable."

Citizenship isn't the only promised benefit Tibetans in India struggle with. At the state level, application of federal statutes intended to ensure protection of the Tibetan refugee community—like school access and home ownership—is woefully uneven. In 2014, the Indian federal government issued a decree intended to close this gap. Known as the Tibetan Rehabilitation Policy, the order sought to bring uniformity to how Tibetans are treated, and called on state governments to ensure that Tibetans are afforded the same rights as citizens to work, vote, lease land, gain citizenship, and access federal welfare schemes.

Lobsang Sangay, the prime minister of the Tibetan government in exile, has insisted that the Indian government's policy will bring "clarity in India" for the Tibetan diaspora. He told me in October 2014 that Tibetans "might have some insecurity as for their status, their job prospects, things like that" before the rehabilitation policy. But with the document in place, "it's pretty clear, [our] status is clear."

———

A few days after my walking conversation with Tenzin, I invited Pala's eldest son to join me for an interview with his father at his childhood home. Ostensibly I needed a translator, but I also wanted Tenzin and his father in the same room, to learn what I could about the family dynamic. Over a bowl of rice and lentils, with Tenzin as my proxy, I asked Pala personal questions about his life, his family, and the patriarch's own hopes and dreams for his children, including the one sitting cross-legged across from me.

"What do you want for your children? Are you proud of them?" I pondered aloud, nodding for Tenzin to translate my every word.

Laughter. Tenzin and his wife, who had joined us for the visit, rocked back and forth uneasily, pointing fingers at the other as if to say, "I'm not asking that, you do it." The question apparently crossed an invisible guru-disciple line that informally governs Tibetans' relationship with their parents.

Tenzin tried to answer on his father's behalf, without posing the question. "All parents want the same thing, I think, for their children: to be educated," the son said.

"What about citizenship?" I pushed him to ask his father. "What would your dad say about your decision to not pursue it in India?"

More laughter.

"If His Holiness says 'Stay here,' then all Tibetans should stay," Tenzin eventually said, composing himself to again speak for Dorjee. "If His Holiness says that all Tibetans have to go back home, we will follow his orders."

Relatives, it turns out, make lousy translators in Little Lhasa. I thanked Tenzin and his wife, and I arranged to return to Dorjee's house the next day, this time with a professional translator to probe more easily into his views on raising children in exile. The subsequent conversation was only slightly more personal, but his answers underscored what many first-generation Tibetan refugees say they feel about their culture in exile: it's on the move again, and not in good way.

"What's best for your children—to stay in India, as four of them have, or to try and build a life abroad, like your youngest daughter?" I asked (this time, thankfully, to contemplative silence and no snickers).

"Son, daughter, the same: stay in one place, focus on work and slowly, you get better. If they choose to stay in India, then make roots. But regardless of where, stay in one place rather than go to all different places. I've been here, McLeod, for so many years, since the beginning. They should follow my lead, settle in one place, and make it their own."

By this measure, Tenzin—a self-taught plumber who once thought college was a waste of time—was exceeding expectations.

"For Tibetans, unlike Indians or foreigners, who want their kids to be doctors, or lawyers, for us, it's nothing as big. For us, we just want our children to be good. Good, and successful. Someday, when I'm not here, all of these properties will be given to my children. When I'm not here, I just want them to be . . . successful and good."

Dorjee's insistence that to be "good" his children must "stay in one place" might sound simple. But for Tibetan "foreigners" in India, life rarely is. Sometimes it's Indian citizens themselves pushing Tibetans to leave.

In April 2012, an Indian resident of Himachal Pradesh named Pawan Kumar filed a civil petition with the state's high court in Shimla, alleging that Tibetans living along Bhagsu Road in McLeod Ganj were squatting on protected forestland.[7] The suit claimed that hundreds of Tibetan refugees, the religious and touristic lifeblood of Little Lhasa, were illegally occupying land in violation of the federal Forest Conservation Act of 1980, which forbade most development. Demolition crews were mobilized, and according to the United States–based Tibet Justice Center, the notices were part of an effort to use the Indian courts to challenge Tibetans' habitation of the subcontinent.

The house in which Tenzin was raised—the very one I had stayed in during the winter of 1997, with its pink-painted concrete walls, blue balconies, and squat toilet—was among those slated for demolition. The house sits amid a sea of refugee-inhabited concrete, and the only outwardly "forested" elements are a few conifers clinging to the hillside. Tibetans began building homes in the early 1960s, on parcels originally gifted by the state government. There they constructed shacks of tin and tarp, and by the 1980s most had been replaced by buildings of steel, brick, and concrete. Today, there is nothing temporary about them.

Judges considering Kumar's petition wrote that upon hearing arguments they were "not only concerned with the encroachment cases of forest land by the Tibetans but also by Indian citizens." The court ordered the regional forest department to produce "a detailed list of all the encroachers." The judges also called for local officials to identify "what steps have been taken by them to ensure that the rocks and big boulders are not defaced and that the persons who have either carved on the rocks or have painted the rocks are dealt with in accordance with law."[8]

The following month, the court reported "a shocking state of affairs," as further investigation revealed some 1,090 homes had been built on thousands of acres of the state's "forested" property.[9] In most of those cases, eviction orders were drawn up. Bulldozers arrived. Tibetans were given until March 31, 2013, to move.

This should have been the end of the road for the Tibetan homes of Bhagsu Road—including the cold, dark, fourth-floor room behind the brown metal door where Tenzin had once studied for his future. Should have been, but wasn't. Local officials managed to put off the demolitions, and in early 2015, the state government ordered an indefinite stay of eviction,[10] overruling the lower courts, and confirming that it was the Tibetans' status as "foreigners" and *not* citizens that saved them. One media report concluded that the government of Himachal Pradesh didn't want to follow through with the evictions "as their culmination may create law and order problem(s) and the issue could have serious international ramifications."[11] Pushing out Tibetans, which might have been seen as a boon to China, would have caused serious political headaches for New Delhi.

Officials of the Tibetan government in exile later told me it was Tibetans' nonlegal status as guests that, ironically, allowed for the reprieve. Hundreds of homes were targeted for demolition, including over a thousand dwellings owned by Indians. Many of the Indian-owned structures were indeed taken down. None of the Tibetan dwellings were touched. "If those 218 Tibetan families are Indian citizens, then the law will be equal to them, they will be evicted," Sonam Dorgee, the Tibetans' settlement officer for Dharamsala, said. "But because the 218 Tibetan families are 'refugees,' [they] have a special status that doesn't allow them to be evicted; Tibetans are treated as the esteemed guests of this country."

Implicit in Sonam's analysis was the belief that evictions would have had political costs for India. But they also would have meant that the Tibetan government in exile wasn't able to protect its own people, which in turn would have raised doubts about the legitimacy of the Dalai Lama and his Central Tibetan Administration—a failure Tibetans and their supporters cannot afford and New Delhi has yet to advocate.

"When it comes to Tibetans having Indian citizenship, you'll find benefits and advantages to the individual, but disadvantages to the community," Sonam concluded. "That's how we look at it. We have no objections, but at the same time we never encourage Tibetans to get citizenship."

In other words, it's the Tibetan administration itself that has the most to lose should Tibetans en masse hand in their RC cards for the navy and gold of an Indian passport.

———

Tenzin was in a more talkative mood the next time we met, for an early dinner at a guesthouse up the hill from the path we had walked a few days earlier. Before we had even ordered, he was speaking slowly into my microphone, answering some of the same questions he had been too shy to ask his own dad—about dreams, passions, fears, and hopes for his family and the Tibetan people. We talked for hours over plates of steamed vegetable dumplings, stuffed pastries, and rounds of lemon honey ginger tea.

He spoke passionately about friends, family, and being a father. His young daughter, who had joined us for dinner (and spent most of it eating ketchup with toothpicks, picking the cheese out of her momos with her hands, and playing an obnoxious dice game on her dad's cell phone), was a source of pride, and frustration. "She doesn't listen to anything I say," Tenzin said, expressing a fatherly concern the world over. "She's always fighting with me."

But his commitment to her future was resolute. "I have the responsibility for my two daughters. My duty is to give them a good education. Whether they want to be a singer, an engineer, that's up to them. My duty is to help them get an education . . . the best education. What they do in the future, that's up to them."

I asked him whether securing the future he envisioned was easier now that he had managed to escape working in his father's shop and landed a good job with the Tibetan government.

"Working for CTA? It's good. We get a salary, we are not volunteering, and on top of that, I am doing something for my country. I mean, I'm not burning myself for Tibet; but working in the CTA, I am doing something for my country, providing a basic need for the people. . . . It's a small contribution from my side."

As the final plate of steamed dumplings found its way to our corner of the restaurant, I prodded Tenzin one last time on his long-term plans. Tibetan government types had their views regarding Indian citizenship. But individual security was surely something Tibetan parents like Tenzin must consider, for their children at least. China will certainly push India to distance itself from the Tibetan diaspora once the Dalai Lama is dead, I suggested. Wouldn't an Indian passport protect his family from this fate?

"I worry about this town after His Holiness is gone," I conceded. "Don't you worry about what comes next?"

"Sometimes I worry, yeah, when I think about His Holiness not being with us. What will be the things that are going to change? Is it going to be worse, or is it going to be better? I don't think it's going to be better. But I don't dwell on this. It's going to be okay. After all, His Holiness has said things will change, and I have full faith in him that things are going to change in his life. We will go back to our country, in his life."

He continued: "His Holiness meets world leaders everywhere, all the leaders. He talks to them, and he knows what they think about the Tibet issue. So if the Dalai Lama says things are going to change, there is a reason that he is saying it. We don't know what's going to happen tomorrow. Nobody knows what's going to happen tomorrow. But when His Holiness says things are going to change, yeah, things will."

"I hope he's right," I said as I stood up to find the waiter and pay the bill. "I hope you're both right."

Unlike in Nepal, Beijing doesn't appear to dictate immigration policy to New Delhi, and Tibetans in India cannot directly blame China for their current legal ambiguity there. But Tibetans' unflinching devotion to their leadership's political skills, coupled with Beijing's unwillingness to engage diplomatically, has created a dangerous stalemate. As Tibetans bet on détente in lieu of citizenship, they risk passing the badge of statelessness on to their children. Leaving such matters to faith is one leap these refugees may come to regret.

It was about a year after my visit with the Dalai Lama that Tibetans inside Tibet began immolating themselves to prove a point. By March 2011, issues like China's restrictions on religion and bans on the use of the Tibetan language in schools had pushed some Tibetans to search for new ways to express their outrage. To many, fire had an intoxicating appeal.

I was living in Abu Dhabi working as a journalist at the time, and editors at my newspaper in the United Arab Emirates—a short three-hour flight from the Indian capital—saw similarities between Tibetans' self-immolations and the wave of burnings that were rippling across the Middle East during the Arab Spring. They wondered whether Tibet, and therefore China, were headed toward its own "spring" of destabilization. I wondered whether this type of protest, for a marginalized minority with slowing growth rates, was self-defeating.[1] In February 2012, I returned to McLeod Ganj to look into both.

One of the freshest immolation deaths that winter was by a young man and former monk named Losang Jamyang. On January 14, 2012, in the Eastern Tibetan city of Ngaba, Losang locked himself into a dingy bathroom near a public square, pulled a bottle of kerosene from his cloak, and took a drink. He splashed the remaining fuel on his clothing, and when he emerged from the stall seconds later, tentacles of flame trailed his wiry, twenty-two-year-old frame. Cameras clicked surreptitiously as he ran through the Ngaba town square, shouting prayers for the Dalai Lama's long life and safe return to Tibet. Less than a minute after lighting himself, Losang dropped to his knees, gasping for air that wouldn't come. A man-eating blanket of flame engulfed him.

Tibetan witnesses described what happened next: Chinese public security police surrounded the charred figure, but instead of extinguishers or blankets they brought batons. When onlookers moved in to collect Losang's lifeless body, authorities blocked their path. Demonstrations turned violent, and dozens of Ngaba residents were injured in the ensuing scuffle. Two were reportedly shot.[2]

Weeks later a video surfaced online of Losang's final moments.[3] The composition is shaky, the sound poor, and the authenticity of the footage uploaded to YouTube impossible to verify (it was obtained and posted by Free Tibet, a UK-based advocacy group, three months after it was reportedly filmed inside Tibet). Advocates say it depicts Losang's final moments, recorded from the upper floors of a building in the Ngaba main square. As the camera rolls, food vendors and shopkeepers mill about in the mid-morning chill. In the foreground, people out for a Saturday stroll amble into the center of the frame. One maroon-clad monk pushing a vegetable cart pauses to crane his neck as a crowd gathers near a busy intersection. A young lady in a pink jacket pushes forward for a better view.

By the time Losang appears on screen it's as a human fireball. Five seconds into the video, a police car rolls up. At eight seconds, the monk pushing the vegetable cart stops walking. Two seconds later, a blast of orange and black rises from the street, and the girl in the pink jacket—her back to the camera—stands motionless as she gets swallowed by the crowd.

A few thousand miles away, on the other side of the world's tallest mountains, a young man about Losang's age awaited news of his friend's fate. Tenzin Norbu, a twenty-two-year-old refugee who escaped to India in 2004, grew up in the same town as Losang in Tibet.[4] And in the winter of 2012, Tenzin had a message to deliver to the world on behalf of the recently departed.

By the time I had arrived in McLeod Ganj, Tenzin was ready to talk about his friend's sacrifice. He asked a local human rights group if any foreign journalists were in town. The media director of an advocacy group I had worked with previously gave Tenzin my number. Minutes after my phone rang, I was seated at a table across from an anxious, wiry figure at a restaurant a few paces from my guesthouse.

Tenzin and I sat in a low wooden stall near the café's front door. A young, rosy-cheeked waitress floated around the stools with mugs of steaming lattes topped in artistically drawn foam. A few booths over, a middle-aged Westerner was attached to an iPod, his head buried in a computer and a plate of eggs. Outside, beyond the picture window, scenes unfolded in a sea of red and marigold: camera-toting tourists and dreadlocked trekkers mingled with Indian pilgrims and Buddhist monks.

As we sipped one round of lemon honey ginger tea after another, in the relative calm of exile, I could sense Losang's rage burning through his proxy. Tenzin explained why he thought his friend had lit the match that day.

"Why did he do it, self-immolation?" Tenzin said. "I don't think he saw any other option. If you raise your voice, you are going to be kicked down. If you say the truth, China is going to put you in prison. There is no other way to raise your voice." For Losang, Tenzin said, death was the only way to "do something special" for Tibet.

Tenzin had pieced together his friend's final days through conversations with people back home—WeChat conversations, e-mails, the occasional phone call, all unsecure forms of communication that carry great risk for people inside Tibet. There are plenty of holes in Losang's story. Tenzin can't return to Tibet to fill them in, and foreign journalists have had their access to the region curtailed since the unrest and subsequent crackdown in 2008. Moreover, Losang told no one of his plans to sacrifice his body, and offered only cryptic bread crumbs for people to follow once he was gone. Some believe he died to make a statement against Chinese bans on the teaching of the Tibetan language. Others believe it was an act of youthful rebellion. Others still see ties to his former monastic days as the fuel.

Yet this much is certain: of the 143 Tibetans who immolated themselves between February 2009 and September 2015, only a handful had their stories retold with any frequency. Losang was an exception. His name was circulated in Congress, inked in newspapers from Abu Dhabi to Washington, and blurted over airwaves around the world.[5] Losang's defiant act lives on. His friend, Tenzin Norbu, is the reason why.

——— ——— ———

Losang woke early on the day he delivered on his promise to "do something" special for Tibet. Before dawn he asked a neighbor to drive him to town, stopping on the way to circle his old monastery. He rambled on about the importance of keeping Tibetan culture alive amid unrelenting Chinese oppression; he was particularly concerned about the future of the spoken Tibetan language. When they stopped to stretch their legs, Losang counseled a recently divorced couple to get back together. At around 1:30 p.m., as his companion finished eating at a restaurant in Ngaba, a city of monks and nomads on the eastern edge of the Tibetan Plateau, Losang excused himself to go to the bathroom. Moments later he streaked violently toward the city's main square.

Losang wasn't the first Tibetan from Ngaba (which the Chinese call Aba) to immolate himself. He was the twelfth. But he was the first non-monk from central Sichuan Province older than twenty to use fire to protest China's policies in Tibet (though he had lived as a monk as an adolescent, he had left the monastery a few years earlier). Days after he died, people began arriving from hundreds of miles away to pay their respects. "The family was being sent gifts from Kham, and people were coming from as far away as Lhasa," Tenzin said.[6] It's a bone-shaking forty-hour drive from Lhasa to Ngaba, a duration Tenzin believes underscores the sense of solidarity that his friend's act of sacrifice inspired. In Tibet, violent deaths were becoming a unifying balm.

Losang Jamyang was not born a martyr; he was made one. Raised in a simple mud-and-timber home beneath the snowy peaks of the eastern Himalayas, he spent his childhood toiling in the fields, an extra set of hands to feed the family. During the summer, when the barley was waist-high and warm mountain breezes kept the snow away, Losang and his three siblings would join their parents in the steppes above the village, living in yak-hair tents as they foraged for medicinal herbs to sell to Chinese traders. Like most of the 150 or so families who made up their cloistered community, his family was poor; herb harvests were the principal source of income for the entire year.

As a boy Losang was scrawny, stooped and slight, the opposite of his father, Gyatso, a brawny and barrel-chested farmer of over six feet. One photograph of Losang, taken not long before he died, shows him seated hunched in the saddle of a cherry-red Honda motorcycle, no helmet to cover his flop of jet-black hair. He couldn't have weighed more than 120 pounds.

When he was eleven, his parents enrolled him at the small Gelug Andu monastery a few hours away from his village by motorbike. And like all Tibetan boys who leave home to become monks, he spent much of his days collecting water, serving tea, and meditating on the scriptures of the learned masters. For half a decade, focusing the mind became his discipline.

But at sixteen, Losang hung up the robes, in exchange for life as a layman and a student. He was pulled more by worldly pursuits than mindfulness and meditation. For a time he lived with friends in Ngaba, closer to his new school than his village. With the regimented schedule of monastery life over, Losang was free to roam. At night he would join mischievous monks to watch Jackie Chan films screened secretly at a small theater in the village. For the first time in his life, Losang could be a boy.

The freedom was short-lived, however. In March 2008, the banality of daily life—girls, movies, and school—was once again consumed, this time by a wave of Tibetan nationalism rolling over the plateau. Swept up in the moment, Tibetans used the Beijing Olympics to draw attention to their lives under Chinese rule. Losang and other Tibetans, some who had only heard stories from their parents of national resistance, were galvanized by the renewed sense of solidarity and defiance. Restrictions on Tibetan language, culture, religion, and politics were fuel for the demonstrations that spring. The games China was hosting were the spark.

As the Olympic torch wound its way across China, inching ever closer to the Tibetan capital, frustration among Tibetans reached a crescendo. Tibetans young and old took to the streets by the thousands, massing in the largest demonstrations inside Tibet since 1989. Beijing responded forcefully. Not far from Losang's village, Chinese police and security agents fanned out to quell the uprising. Helmeted soldiers and riot police stood shoulder to shoulder along the unpaved streets. Men with batons encircled the mighty Kirti Monastery, which was founded in the fifteenth century and once housed some twenty-five hundred monks. Mass arrests, shootings, beatings, and public shaming sessions intensified as spring went on. Some of the casualties were Losang's classmates.

The list of Tibetans' grievances that spring was long—bans on possessing the Dalai Lama's photo; Chinese control of Tibetan monasteries; the forced relocation of nomads from Tibet's sweeping grasslands into dreary communal housing blocks. But for many young Tibetans, including Losang, the most debasing policy was a plan Beijing had begun to implement to limit the use and study of the Tibetan language. In the Tibetan part of Western China where Losang was raised, Mandarin was replacing the Tibetan language in state-run schools. In one protest in November 2012, at a medical school near Tongren in Qinghai, more than one thousand students rallied after the distribution of Chinese-language textbooks that claimed in their introduction that the Tibetan language was "devoid of relevance" in modern China.[7]

Kate Saunders, a policy analyst at the International Campaign for Tibet, said that many of the self-immolators "raised the language issue as the bedrock of their grievance." One twenty-two-year-old self-immolator from Qinghai, Ngawang Norphel, seemed to speak for a generation when he declared from his hospital bed on June 20, 2012: "My people have no freedom of language. Everybody is mixing Tibetan and Chinese. If we don't have our freedom, cultural traditions and language, it would be extremely embarrassing for us. Every nationality needs freedom, language, and tradition. Without language, what would be our nationality? . . . Chinese or Tibetan?"[8]

Immolation was not Losang's first answer to those questions. In 2010, he and a group of friends started a program to encourage Tibetans to speak more Tibetan in their daily lives. It was civil disobedience with practical appeal. Friends who grew up speaking Mandarin reengaged with classical Tibetan script. With Losang's help, schoolchildren worked to become better communicators in their ancestors' tongue. Elderly *mo-mos* and *po-pos*—grandmothers and grandfathers—who hadn't studied traditional Tibetan for years began to dust off their vocabulary, inspired by Losang's nonviolent attempt to promote Tibetan tradition.

"They came and gave an examination about speaking the pure Tibetan language," Tenzin said. "This became so famous. Many, many people came to take the exam. Even my mother, who is in her sixties, she tries to speak pure Tibetan language. The impact of that program was so huge."

But there was a downside, too, which was proportionate to the program's success: just as some Tibetans were reconnecting with their linguistic heritage, Losang was discovering what it meant to be a wanted man in Chinese-controlled Tibet.

Chinese law officially protects minority languages, including Tibetan dialects. In autonomous regions (parts of Western and Northern China where Han are not the ethnic majority) this means that on paper, China's minorities should have more latitude in shaping language policies for education, business, and commerce. Article 4 of the Constitution of the People's Republic declares (somewhat hopefully) that people of all backgrounds "have the freedom to use and develop their own spoken and written languages, and to preserve or reform their own ways and customs." Taken alone, this might suggest that China is more enlightened than many modernizing countries that preceded it. The United States' Bureau of Indian Affairs, for example, suppressed the use of indigenous languages in federally run schools during the nineteenth and twentieth centuries, while the government of Turkey banned Kurdish songs and language in the Kurdish part of that country until 1991.

But Article 19 of the 1982 constitution undercuts many of the protections Article 4 would seem to enshrine. The later article declared that Mandarin (*Putonghua*, which means "common speech" and is based on Beijing pronunciation) should be promoted nationwide,[9] a declaration some have interpreted as a way to encourage "a supra-ethnic identity as 'citizens of China'" to emerge nationally.[10] And it is this law that has pushed minority dialects to the margins through linguistic "chauvinism."[11]

As far back as the Qin and Han dynasties (221 BC to AD 220), China's rulers pushed the dominant Han language and Confucian ideology in non-Han areas of the South and East. During the early years of communism, minority languages were initially encouraged, so long as their speakers remained active participants in the socialist project. But by the late 1950s, minority languages were deemed an impediment to unity by Mao. Propaganda at the time suggested minorities had "a new high tide of enthusiasm for learning Han" as they sought to erase "the linguistic hindrance to learning advanced ways."[12] Assimilation policies of the Cultural Revolution during the 1960s and 1970s put a further strain on minority culture, identity, and language.

Today, preference for Mandarin means that other languages—particularly those with political connotations, such as Uighur and Tibetan—are disadvantaged by default. The biggest challenge to the survival of Tibetans' linguistic heritage in particular may be practical. "Tibetans who are fluent in Tibetan find it hard to get good jobs, even in Qinghai," which is heavily populated with ethnic Tibetans, says Columbia University Tibet expert Robert Barnett.[13] "So in the longer term this is likely to act as a general economic disincentive for the future of Tibetan language, and the current renaissance faces serious risks and challenges unless progressive policies are introduced."

Tibetans in parts of historic Tibet—areas outside the Tibet Autonomous Region, where legal protections have received less attention—have made an effort to revitalize literary and spoken traditions. Tibetan poetry, music, religious texts, literature, and film even experienced a period of revival during the 1990s. But more recently, the increase of Han migration to the Tibet Autonomous Region, and rules mandating the use of Mandarin in school curriculum throughout Tibetans areas, have had a chilling effect on Tibetans' native language abilities. A 2015 rule by the Chinese Ministry of Education to "make sure that minority students master and use the basic common language" inflamed many young Tibetans further.[14]

This is the context in which Losang launched his Tibetan language education effort.

Eventually, though, his program was deemed illegal, and defiant participants were followed and threatened by police, Tenzin recalled. As the pressure mounted, friends and family members were also targeted, and an innocent attempt to reconnect people with their linguistic roots became just another failed attempt to respond to China's advances through nonviolence. With his Pure Tibetan Language Association no more, Losang, then twenty-two, faced a choice: concede defeat or continue to lead. In his mind, immolation was the only way to carry on.

———

If the point of self-immolation is to inspire solidarity—and sociologists say it can be—Losang was among a committed core. Over 125 Tibetans followed in his fiery footsteps, bringing to 143 the number who immolated themselves between February 2009 and September 2015. Forty-five of those hailed from Losang's hometown of Ngaba, in the Chinese province of Sichuan. Most were monks; Lobsang was among the first who wasn't.[15]

But mothers, fathers, goat herders, shopkeepers, shepherds, and high school students have all joined in the Tibetan parade of death. The youngest to die was a bright-eyed fifteen. The oldest, a farmer in his sixties, killed himself while circumambulating one of Tibet's holiest temples.[16] Some drafted letters to explain their actions. One, a twenty-six-year-old Tibetan refugee based in India named Jamphel Yeshi, wrote that he was choosing to die so that the world would wake up to Tibetans' suffering. Yet most Tibetan immolators appear to have acted with a very different audience in mind. Wang Lixiong, an expert on China's ethnic policies, says, given the few final statements that have been drafted, most Tibetans were directing their actions toward fellow Tibetans, not the international community. While Tibet's refugees have long sought global support, "Tibetans inside Tibet have finally realized that the struggle has to be on their own," Wang says.

People have traded their bodies to defend their beliefs for centuries. In Greco-Roman mythology, Heracles and Dido are believed to have ended their lives with fire, and legend holds that Croesus—king of Lydia, the ancient kingdom of Anatolia—did the same after his defeat to the Persians in the sixth century BC. Secular and highly visible self-sacrifices were also common during medieval times, when conscripts and consorts, barons and bodyguards all tossed themselves into the pyre at the cremation ceremonies of their kings and rulers—believing their oaths of fealty extended beyond this world and into the next.[17] In ancient India, Hindu women tossed themselves on their husband's funeral pyre in a similar fashion, practicing a now obsolete death ritual known as *sati*. More recently, poor Chinese workers have used their own suicides to bring attention to deplorable working conditions in factories that manufacture goods for Western markets.[18]

But it was Buddhists who perfected the fiery suicidal protest as a form of civil disobedience. The most enduring modern moment of Buddhist self-immolation took place in 1963, when Vietnamese monk Thich Quang Duc lit himself ablaze to protest the anti-Buddhist policies of Ngo Dinh Diem, the US-backed president who favored Vietnam's Christian minority. Yet the tactic has been popular for far longer. In imperial China, self-immolations were advertised and attended by officials and crowds of cheering onlookers. Monks martyred themselves to protest foreign invasions, or to show displeasure with declining support of patronage from the ruling classes. Some would swallow fragrant incense to ease the passage of their souls into the afterlife.[19]

Chinese scholars of Tibetan history argue that self-immolation is counter to the Buddhist doctrine of nonviolence. But Tibetan Buddhism has a rich if esoteric tradition of self-sacrifice. When only the immolator is harmed, death can be seen as a high form of religious devotion. The Lotus Sutra, a sacred text in Mahayana Buddhism, explains that only the most learned masters practiced self-sacrifice for the sake of protecting the dharma. An entire chapter of that text is devoted to self-immolation; the story of the so-called medicine king inspired Japanese Buddhists to immolate themselves as early as 1026.

And the Jataka Tales, Sanskrit volumes that tell the stories of the previous lives of the Buddha—and which are the subject of teachings that the Dalai Lama gives each spring from his monastery in McLeod Ganj—recount one incarnation who sacrificed himself to feed a starving tiger and her cubs. Legend has it that the Namo Buddha temple in Eastern Nepal is built atop the bones and hair that remained after the cats were finished feeding. It draws thousands of Tibetan pilgrims annually, including many who sneak across the Tibetan and Indian borders for a chance to pray in its shadows.

Today's Tibetan refugees treat self-immolators with a similar veneration. At the Martyrs' Memorial near the Dalai Lama's residence, names of Tibetans who have sacrificed their lives are etched in stone. Nearby, artistic sculptures show Tibetans with their fists raised and robes burning in defiance. Throughout town, monks meander the streets with "Tibet is burning" stitched onto their bags. Together they are physical reminders of the flesh-and-bone bonds between Tibetans in exile and their brethren across the border.

For the most part, however, self-immolations inside Tibet have been low-key, off-camera, and nearly invisible, nothing like the public entertainment of ancient times. Unlike Mohamed Bouazizi in Tunisia, whose death by fire was recorded by dozens of cameras and launched the Arab Spring in 2011, most Tibetans have died without fanfare. No more than a few hundred witnesses watched Losang Jamyang take his life in January 2012. China has never officially acknowledged the event. "Sharing information can get Tibetans killed," Kirti Rinpoche, the exiled abbot of the monastery in Ngaba, told me. "The local Chinese government sentences people who share information. Even if they are suspected of information sharing, they can be imprisoned."

— — —

How did it come to this? Why would Tibetan men, women, and teenagers take such pains to calculate their last breath in a horrific, desperate display of public sacrifice? And what was it about life inside Tibet that had made death a better option?

Tibetans' modern anger is rooted in decades of subjugation at the hands of the Communist Party of China. Following China's invasion of Eastern Tibet in October 1950, Tibetans, outgunned and outnumbered by Chinese forces, sent a team of delegates to Beijing to negotiate a way out of the impasse. Western democracies and the United Nations had already turned their backs on supporting Tibet's legitimate claims of sovereignty, and by May 1951, the Chinese government and delegates of the Dalai Lama reached an accord known as the Seventeen-Point Agreement for the Peaceful Liberation of Tibet. It was, in many respects, *zhi lao hu*—a paper tiger.

On its face, the document appeared sensitive to Tibetans' demands—it called for the continuation of Tibet's traditional social, political, and religious systems of governance, and in return asked for Tibetans to acknowledge that Tibet was an inalienable part of the Chinese "motherland." Yet almost immediately the document's lofty rhetoric fell short; China's plan for control of Tibet through "democratic reforms and socialist transformation" hinted at Beijing's true intentions.[20]

For one, the deal allowed the People's Liberation Army to establish military and administrative committees inside Tibet, seeming contradictions to previous vows of Tibetan autonomy. The document also legitimated a fracturing of historic Tibet, a costly miscalculation for Tibetans that saw huge swaths of Eastern Tibet (including Amdo and Kham) divided into subdistricts within Qinghai, Sichuan, Gansu, and Yunnan Provinces.

Despite these early signals, Mao Zedong and his communist colleagues continued to assure the Tibetans that the Chinese presence would be noninvasive and complementary. But realities on the ground suggested otherwise. Tibetan place names were replaced with Mandarin. Official histories were rewritten to denote Tibet before the communists' arrival as a feudal "hell." And propaganda tools—such as newspapers, magazines, books, and free outdoor movie screenings—were deployed to recast Tibet's religious history. In Mao's new China, class—not religion—was the defining characteristic of the masses.[21]

Yet Mao's plan for appeasing Tibet's masses—to show them the error of their Buddhist ways by unveiling a new class consciousness—backfired badly. Nationalist sentiment spiked, and in parts of Kham in Eastern Tibet, an organized resistance was mounted against the Chinese presence. During one confrontation in the spring of 1956, in Lithang (in today's southern Sichuan Province), Chinese attempts to arrest religious leaders from a local monastery led to a fierce standoff. During the fighting, the Chinese army called in airstrikes, destroying the monastery and killing hundreds of monks and lay people in the siege. As one Tibetan resister later recalled of the event, "massive fighting" erupted between the Tibetans and the Chinese, turning the river "red with blood" and the sky "yellow from all of the explosions and gunshots."[22]

Episodes like Lithang toughened the Tibetan resolve, and by the late 1950s, areas to the east of Lhasa had begun to revolt.[23] Leading the rebellion was the Chushi Gangdruk (which means "Four Rivers, Six Ranges," and is the traditional name for Kham), a collection of Tibetan fighters who drew support mostly from men and monks in the East but also from a handful of former Chinese Nationalist soldiers, spies, and even a few Xinjiang Uighurs.[24] Aided by covert support from the American CIA—which initially included communications training but eventually armaments, medical supplies, and radios—the Tibetan fighters engaged in a guerrilla-style campaign.

Early on, the Tibetan fighters chalked up some success. But by March 1959, the tide shifted in China's favor. On March 10 a Chinese invitation to the Dalai Lama to attend a theater show at a PLA military camp caused panic among the Tibetan public. Rumor spread of a Chinese plan to kidnap the Tibetan leader if he accepted. To ensure the Dalai Lama's safety, huge crowds of Tibetan monks and laypeople surrounded the Norbulingka palace in Lhasa, his summer residence. For days Tibetans held a vigil. On March 17, the Chinese military opened fire, lobbing two mortar shells that fell harmlessly near the palace's northern gate. But bloodshed was imminent. That evening, the Dalai Lama, in a bid to encourage the crowds to disperse and avoid a massacre, slipped out of Lhasa, dressed as a layperson. Three days later, Chinese troops began their siege of Lhasa, and then moved to control the rest of Tibet. Though precise casualty figures are not known, Chinese historian Jianglin Li estimates that at least 15,000 Tibetans were killed.

After the events of 1959, China's position hardened. The pace of reform efforts accelerated, and traditional elites—treated as allies prior to the uprising—were marginalized. Senior religious leaders, especially the Panchen Lama, were viewed with even greater suspicion. As the Communists' attack on traditional Tibetan values and institutions intensified, so did Beijing's slandering of the Dalai Lama. Between 1959 and 1962, as the dust of the failed uprising settled over the country—and with social and economic reforms being implemented across China—Beijing moved in on Tibet with an iron fist. The monasteries' role in the March 1959 revolt—monks were among the first to stand guard at the Norbulingka, and the last to leave—no doubt played a role in recrafting Chinese policy.

The Cultural Revolution that swept across the Chinese heartland in June 1966 landed on Tibet's doorstep in August of that year. Hundreds of thousands of Red Guards on the Tibetan Plateau targeted the "four olds" of ideology, customs, culture, and habits. By the time that dark period of Chinese history had ended a decade later, Tibet's religious and cultural institutions lay in ruin. An untold number of monks and laypeople were killed, or committed suicide. "People were physically attacked in the streets for wearing Tibetan dress or having non-Han hair styles," one historian of the period notes. "An attempt was made to destroy every single religious item. All but a handful of monasteries and temples (the figures range from 2,000 to 6,500) were destroyed, many taken down brick by brick until not a trace was left."[25]

With Mao's death in 1976, Tibetans saw a slight improvement in their fate. Tibetans were again permitted a dose of religious freedom. Monks imprisoned following the revolt of 1959 were released. And temples and monasteries destroyed during the Cultural Revolution were rebuilt. Chinese leaders even extended an olive branch to the Dalai Lama in a bid to start talks on his possible return.[26] Over the next decade, as Deng Xiaoping's government admitted errors of past policies, Tibet experienced a period of profound political and economic change. Government subsidies poured into Tibet, agricultural production quotas that applied elsewhere were waived, taxes were frozen, and tourism was encouraged.

By 1983 the Dalai Lama, buoyed by talks with the Chinese, expressed confidence that he would be back in Tibet soon "to see with my own eyes what the situation is."[27] But optimism waned soon after, and in September 1987, ordinary monks again took to the streets to protest life in Chinese-controlled Tibet. They were the first public demonstrations in Tibet in twenty-eight years.[28] One large demonstration on October 1—China's National Day—ended in bloodshed. By the time pro-democracy protests had erupted in Beijing and Tiananmen Square during the summer of 1989, hard-liners in Beijing had already called for the return to a tougher stance on Tibet.

The cycle of openness followed by protest and eventual crackdown has persisted in the decades since. When I visited Tibet briefly as part of a student group in the late 1990s, Tibetans still seemed—outwardly at least—in control of their religious destiny. That I was able to visit at all was testament to another thaw. Although CCTV cameras tracked our every move, and in Lhasa soldiers frequently patrolled the wide-open plaza in front of the Potala Palace, Tibetans more or less maintained an air of self-determination. During our visits to monasteries outside the capital, Tibetans would pull me and my classmates aside to inquire about the status of Tibet on the international agenda, or secretly show us small photos of the Dalai Lama that they had discreetly tucked into their open-air altars.

But by March 2008, a cold political wind once again blew across the Roof of the World. Tibetans took to the streets in Lhasa ahead of the Beijing Olympics, and the resulting violence led to the destruction of dozens of Chinese shops and the death of nearly two dozen Han Chinese. In response, provincial authorities deployed thousands of military personnel to the streets, surrounded monasteries with armed paramilitaries, and installed more video surveillance and gun-toting sentries in some of the city's most sacred spaces. Martial law was announced and remains in effect.

For many Chinese, the ongoing agitation by Tibetans must seem like a slap in the face. Economically, Tibet is a rare exception in China—a relative backwater spoiled with government largesse. China has spent billions on Tibet's development since the 1950s, including an estimated $45.4 billion in infrastructure improvements in the TAR between 2001 and 2010, according to the central government.[29] A train line connecting Lhasa with the rest of China has helped bring cheaper goods and services to Tibetans and Han transplants. Additional rail links are in the works (including one line that would terminate in Purang Dorjee's hometown).[30] Chinese leaders point to an "economic miracle" that has pushed a once-feudal buddhocracy into the modern era. To this day Beijing's diplomats take this message of largesse on the road; in April 2017 a delegation from the National People's Congress visited the United Kingdom to discuss China's development strategy for Tibet with university students and members of Parliament.[31]

Yet despite all the money, Tibetans have not been mollified. Part of the reason, says economic historian Andrew Martin Fischer, is that Beijing has overlooked the value of culture and the importance of inclusion in its development model. Tibetan monks and nuns are repeatedly forced to denounce the Dalai Lama, a requirement that Fischer says is "tantamount to the most cardinal of sins, condemning one to countless eons of 'vajra hell.'" Campaigns to relocate Tibetan nomads from sensitive grazing lands have also spurred anger, as have unofficial policies that favor non-Tibetans in the job market. But Fischer believes that Beijing's "top-down" approach to development inside Tibet is an overarching reason why tempers still flare. Developmental "marginalization," he contends, is a key reason why Tibetans have not been pacified by China's spending spree.

The pace of self-burnings has slowed in recent years, but not because Tibetans have been appeased. On the contrary, security measures have only tightened. In 2012, the central government made "organizing, plotting, inciting, compelling, luring, instigating, or helping others to commit self-immolation" a criminal offense, punishable as "intentional homicide" under Chinese law. According to the US State Department's 2016 report on human rights, local officials in certain areas even "withheld public benefits from the family members of self-immolators and ordered friends and monastic personnel to refrain from participating in religious burial rites or mourning activities for self-immolators." Nearly one hundred Tibetans were punished for alleged association with a planned or actual self-immolation.

By 2015 the pace of self-immolations had slowed considerably; seven laypersons and Tibetan clergy killed themselves with fire that year. That was down from eleven in 2014, and a steep decline from 2012, when eighty-three Tibetans—Losang Jamyang among them—took their lives this way.

Tenzin Norbu's own journey from a faceless minority to a dead man's spokesman began in early 2003, when at fourteen he and his sister, Dawa, began plotting their own, less fiery exits from Ngaba. Poverty and political repression were motivators for their flight, but it was the promise of a Tibetan-style education outside Tibet that pushed them to leave their family and head for India.

Like Losang, Tenzin was the son of farmers who provided enough for the table but little in the way of a financial future for their children. And like Losang, Tenzin and his sister would climb the hills and rocky pastures to the grasslands above the village in search of *yartsa gunbu*, a caterpillar fungus valued by Chinese herbalists. Picturesque and idyllic to some, Ngaba was a dreamer's dead end.

But it wasn't an impossible place to leave. A monk they knew from a local monastery told them of a place, high over the Himalayas, where dreams not only come true, but were paid for. In India, a Tibetan education—including tuition, housing, food, even uniforms of bright blue trousers and heather-gray sweaters—was there to be had at no cost. All a Tibetan child needed to do to be availed of this generosity was to travel, by any means possible, fifteen hundred miles from home.

And the monk told them something else: he could guide them.

Many had dreamt this dream before them. Since the 1960s, Tibetan refugee camps in India and Nepal have offered schooling to every Tibetan child arriving on their doorstep. The arrangement has had sweeping appeal; tens of thousands have navigated the snowy peaks and icy rivers for a chance to study in high school and, later, attend college in India, where a quota system allows Tibetan refugees a competitive advantage. According to data obtained by the US Embassy in New Delhi, over eighty-seven thousand Tibetans left Tibet between 1980 and 2009.[32] While more than half of them eventually returned to Tibet after a short pilgrimage and audience with the Dalai Lama, the majority who stayed were children who enrolled in school.[33]

India isn't the only option for young Tibetans in search of an education, and it may not even be the best. China's educational opportunities have progressed by leaps and bounds over India's strained system, experts say. And yet, for many minorities in Western China, schooling is undesirable, costly, and short on cultural and linguistic immersion. Grade schools are often taught exclusively in Mandarin, and college placements are limited. High tuition fees and a selection process that favors Han—the dominant ethnic group in China—mean fewer opportunities for even the most gifted Tibetans. Moreover, a college degree is of little practical use in the poorest parts of Tibet. For farmers, their children are free labor; time spent in the classroom is money and food lost at harvest.

But the monk had planted a seed in Tenzin and his sister, and it would only grow as spring turned to summer.

By September 2003, leaving Ngaba became an obsession. It wasn't merely the prospect of life behind a plow that pushed Tenzin to look for a way out. In his corner of Tibet, alcoholism, drug use, and violence swallow up young men. The year he left Ngaba, he remembers fistfights, brawls, and stabbings born of boredom killing over a dozen young men, many of whom he knew. Tenzin was committed to avoiding a similar fate.

The going rate in 2003 to be smuggled out of Tibet was 4,000 Chinese yuan a person—the equivalent of about $500 at the time. There were no discounts for teenagers, or for traveling in pairs. It took Tenzin's parents nearly a year to earn enough to smuggle their children to freedom. Tenzin says he isn't sure why his father agreed to fund his escape. Perhaps he saw a bit of himself in his boy, and reasoned that a chance at freedom was the best gift he could give. Or maybe he, too, had once dreamed of fleeing Chinese-controlled Tibet. Too old to leave now, the best he could do was to ensure his children had a better life. "My father is a very strong man," Tenzin said during one of our conversations. "As we were leaving he told me if I can make a difference in India, then go; 'A man who dies in the mountain is the same as a man who dies in the valley.'" The difference, his father said, is what you do before your final day.

On a Sunday morning in September 2003, after giving their father a hug good-bye, Tenzin and his thirteen-year-old sister left Ngaba, very likely forever. With only a few extra yuan of spending money and a change of clothes in a backpack, the children boarded a bus for the six-day journey to Lhasa. They motored through Qamdo and Nagqu, staring out the windows at the Tibet they were leaving behind—massive mountains, sweeping vistas, and blue-green lakes of snowmelt and salt painting an indelible picture in their minds. Aside from the occasional herd of yaks blocking the road, it was an uneventful trip. In 2003, Chinese roadblocks in western Sichuan were rare, and moving between Lhasa and districts to the east was routine for a Tibetan with no Chinese passport.

Lhasa proved more challenging. Frequent protests had tested the city's stability, and Beijing was keeping close tabs on the residents in a bid to maintain control. By 2003 the Tibetan capital was under twenty-four-hour surveillance. Tibetans, once fierce protectors of this holy city, had become caged minorities whose movements were closely monitored. "When we got to Lhasa we had to be very cautious," Tenzin remembers. "If I told anyone I was going to India we would have been caught, and probably put in jail. We had to show no sign that we intended to leave, and just pretend that we are staying in Lhasa. We talked to nobody."

They stayed in Lhasa for two weeks, trying to blend in but moving with purpose. Tenzin and his monk friend, who traveled separately from Ngaba, fanned out across the capital to call on the underbelly of smugglers and counterfeiters who make up a booming flesh trade. Even in Lhasa, one of the most paranoid and security-heavy cities in China, cash still bought forged permits and travel papers good enough to fool Chinese immigration. With these documents, Tenzin and his sister would be able to bypass the numerous checkpoints between Lhasa and Dram, the drab border town that sits in the nook of a deep river gorge on the eastern edge of the Friendship Bridge that connects Tibet and Nepal.

Historically, Tibetans looking to flee Chinese occupation have stayed off the roads for fear of being detected. But the alternative—weeks of trekking through mountain passes, blizzards, and ice fields—was not a safe option, especially for children. In March 1959, the Fourteenth Dalai Lama, twenty-five at the time, needed nearly a month to make the journey, hardship he later described as days of "appalling weather, which threw blizzards and snow glare at us by turns as we straggled along."[34] Tenzin and his sister were not as strong or well equipped; a monthlong hike over the Himalayas would surely have killed them. Smugglers and checkpoints seemed a safer option.

Fifteen days after they arrived in Lhasa, and three weeks after leaving Ng-aba, Tenzin and his sister were on the move again. The monk said his good-byes, but not before arranging for them to join a group of four other Tibetans being slipped into Nepal. For three days they sat squeezed into the backseat of a white Toyota Land Cruiser, with little food and too few rest stops to break the monotony of the gold-and-gray-hued grasslands unfolding beyond the hood. As the would-be refugees motored toward Nepal, Tenzin and his sister rehearsed in whispers what they would say if Chinese police pulled them aside for interrogation at one of the route's numerous roadblocks.

"We'd say we were going to Dram to explore establishing a business," Tenzin remembers, conceding that they never did discuss what type of business they fictionally wanted to open. "Obviously we weren't thinking that far ahead."

The ruse was never needed, as at each stop the papers they had purchased in Lhasa were enough to persuade the Chinese soldiers to wave the travelers on.

The sun was rising when their Toyota rumbled into Dram. Tenzin, Dawa, and the four others were hurried into a windowless room owned by the businessman who had secured their forged documents. They were told not to leave, and not to open the door for anyone.

Dram looks like any other grimy border town in a developing country—a smattering of billiard halls, shady bars, brothels, and police stations. I passed through briefly in 1997, on my return to Nepal from Lhasa as part of the same Tibetan study program that brought me to McLeod Ganj earlier that year. A depressing cloud hung over the border post—gray, transient, and idling with the hum of motorists stocking up on gas, buying snacks, or sipping cans of Pabst Blue Ribbon, China's most popular American beer at the time. But Dram left no indelible mark on my memory.

To an illegal on the run, however, this is where dreams die. It is a minefield of security, and the difference between jail and freedom is one wrong turn or poorly timed encounter.

At 9 p.m. the driver returned, and the six Tibetans were led out of the room under cover of darkness. They walked north out of town, climbing a small hill before turning left toward the Bhote Koshi River, a thirty-foot-wide raging torrent of snowmelt that forms a natural border between Nepal and Chinese-controlled Tibet. The terrain was treacherous; a hill, rising gradually at first, peaked at a cliff that tumbled steeply to the river. At one point Tenzin's sister slipped, almost falling off the cliff before one of the other asylum seekers grabbed her hand. After scrambling up the rocky knoll, they stopped where they "couldn't see the town anymore," Tenzin recalls, about two miles from where they had started.

This was the rendezvous point where they were to hide among the rocks in silence, waiting for smugglers to arrive on the Nepal side to help them across the river.

That first evening, no one came.

As the night turned to dawn, fear of failure began to dull the hope that had fueled Tenzin since he left Ngaba. Out of view from the main part of Dram, the six castaways and their guide were without food or water, and had no choice but to stay low to avoid detection. The sound of the river's crashing water muffled their voices, but on the open cliff face, two miles was not enough distance to shield their silhouettes from the rising sun.

Tenzin's thoughts moved between possible scenarios. Had they been duped? Were they to be handed over to Chinese police, their would-be saviors selling their freedom a second time? What should they do now? Run?

"I was worried, because the guy said it would take only one night. I thought, 'Maybe this guy is going to take our money and then they are going to leave us there.' I had my sister, and we'd paid eight thousand yuan. I thought I had fallen for a trap."

He hadn't. Just before dawn after a second night on the rocks, a young Nepali man appeared from the shadows on the other side of the river. With one
end of a rope fixed to a tree, he used a makeshift sling to toss the other end
high into the darkness across the water. It landed with a thud, a few feet from
where Tenzin and his sister had huddled for warmth. Guides on the Tibet
side knotted the end of the rope, and within minutes the taut line spanned
the Bhote Koshi—a literal piece of string to guide them to freedom. An hour
later, Tenzin and his sister stood firmly in Nepali territory. Tibet, for the first
time in their lives, was behind them.

As the new refugees inched up from the riverbank, Chinese policemen in
Dram spotted the group in the morning light. In a halfhearted trot the police
started toward the Friendship Bridge that spans the torrent of Himalayan
snowmelt. But as the six Tibetans climbed faster, turning into the woods and
out of view, the police slowly faded away. Tenzin turned for a final look into
his native land. The Chinese policemen, specks in the middle of the bridge,
had stopped running.

And just like that, he said, "We were free."

———

Tenzin and I stayed in touch after our first cup of tea in McLeod Ganj. We
spoke by phone when he was studying for college placement exams and
applying to universities in India. We chatted over Skype during his school
breaks and on public holidays. And over the years as we spoke I watched as
Tenzin's dreams for his future began to shift, as if burdened by a duty to make
as much of an impact in life as his friend had in death. During one of our
first conversations he told me he was preparing an application to study at a
film school in the United States. Later he explained how his most pressing
goal was to become an economist, so he could return to Tibet and help his
people become more prosperous under Chinese rule. It was Tenzin's version
of "something special."

Tenzin and Losang grew up in the same village, shared similar hobbies,
and, above all, longed to leave Ngaba. Yet their paths to freedom were as
divergent as life and death. As Tenzin's vision for his own future matured, a
free man in exile, it stood in stark contrast to that of his martyred friend in
Tibet. Had Tenzin taken the path of least resistance—never saying a word

publicly about his friend's death and what drove him to it—China's system of control and oppression might never have cast a shadow on his family's doorstep. His father wouldn't have to look over his shoulder each time he drives his motorcycle to town to pick up farm supplies. His brothers might never have to worry about being among the "disappeared."

But had Tenzin stayed silent, Losang's act of defiance would have died with him. And although it was likely not his intention, the world would never have known what pushes someone to wrap himself in a cloak of fire just when he is supposed to be learning how to live.

Most longtime Tibetan refugees I know have walked the same streets as Tenzin Norbu, eaten at the same hole-in-the-wall noodle stands, breathed the same rejuvenating mountain air, prayed in the same temples, and shopped in the same stores. But they come from experiences vastly different from those of their brethren over the border: nurtured on hope and dal, Tibetans from India and Nepal are as much cultural migrants as they are political refugees. It is in this gray space of Tibetan belonging—between those born inside Tibet and those who are raised entirely in a home that is not officially theirs—that the Tibetan diaspora is increasingly being defined.

A few weeks before I returned to McLeod Ganj once more, this time in November 2014, I stumbled across an old photograph of a young man I had spent many hours with during my first visit to Little Lhasa. Stuffed among the tattered collection of five-by-seven photos in my parents' attic—pictures of former girlfriends, college parties, an orange-and-white vw bus that my brother and I had driven across the United States when we were in our early twenties—was a discolored image of a boy and his dog near a river of recent snowmelt. I had taken it in early 1997 not far from Dorjee's home in McLeod Ganj.

Each day after school that winter, Ngodup Gyatso,[1] whose parents ran a fabric store down the street from Dorjee's shop, would entertain me with walks to surrounding villages; the photo was taken near a place called Bhagsu Nag. I had met his parents through the merchant network Dorjee belonged to, and they had encouraged the boy to practice his English with me during his free time. So on most afternoons we would walk, and talk, turning right at the bus stand and up the hill toward the Lands End tea stall, a small shack perched on a cliff that in the 1990s marked the end of commerce on the road out of town. Ngodup would kick stones along Bhagsu Road as we recited our respective second languages. Quiet but pensive, he was purposeful and naturally kind. Yet even at twelve he carried an air of boredom and idleness— stone kicking personified. In the photo Ngodup is peering at the camera wide-eyed, but his big brown eyes seem to be focused on something else.

By late 2014, the next time I saw Ngodup, little had outwardly changed in his appearance: his face was still round and youthful, his eyes sincere. He sported a short crop of jet-black hair, just as he had some two decades earlier. But his demeanor was more slumped, sadder somehow. The stone-kicking boredom of childhood had matured into an adult's palpable lethargy. I couldn't immediately put my finger on it, but he was distant in a way that even a stranger for nearly twenty years could sense. Though my visit to Mc-Leod Ganj that time was geared toward gaining a deeper appreciation of how Tibetan society was adapting to life under the shadow of an ascendant China, I was also intent on piecing together details of a life that photographs leave out.

Ngodup was twenty-nine by the time we reconnected, and had been the caretaker of his parent's shop for about six years, selling the same woolen hats and woven cloth to different old men and young ladies as his parents had before him. He had assumed command of the store in the mid-2000s, sometime after finishing high school, but isn't certain exactly when. "I never tried to leave here," Ngodup said one day in between puffs on a cigarette. "I like Dharamsala, with my family, my friends. It's home."

I visited him often during that two-week visit, excited to have reconnected with an extended member of my personal McLeod Ganj "family." During our first conversations he seemed content enough. Old classmates streamed into the store to bum smokes and make plans for when Ngodup got off work— around eight o'clock each night. One day a former schoolmate ambled in, Tibetan textbooks tucked under his arm. They were manuals for a placement exam with the Men Tse Kang medical center. The exam was for admission to a six-month training program; over one hundred young Tibetans from across India were competing for the program's two open seats. At least Ngodup was lucky enough to have a job, I thought.

But as the days went on, the clearer it became that "lucky" was not an adjective Ngodup would ascribe to himself. "Overshadowed," "stifled," and "stuck" seemed to better define his worldview. "So much has changed; so many Tibetans have moved to Europe, to the U.S.," he said one day. And he was still in McLeod Ganj, manning the till of a dusty store hawking linen and cotton threads to a new generation of displaced people. Ngodup was—literally and figuratively—toiling in his parent's footsteps.

That fall Ngodup spent most of his waking hours in the store, seated atop a small wooden stool in the middle of a tiny room packed high with boxes of merchandise. From his perch he could make out the silhouette of the Namgyalma Stupa down the street, its bright red prayer wheels and colorful murals erected in 1965 to honor the Tibetan warriors killed fighting the Chinese in their failed freedom struggle. A television tuned to Indian soaps flickered silently in one corner. Business in the refugee fabric industry was, apparently, feast or famine.

Ngodup was a boy of few words, and is a man of fewer. During many of our visits that fall, minutes would tick by with dead air and Hindi television, silence typically filled by drags on a cigarette or the next customer. One afternoon a British artist wandered in, a Tibetan translator in tow, asking Ngodup and me to scribble a "message to the world" on an index card. Ngodup, complying, penned a sentiment in English about "world peace" (I wrote a line about embracing diversity). "The aim," the artist said, pulling out a camera to snap photos of us holding our index cards to our chests, "is to complete the project and have it showing at Glastonbury 2015. The Dalai Lama is going to attend. That's my goal, anyway." Ngodup and I went along, going through the motions.

My morning and afternoon visits went like this for nearly two weeks, and during each one I gained a deeper appreciation of what being a refugee shopkeeper in a tiny North Indian village was like: long days, bad television, lots of tea and cigarettes, friends with jobs and dreams, and a town that stayed the same.

Inside this stew of perpetual motion and monotony sat Ngodup. And in a bottle next to him on the floor was how he had decided to cope.

————

Buses and motorbikes clog the main road leading from the center of Mc-Leod Ganj, and storefront walls vying for eyeballs are plastered with signs hawking rooms, soft drinks, "Free Tibet" movie nights, and authentic Tibetan food. But one green-and-white billboard, placed above a doorway just a few paces from the narrow alley that leads to Ngodup's shop, underscores the challenges descending on young Tibetans of Little Lhasa today. It reads: "Kunphen, Registered under the Society Act—XXI of 1860." It is McLeod Ganj's only private center for substance abuse and dependency. And it is busy these days.

It would be a few months after first reconnecting with Ngodup that I made my way to the small counseling center on Bhagsu Road to inquire about help for wayward Tibetans. On most days that I walked by, the dark offices of Kunphen were closed, hidden behind a metal rolling door and a large padlock. But eventually, with the help of a Punjabi shoe repairman camped out daily on a nearby stoop, I connected with the center's only staff member, a part-time schoolteacher from Eastern Tibet named Ngawang Sonam. Nervous to speak at first, Ngawang eventually opened up and shared his views on the addictions from which Tibetan refugees suffer.

Kunphen's office was a cluttered mess on the afternoon I visited. Dusty brochures offering advice on drug-treatment options and "Basic Facts about HIV & AIDS" littered one corner of the small room. Posters with antidrug slogans—"Turn On Music, Turn Off Drugs"—hung next to signs detailing "basic facts about alcohol" and the five stages of intoxication ("happy," "excited," "confused," "stupor," and "coma"). On the desk, a pile of unfiled papers competed for space with a tattered box labeled "Donation" in English and Chinese. Over the doorway an old photo of the Dalai Lama peered into the room, and next to his image, a small plaque with a quote from Alcoholics Anonymous challenged those reading it to seek help from within: "I need to concentrate not so much on what needs to be changed in the world," it read, "as on what needs to be changed in me and my attitudes."

For a man in a dispiriting, lonely line of work, Ngawang exudes enthusiasm. Slight and serious with an almond face and soft eyes, he portrays a positive tone despite the topic. McLeod Ganj and Dharamsala are actually cleaning up, he says, notwithstanding the obvious challenges. During the late 1990s and early 2000s, the village was practically overrun with nighttime parties, blaring music, and frequent offers of drugs. But by 2014 there was less outward debauchery. Many of the worst offenders—drug addicts dubbed forest people by the locals, because of where they slept at night—had left town, either for treatment centers in cities or easier access to their vices. Yet it wasn't clear if troubled Tibetans were cleaning up their collective acts or simply exporting their addictive tendencies.

Ngawang, who carries a book of prayers to the protector deity Palden Lamo wherever he goes, said that by his count, forty-five Tibetans in McLeod Ganj had died from drug- or alcohol-related causes between 2000 and 2013. Since then, he said, the death rate has slowed. "It's a little bit decreasing. Three years ago there were many youngsters who used drugs and alcohol, and many people sleeping on the road, everywhere. But now, this time, it's less."

And yet even today it doesn't take long for a visitor to be approached by a shady-looking young man offering "smoke, blow, what do you need?" outside the many coffee shops and tea stalls that line the main drag. Fewer people may be splayed out in the road or in the woods, too drunk or stoned to walk, but that doesn't mean the problem has vanished completely.

Tibetan refugees have plenty of company when it comes to drug and alcohol addiction. Researchers have long charted the effects of voluntary or forced displacement on the choices young people make; health experts who have studied refugee populations—from Vietnamese refugees in Hong Kong to Cambodian women in Massachusetts—say that forced refugee populations are almost always at a higher risk of mental and psychiatric disorders, which are in turn associated with a higher frequency of substance abuse.[2] One study from 2003, conducted by an undergraduate student from Emory University, recorded the observations of recovering Tibetan addicts in Dharamsala. She reported that conflicting influences between young Tibetans' Indian upbringing and the cultures of their adopted homeland created tensions within Tibetan families, which in turn fueled substance dependency.

Other studies have found that intergenerational conflict within transnational populations can strain family bonds, polarizing children and parents, which "may lead to delinquency, drug use, and further alienation."[3] It would stand to reason that Tibetans born in India to parents born in Tibet would face similar challenges navigating cultural identities.

Tibetans in exile see China as a source of their suffering, at least indirectly. Beijing's relentless vilification of their spiritual leader, and its continued refusal to consider a political solution to the Tibet issue, have contributed to

Tibetan exiles' sense of isolation and hopelessness. But addiction, as damaging as it is for the fabric of any society, may also be a boon for China's strategy. As Tibet scholar Warren W. Smith Jr. has noted, "ultimately, China believes that it has no need to negotiate with Tibetan exiles because it already has the solution to the Tibetan problem by means of political repression, economic development, colonization and assimilation" inside Tibet. "Many Chinese seem to believe that the demise of the Tibetan political issue will be simultaneous with that of the 14th Dalai Lama."[4]

Looked at this way, anything that weakens the Tibetan exile community from within would benefit a wait-and-see strategy.

The discussion with the Kunphen office director eventually veered in this direction, toward China. In 2011 a young Tibetan filmmaker, Tenzin Seshi, told the human rights activist Maura Moynihan that Tibetan refugees were experiencing an uptick in heroin addiction, and that Chinese agents, sometimes posing as monks, passed out heroin and needles to Tibetans in Nepal.[5] This seemed beneath even an increasingly aggressive China. No Tibetan official I've ever met has so much as hinted at such a claim.

Ngawang dismissed the theory quickly. Tibetans alone must take responsibility for their addictions, he said. "Inside Tibet and outside Tibet, the situation is totally different. Inside Tibet, it's true, there are cheaper prices for cigarettes, and the alcohol is very cheap. But in India, Nepal, and Bhutan, all this is not influenced by China." Rather, he said, Tibetans should look in the mirror.

"You know that this place is a little bit crazy," he said of McLeod Ganj. "Many foreigners come here and stay here, two weeks, three weeks, and during that time they are enjoying, and during that time those kids are also enjoying with those foreigners, getting benefits from the foreigners. That's the problem . . . they are taking ganja, heroin. It's easy to get it here. And Tibetans, they are taking from the foreigners a little bit of money, going to buy, and then [taking] a little bit off the top."

Alcohol and tobacco are among the most commonly abused drugs in Tibetan exile, advocates says, but prescription painkillers, marijuana, heroin, hashish, and, increasingly, inhalants, are all competing for young brain cells.

Among the biggest scourges Ngawang says he contends with is "huffing"— the act of inhaling vapors. Little Lhasa's school-age children are easily lured by cheap, addictive, powerful inhalants, he said. "Everything from Wite Out and rubber glue—like the kind used by the repairman to fix shoes—to gasoline. They are so strong." Ngawang, who works part time at a private elementary school in town, said he has seen abuse close-up, in the classroom. "Some kids will soak their clothes in gas and take whiffs of it during the day," he said. I had heard similar stories of abuse from a Westerner who works closely with Tibetan government officials on refugee assistance programs.

The Dalai Lama has often stressed the need to combat addiction with education. During a five-day conference on craving and addiction in late 2013, His Holiness talked about how the mind can be conditioned to defend against the desires that lead to material suffering—including the desire for drugs. And schools, he explained, should serve as environments that teach children connectedness and purpose, passion and pride. "We must bring to children a sense of wonderment about the world, rather than so much negativity," he said. "And we must bring more simplicity."[6]

Yet when education fails, or worse—when schools become the center of abuse—even inspirational rhetoric fails. Namshey Chigangtsang, a former school guidance counselor who has worked with drug addicts in the Tibetan settlements, says a huge percentage of grade-school students are experimenting with drugs and alcohol in Tibetan areas. In one Tibetan school in Jogindernagar, two hours southeast of Dharamsala, she found that as many as a quarter of students in grades six to ten had experimented with tobacco, alcohol, inhalants, or harder drugs.

More troubling, she said, was how school administrators responded when she presented the data. "I discussed the findings with my school authorities, and I was not very happy with their response," she said. "They took it very lightly. They didn't see it the way I saw it." When she proposed posting the findings on a school notice board to alert teachers and parents to "what is happening in our school," the school's headmaster said "no, a big no for that. I didn't feel good about that."

Unfortunately, Chigangtsang has few advocates in her search for solutions. A lack of funding and a dearth of treatment options for substance abuse in Tibetan communities mean many Tibetans are on their own. The Tibetan government in exile does offer support to those seeking treatment but suffers from a shortage of personnel to administer programs. Moreover, a lack of postrehabilitation treatment centers in India means high rates of recidivism among recovering addicts, counselors say. The lack of centralized support has opened the door for private clinics, but these have also largely failed to deliver. Kunphen is the only private center offering support in Little Lhasa; staffed largely by untrained volunteers (and it isn't without its critics), it operates on a shoestring budget fueled by donations.[7] A second NGO, called Choice, which focused primarily on HIV and AIDS advocacy, shut down in August 2013. Officials cited a "lack of human resources and the dwindling source of funds" as one reason for its closure.[8]

——

Had I been more invested in slowing Ngodup's downfall I would have been too late anyway; by the time I returned to McLeod Ganj in early 2016, after first reconnecting with him in November 2014, friends had already staged an intervention. As he was unwilling to enroll in a treatment program independently, they forced him to go. By January he was already a few months into a six-month-long detox stint at an Indian-run rehab center in Dehradun.

In truth, I hadn't realized the extent of Ngodup's addiction during our initial visits. I had even bought him a beer once—his preferred Indian-brewed brand, Kingfisher, sold as "premium" or "strong," depending on its alcohol content—a gift I now regret. It wasn't until speaking with those who knew him better that I reflected on the clear signs I had missed: daytime beer breath, frequent hangovers, glassy eyes, vacant stares, and random bursts of energy. During most shifts, and definitely by early afternoon, he was drunk.

Ngodup Gyatso, "he's always drinking," Kunphen's Ngawang told me (apparently not bound by the same patient-counselor confidentiality rules of his Western counterparts). "His family is good, rich compared to other people. I would tell him if he needed help I could arrange for him to go to a rehab center, stay there for six months, and then come back. But he never listened. He told me, 'Fuck you, I don't want to go there, why you talking to me about this?' Then I just gave up."

But his friends didn't give up. "By force we have to send him," one former classmate, who wanted to remain anonymous, recalled. "When he comes back we will accept him. We are not going to neglect or ignore him. We are going to try and do our best to improve him, to make him a good man."

Another longtime friend is equally committed. When we spoke by phone—she was living in New York City at the time—she was quick to comment on

Ngodup's predicament. "We are always advising him, but what to do? I told him that if he were to go to France, or to Switzerland, or the Unites States" it would be better. "He just said 'No, I don't want to move anywhere. I like it here.' He thinks like that. I asked him is there something in your mind? And he said, 'No, I don't have any problem.' And I say, 'If you don't have problem, why are you drinking so much?'"

"I will help him," she continued. "If he needs any money I will send to him. Anything he needs I will do. I do wish we could show him the good way, the good path. I'm also hoping that one day he will change. I'm waiting for that day to come."

It remains to be seen whether the strategy of intervention and love will pay off. Ngawang says that even with the best intentions, rehabilitation centers in India are often ineffective. "Most of the centers are doing business only," he said. "If your son is using, you just send him to a rehab center, and then give them money. But after two or three days, when you call, they might say, 'Okay, your son is missing, and we don't know where he is.' That is just business [not rehabilitation]. Most of the rehab centers are like this."

And even if the center Ngodup enrolled in does function legitimately, he will face long odds being fully accepted back into the Tibetan exile fold once he returns. Staying strong in a small town like McLeod Ganj, where everyone's business is an open secret, will not be easy.

"In our society, the thinking is a little bit wrong," the Kunphen director said. "They think, maybe users are enjoying, and thinking that life is just rich, but they never think that this is a disease. But we are always telling people, please, don't talk with these people softly. Help them. It's very easy for them to be hurt, and then again they are using more and more. That's our Tibetan society."

For now, at least, Ngodup is making the most of his second chance. In early 2017 he had completed the rehab program and was back in McLeod Ganj, manning the till at his parent's small fabric shop. Best of all, he was beating the odds and remained on the wagon.

―――

Many other Tibetan refugees—especially those born and raised inside Tibet—have a far harder time when addiction captures them. Faced with language barriers, no family support systems, crippling unemployment, and a refugee structure that is dominated by longtime settlers, fresh-from-Tibet Tibetans (so-called new arrivals, in Tibetan exile parlance) face longer odds than their established brethren.

In *Dharamsala Days, Dharamsala Nights*, one of the only detailed accounts of the vast social and cultural gulf that has emerged between Tibet Tibetans and Indo-Tibetans over the last few decades, a Canadian activist and author who spent years researching Tibet Tibetans' integration into Indian exile found that "new arrivals" often struggled financially and socially, so much so that many of them returned to China voluntarily. Those who stayed in India were subject to the pull of depression, despair, addiction, or worse.

"Unemployment and the lack of access to higher education and other opportunities drove some of the brightest newcomers to the brink of madness," the author, who wrote under the pseudonym Pauline MacDonald, concluded in her 2013 self-published work. "Others cultivated carefree and sometimes arrogant public images, but in private they would occasionally admit to feelings of despair and humiliation. Binge drinking and alcoholism were widespread. Counseling was unavailable, but I was told that the exile government gladly paid for bus tickets back to Tibet."

Similar integration challenges await those Tibetans who emigrate from China or India to the West (despite China's near-total lockdown on overland escape routes between Tibet and Nepal or India, Tibetans continue to leave, often by air, using forged documents and false pretenses). One Tibet scholar, who spent the summer of 2016 working closely with exiled Tibetans in Paris, said that while English-speaking Indo-Tibetans are often able to adapt to their new surroundings, Tibet Tibetans have a much harder time. In France, new arrivals from Tibet are "completely insular" in their group dynamics, with "zero integration, zero assimilation" into their new environment, he said. These fresh-from-Tibet Tibetans operate by finding other Tibetans from their region who speak French, or somebody who speaks Tibetan who is French. In this way they are completely dependent on others. And if they fail to find these key enablers, they can end up in very dark places.

"My French friends who speak Tibetan are working day and night helping all these Tibetans with medical problems, passport problems, job problems, psychological problems, because they don't interact with the community at all," the scholar told me. "Last week, my colleague here who is fluent in Tibetan . . . called in late for a meeting because she had to go to the morgue to try and help the French morticians deal with a Tibetan that had been brought in dead, because he had committed suicide. Nobody knew this person. They didn't know why he committed suicide, or who his friends were. He seems to be someone who was completely isolated. He had failed to keep with the Tibet community, and killed himself."

It was not an isolated happening, the scholar added. "This was just one of the awful stories we get" regarding Tibetans unable to adjust to life in exile.

The Tibetan term *phuntsokling* translates to "abode of plenty and happiness." In the 1960s, when the Tibetan refugee camp that bears this name was born, Phuntsokling was both. Deep in the jungles of India's Orissa State, four hundred miles southwest of Kolkata, the camp's red, earthy soils and rows of carefully cultivated corn complement the four hundred or so tin-and-timber shacks that house the nineteen hundred Tibetan refugees who reside there. But in the spring of 2012, when a long-simmering land dispute in this idyllic setting went public, Tibetans received a poignant reminder that even after six decades in India they remain very much on shaky ground.

Orissa began as an oasis of good fortune. Most of the camp's earliest inhabitants came from oft-deadly jobs constructing roads, dams, and buildings in Chamba, Dalhousie, and Bomdila in the North, or from the Chinese-occupied valleys and cities of Southern and Western Tibet.[1] Realizing that road camps were not a viable long-term solution to their displacement, the Dalai Lama's administration approached the Indian government to secure land for semi-permanent, self-contained settlements. In turn, rural states with large tracts of relatively undeveloped land began to permit the first wave of Tibetans to settle as farmers.[2] Three refugee settlements—Bylakuppe in Karnataka, Mainpat in Madhya Pradesh, and Phuntsokling in Orissa—were born.

Early on, Tibetans struggled in India's hot, arid, low-lying jungles. George Woodcock, a Canadian author and historian who studied life in Bylakuppe, noted that for the first Tibetan settlers, weather was a minor challenge. More difficult were the beasts that roamed the jungles—"the kind of special difficulties" associated with India's interior. "At Bylakuppe," he wrote, "early crops were destroyed by elephants, and several Tibetan settlers were killed in attempting to drive the animals away."[3]

By 1964, foreign aid and a team of Swiss agriculturalists had arrived at Bylakuppe. There, the results were almost immediate—better crops, healthier people, fewer run-ins with large mammals.

By contrast, at the two other early settlements, including Phuntsokling, foreign agricultural support didn't arrive until some time later. Tibetans there continued to muddle through their relocation. "At both these settlements the inhabitants are still dependent on food rations and monetary subsidies, and are psychologically depressed in comparison with the people at Bylakuppe," Woodcock concluded in 1970.[4] Even today these settlements are remote, isolated, and poorly connected to Indian rail or air services.

In time, Swiss experts did arrive in Phuntsokling.[5] Soils tests and local market studies were conducted, as were irrigation and mechanization surveys. And eventually corn, one of the world's most consumed and cultivated grains, which is easy to plant and offers decent profit margins, was identified as a suitable cash crop for Orissa's jungle soils.

By the late 1990s, the camp that began slowly was fully functional. Vast orchards of guava, papaya, and jackfruit bordered rows of towering maize. Once-uninhabited forests were home to two primary schools, a high school, banks, flour mills, handicraft centers, a noodle factory, convenience stores, and a hospital. Back then the biggest threat to Tibetans, at least on the surface, appeared to be diminished rainfall during the monsoon. Each afternoon as the skies darkened and thick cumulous clouds gathered for a possible thunderstorm, Tibetan men wrapped in muddy sarongs took cover under canopies of teak and bamboo in soggy anticipation. More often than not, though, the skies never opened.[6]

But corn, for all its benefits, has a negative side: it is all or nothing. Disease or one bad storm can wipe out an entire year's crop, and even when yields are good, it's harvested just once a year. When the stalks are picked, Tibetans either descend into long periods of idleness, or leave in search of more work (selling hand-knit wool sweaters in India's biggest cities is a Tibetan specialty). And once they leave, the lure of leaving permanently is inescapable. When Phuntsokling opened in the early 1960s, some 3,000 refugees were registered as residing there. By 2009, the last time an official census was released, the settlement's total numbers had shrunk to 1,885. Most of those remaining see the cultivation of corn as problematical.[7]

It was within this context that I arrived in Phuntsokling in March 1997, a few weeks after saying goodbye to Purang Dorjee in McLeod Ganj. I had set out for India's farm belt that spring to study why Tibetans were leaving farming settlements in droves, and to consider ways to reverse the migration trends. I spent the days on a work-study project helping Tibetan farmers find ways to deal with erratic rainfall, and new ways to make the soil work for them.

An affable Tibetan bureaucrat named Tsering Phuntsok (he insisted that people call him "Uncle") was my guide for the month. With chubby cheeks and a thick black goatee, Uncle was a thinner doppelganger for Dom DeLuise, the TV and film comic, and had a jovial manner that made our daily sojourns aboard his Enfield 350 motorcycle pass easily. Together we canvassed the camp's twenty-five hundred acres in search of supplies for an overhead irrigation sprinkler system prototype. Our idea was simple: fashion rusty pipes, rubber hoses, or anything else we could find along those lines into a workable watering system, that, with the help of Swiss-made sprinkler heads, would give farmers the ability to remain in Phuntsokling year-round, weathering the dry season by irrigating a second-season crop once the corn harvest was complete.

Four weeks later, the first trickle of water splattered onto the scorched earth in murky anticipation. It was April 14, 1997. The pump at the water's edge sputtered violently, sending a silted stream to the waiting pipes. A muddy mist flickered lightly on the wilted rows of tomatoes, chilies, and potatoes. It was my last day in Phuntsokling, the culmination of a month-long salvage effort. And its inauguration felt like another brick had been added to the wall of Tibetans' semipermanence in Phuntsokling.

But it was, like so much of the Tibetans' exiled existence, a mirage. Fifteen years later, a string of newspapers headlines summed up how little had changed for the refugees of Orissa. "Tibetan Settlers Asked to Surrender 'Occupied' Land," read one headline. And another: "Tribal People Up in Arms against Land Grab." With each news item, Tibetans' sense of permanence was eroded like nutrients from a poorly plowed field. But this time it was local politics, not Mother Nature, causing the storm.

As Purang Dorjee and the Tibetans of India's North battled legal challenges to their right of habitation—including claims that they were residing on "forested land"—Tibetans in India's East faced an even more immediate threat. In May 2012, hundreds of local villagers marched into the camps at Phuntsokling and vowed to take back leased farmland, by force if necessary. Photos of the protests showed women wrapped in saris hoisting the red-and-white hammer-and-sickle flag of the Communist Party of India (drawing parallels to the poor farmers who fueled China's Maoist-led revolution, waging a class-based uprising against the privileged bourgeoisie). The *Hindu* newspaper, which reported on the colorful protests, wrote that hundreds of "tribal people from 23 villages of Chandragiri"—the Indian township that borders Phuntsokling—marched on the Tibetan refugee area and demanded that Tibetans stop farming it. They brought "200 traditional bullock-driven ploughs with them." And when the marchers arrived, led by local and national Communist Party officials, they planted their flags in the Tibetans' fields and began plowing in protest.[8]

When Tibetans were first settled in India's South and East, the welcome wasn't warm, but it wasn't hostile either. Local politicians and landowners expected a gold rush to come their way as a result of the new arrivals. Many Indian leaders were under the impression that their guests would return to Tibet after a few years, leaving the land they cleared and infrastructure they developed in possession of the local community.[9] Tibetan refugees were tolerated as the flood of government and donor dollars poured into penniless areas of India.

But when leaving became less likely, and China's position in Tibet solidified, tensions for Tibetans in India began to mount.

The following February, in early 2013, a few months before the start of the next growing season, tribal and Communist Party politicians again threatened to take over farmland leased to Tibetan refugees.[10] As Dandapani Raita, a Communist Party member from Orissa,[11] told one Indian journalist: "We are not against the Tibetan settlers but we want that each of their families should have one acre of land as per the norms. They cannot possess land through means of deceit while the local tribal and Dalit people remain landless." The *Hindu* later wrote that "it is an irony" that Adivasi [aboriginal] and Dalit [oppressed] people had no legal right to lands that they had lived on for centuries, "while the Tibetan settlers continue to hold illegal possession on government land in the area."[12] For two seasons the fields of Phuntsokling lay forcibly fallow, held hostage by Indian Maoists' anti-Tibetan demonstrations.

Eventually, local officials agreed to reallocate roughly 130 acres of farmland that had been cultivated by the Tibetans. According to one press report, landless Indians in surrounding villages were "appeased" with an acre of land each, as well as government promises to enroll more tribal children in schools, improve road infrastructure in the region, and enhance local health facilities.[13] The strategy of challenging Tibetan refugees—and garnering substantial media coverage for it—was an effective one. In May 2013, the Tibetan administration struck a deal with local Orissa officials, and individual Tibetan farmers were again given clearance to cultivate.[14] Tibetan leases were renewed once more, but in the process, Phuntsokling had shrunk.

Corn remains a troubled crop for Tibetans in Orissa, but the political drama surrounding its cultivation appears to have subsided. Sonam Topgyal Khorlatsang, the Tibetan government in exile's home secretary, said in early 2016 that the Phuntsokling saga was "all local politics" that had swept Tibetans into its vortex. "Once that incident took place," he said, "immediately after that I personally visited the area and met all the Indian officials in Bhubaneswar," the state capital. "It doesn't seem there is any influence from any other quarters than the [local] Communist Party."

Chonor Samdup, the settlement officer of the Tibetan government in exile in Phuntsokling, was similarly dismissive when I reached him on his cell phone in June 2016. While it was still a "sensitive" topic for the local community—one he didn't feel comfortable discussing in detail over the phone—the worst appeared to be over. "You can say that it's been settled," he said simply.

———

During the exiles' first few decades in India, when Tibetan-host conflicts were rare, anthropologists determined that mutual economic benefits had "gone a long way in developing more positive Indian attitude towards the Tibetans."[15] Surveys of Tibetans and Indians in North India during the 1980s, for example, found that for the most part attitudes toward each other were positive and constructive.[16] Tensions, if they did exist, were more opaque, and far below the surface.

Today, though, Tibetans can be a source of resentment in some parts of their adopted homeland. Visit any Tibetan town in India and it's easy to see the difference in relative wealth: with their gilded monasteries, jade jewelry, and fine wool woven carpets, Tibetan settlements strike a stark economic contrast to many of the indigenous Indian communities that they border. At times, Tibetan officials say, this disparity has made them targets, especially in the courts.

Tibetans in India have been sued for a long list of alleged infractions—such as wrongfully holding parliamentary elections (on the grounds that Tibetans are not citizens and therefore cannot constitutionally cast ballots)[17]; building homes (in Purang Dorjee's case, on land gifted to him by the state); and carving rocks with religious symbols. During one visit to McLeod Ganj, I asked Sonam Dorgee, the Dharamsala settlement officer, why he thought cases like these kept cropping up, and what could be done to alleviate the tension. Surely Tibetans win no local fans when the Indian federal government swoops in to offer them special protections that are not bestowed on others.

"There may be some Indians who are playing into the hands of the People's Republic of China," he said. "There may be some cases where Tibetans are doing quite well in business, in hotels and restaurants, and they [Indians] don't want Tibetans to be so successful. So there can be many reasons.

"There is," he concluded, "a growing [anti-Tibetan] feeling among Indians."

Whether that is true is impossible to judge with any objectivity. What is clear, though, is that Tibetans in India have staked their future on a country that hasn't always embraced them. Only one Indian state, Karnataka, allows Tibetans to register property in their own names, a relatively new development.[18] In 2016, the top Tibetan official of that state's largest settlement, Mundgod, said he was optimistic that the new lease agreement would lead to greater opportunities for Tibetans to access Indian sources of funding—like farm subsides and loans (roughly a third of the settlement relies on farming to make a living). But others, including the head of the local agricultural cooperative, complained that at twenty years, the lease term was too short and would discourage any effort to attract investment for bigger projects or longer-term stability.

Still, any land deal is better than what many Indians in the area are entitled to. In late 2008, a local Indian opposition group emerged to challenge what it viewed as favoritism to Tibetans on land issues. In a petition filed by Nagarika Hritheyrakshana Vedike Mundgod Taluk (which translates to "Mundgod Citizens' Interest Protection"), the group argued that Tibetans were being treated better than citizens.

"They have constructed their camps into a mini-Tibet," the group wrote in their native Kannada language. "Our neighboring people have given sufficient help and compassion to these foreigners. But, these ungrateful people who benefited from our help are mistreating us. Their earlier behavior [of humility] is no more visible these days. New people are coming here daily. They buy our land and [build] illegal construction. The question is: Who gives them the permission to build? If we look at the current situation, we feel as though we have become refugees ourselves compared to them."[19]

To be sure, land disputes in India are not a uniquely Tibetan problem. Sanjoy Chakravorty, a professor of geography and urban studies at Temple University, and an expert on land use in India, says the average holding size for an Indian farmer is less than three acres, compared to 450 acres in the United States, or 200 acres in Europe. With such small landholdings, "it's virtually impossible to make a living off the land. It's the root cause of India's poverty, the inability to transition to an urban economy."

For local politicians, especially in agricultural areas, their choice appears clear: support your constituents, no matter what policies the federal government might be pushing. "You cannot say in India that you are against the farmer or you are not pro-farmer. It's just not a tenable, viable, political position," said Sanjoy. It is how much are you *for* the farmer, that really is the question. There is no doubt that at the ground and the national levels, land politics is big politics, big-time politics." And in this context, Sanjoy said, "if Tibetans have gotten the squeeze, it is unsurprising because they are easily identifiable as the 'other,' not one of us. They are the easiest group to organize against."

And yet, dueling plows, angry petitions, and lawsuits over painted slate are manageable problems. Violence, though rare, presents more nuanced challenges.

Occasionally, Tibetan businesses have been targeted directly. In 1994, five years after the Dalai Lama was awarded his Nobel Peace Prize, Tibetan-run businesses in McLeod Ganj were the targets of mob violence following the stabbing death of an Indian teenager. Demonstrators set fire to Tibetan storefronts and the Dalai Lama's government offices, demanding that the permanent guests be shown the door.[20] Although Dorjee's Shop No. 5 was spared, fifteen people were ultimately injured in riots that lasted two days.

Then, in July 1999, nearly 140 Tibetan shops and market stalls in Manali, a seven-hour drive from the Dalai Lama's residence, were burned and "razed to earth by an infuriated mob consisting of thousands of local residents." The *Tribune* reported that the attack followed another altercation between Tibetan and Indian students, and prompted the deputy police commissioner to request additional forces to protect Tibetan refugees.[21] Following that incident, the Dalai Lama briefly considered moving some government offices and his personal residence to a suburb of Delhi, "as the growing tension between the locals and the Tibetans is becoming a cause of worry."[22]

The Dalai Lama stayed, but nearly two decades on, tensions remain. Tsepak Tenzing, a Tibetan American whose parents live in South India, believes that "today, there is resentment of Tibetans" in places like Karnataka, the South Indian state with the largest Tibetan refugee population, "because land is now so scarce and expensive."[23] In her 2013 self-published travelogue *Dharamsala Days, Dharamsala Nights*, Pauline MacDonald noted that there is "a lot of bad blood" between local Indians and Tibetans, fueled mostly by "the Tibetans' perceived economic prosperity."

To this day "bad blood" continues to boil. One murder in McLeod Ganj was still fresh when I visited in January 2016.[24] On the main street a pile of rocks marked the spot where, a few months earlier, a young Tibetan man was stabbed in the abdomen and killed after a late-night altercation with three local Indian men. Photos of the crime scene online show stained pavement and pools of blood seeping into a drainage ditch. Such incidents have even prompted Tibetans to ask the once unthinkable: "Is Dharamsala safe for Tibetans?"[25]

--- --- ---

To answer questions like that one, the federal government in 2014 unveiled its long-awaited "Tibetan Rehabilitation Policy," to bring national uniformity to the legal protections afforded Tibetans in India.[26] Among the benefits that New Delhi wanted to extend to every Tibetan in the country were access to health care, the right to secure a bank loan, access to educational grants and food subsidies, and consideration for state and federal jobs in sectors traditionally reserved for Indian citizens, like education. At a November 2014 unveiling of the rehabilitation plan, the Indian minister of state for home affairs, Kiren Rijiju, said that extending India's "welfare related program and policies [to] our Tibetan friends" was the right thing to do.

"The benefits [that] we envisage for our Indian citizen should reach to our honored guest," he said. "And sometimes we need to go beyond."

Yet for all the proclamations of official support, extension of benefits, and pledges of equality, Tibetans still face difficulties integrating at the local level. Tibetans are scattered across ten Indian states, and laws on incorporating noncitizens into the social fabric vary widely. At the same November 2014 occasion, Rijiju and other federal officials seemed to be selling the measure to state governments more than unveiling it. Attendance was voluntary, and according to one accounting of attendees, three states with Tibetan constituencies—including Orissa, where Phuntsokling is located—had no representation at all.

The empty chairs were a poignant reminder of how uneven political support for Tibetans in India truly is.

If parts of South Asia are tiring of Tibetan refugees, the gritty urban jungles of Western capitals offer more allure. In a suburb of Paris, where Purang Dorjee's youngest daughter works at a beauty salon, Tibetan immigrants share cramped flats with other transplants from Africa, Asia, and Eastern Europe. In Germany, Switzerland, and the Czech Republic, municipal governments fly the Tibetan flag in solidarity with their small Tibetan communities during sensitive anniversaries. On the banks of the River Thames, London's small but growing Tibetan population gathers frequently to dance, sing, and mark key dates on the Tibetan calendar.

And along a stretch of busy highway in Woodside, Queens, just a short subway ride from the United Nations, the largest community of Tibetan exiles outside of Asia is spending millions to convert an old garment factory into a community center for religious, cultural, and educational programming.

Tibetans have been migrating to the United States for decades, but their presence was solidified in 1992, when one thousand refugees from India and Nepal were granted visas as part of a onetime resettlement program authorized by Congress. For over a decade afterward these well-connected few maintained tight bonds and a small community—raising awareness of their plight, sending cash back to their families, and challenging China from afar.

By the mid-2000s, with the original wave of emigrants firmly established in New York's ethnic melting pot, the number of Tibetans in the United States and throughout North America began to surge on the backs of family reunification. By 2009, the Tibetan government in exile in India counted over nine thousand Tibetans living in the United States, with the majority of those calling the tristate area of Connecticut, New York, and New Jersey home.[1] In 2012, with the New York Tibetan community ballooned but dispersed, Tibetan leaders began looking for a building to serve as a focal point for their people, culture, and faith.

Four years later, inside a boarded-up linen mill, Tibetans' new center of gravity had an address.

I first visited the Phuntsok Deshi Tibetan Community Hall in Woodside in March 2016, long before it was officially inaugurated. Fifteen minutes on the R Train deposited me in an industrial part of Queens that is the urban and cosmopolitan opposite of Midtown Manhattan. Low-rise factory buildings sit next to used-car showrooms, and busy tire stores line the walk from the Northern Boulevard subway station to the center at 32–01 Fifty-Seventh Street. As I walked east past a small Dominican deli and a (closed) late-night disco, planes roared low overhead en route to nearby La Guardia Airport, and the *clack-clack* of power tools banged from a row of auto-repair shops in the vicinity.

Sonam Gyatso, president of the Tibetan Community of New York–New Jersey, was waiting for me when I arrived. We met in a garbage-strewn parking lot beside a two-story concrete-and-brick building. Piles of metal beams and plastic tabletops leaned against a graffiti-covered facade. He had just handed over the keys to the general contractor, so we couldn't go inside, but from the exterior I could imagine wide-open spaces of concrete and exposed wiring, where looms and stitching machines once turned out aprons and uniforms for workers across the city. Photos online do the space more justice—covering up the empty walls and stark beams are huge, colorful brocades of crimson and gold, and at one end of the empty hall stands a tiny stage adorned with red-and-green bunting, butter lamps, and a huge photo of Lhasa's Potala Palace. But from where Sonam stood on that late-winter day, Tibetans' New York meeting hall looked more like a dark, drab, cinderblock clean slate.

We talked in the parking lot as the sun slowly slipped below the horizon. Sonam explained why he thought Tibetans in New York needed a dedicated multimillion-dollar space to congregate. As the struggle with China continues, "we are losing a lot" as refugees, especially when it comes to the younger generation's knowledge of language and Tibetan scripture, he said. And the best way to preserve these assets is to ensure that New York's Tibetan Americans have a facility to serve as the center of their cultural and religious activities—a church, a synagogue, a temple to their culture. Once renovations were complete, at a cost of roughly $3.5 million, the hall would accommodate an eight-hundred-seat theater and permanent stage on the ground floor, and thirteen classrooms and a kitchen on the lower level. A Tibetan language school was expected to move in, serving some five hundred tristate students weekly. And according to the project's website, the space will "serve as a backbone and/or a support system for all Tibetans . . . where all individuals can unite as one and learn from one another."[2]

Pledges of unity in exile stand in stark contrast to where Tibetans started. Tibet of old was, like most societies at various points in history, a fragmented, unequal place, where religion, geography, and class collided to create an often unstable mix of social friction and rivalry. Far from the paradise of harmony and equality that Hollywood has at times presented,[3] Tibet had many challenges. Indeed, the reality that Tibet was a splintered, feudal society of the landed and landless presented China with a means to rationalize its occupation. In the Chinese version of history, the arrival of Mao's soldiers in 1950 led to the emancipation of Tibetan "serfs" from the grips of monastic oppression. Much of China's early efforts to gain favor in Tibet were aimed at coopting some elites, while encouraging Tibet's proletariat to revolt against others—the "serfs" against the monks, lamas, and landed gentry.

Western-trained observers are more conflicted in their terminology; some have substantiated the idea that Tibet practiced an "institutionalized inequality that can be called pervasive serfdom."[4] Others suggest that historic Tibet was governed more as a "caste-like social hierarchy."[5] But whatever one calls it, there is little question that Tibet before 1950—not unlike preindustrial (and much of industrialized) Europe, America, or China, for that matter—was far from equitable for most of its residents.

That inequality did not vanish when Tibetans became refugees. Rather, it migrated with them.[6] In *Red Star over Tibet*, the late Tibetan historian Dawa Norbu recalled his family's uncomfortable relocation to India in the 1960s. Poor families like his were forced to beg for food or sell their most prized possessions to make ends meet. Especially difficult to comprehend, he recalls, was how Tibet's wealthiest responded to the needs of its poorest once in exile. "We children were skinny, pot-bellied, pale and yellow-complexioned through malnutrition. We had sores all over our bodies, due to unhygienic conditions, and an inability to adapt quickly to our new environment," Norbu wrote of those days.

"But the foreigners treated and nursed us like real parents, without a patronizing air or any sign of revulsion at our unhealthy state; whereas our own kin, the sons and daughters of Tibetan aristocracy and wealthy Tibetans, studying in colleges or working around Darjeeling [India], did not come to help us. Perhaps they were ashamed of us."[7]

Class wasn't the only dividing line for Tibetan refugees just arriving in India. Geography and religious allegiances also tested the exiles' unity. One of the most significant early splits emerged in 1965, when refugees from Eastern Tibet protested the Tibetan administration by refusing to pay taxes or support the legitimacy of the refugee movement. The grievances were partly over culture and tradition, which vary among regions. But there was also concern that the CTA—made up primarily of Lhasa-based aristocrats—would trade Eastern Tibet to China if pushed.

Today the Tibetan diaspora is more outwardly unified and egalitarian than historical Tibet ever was. For young Tibetans, the rifts of their parents and grandparents seem like distant memories, and among most second- and third-generation refugees the "Tibetan nation" is culturally, religiously, and politically alive. Historical divisions—along geographic, linguistic, cultural, or religious lines—seem less important to modern Tibetan refugees. And yet, the lingering challenge is how best to construct a sense of Tibetan identity that is transnational and meaningful.

Tibetans have taken steps to address this challenge. Since arriving in exile, Tibetan leaders have discouraged migration out of Asia, pushed for limited acculturation in the places they live, discouraged citizenship, and generally looked down upon marriage with non-Tibetans. London-based Tibet scholar Dibyesh Anand says these and other forms of ethnic identification are a means of "communal border patrolling," of inscribed cohesion that finds parallels in the Israeli and Palestinian communities.[8]

The community space being created among the used-car dealers and Dominican delis of Woodside, Queens, may be one of the best places in the world to see how well the ideal is mixing with the realities of the modern.

—— ——

After our tour of the community center property, Sonam led me through the backdoor of an adjacent building, a two-story white clapboard house that serves as the unofficial headquarters for Tibetans in North America. Inside, it was clear why Tibetans were building a new, spacious center next door: they're bursting at the seams. On the day I visited, the house was a cluttered jumble of religious relics mixed with the trappings of modern political life. At a small desk the local cultural affairs coordinator, Tsultrim Gyatso, counted receipts amid a pile of "Green Book" applications (an identity document issued to Tibetans by their government in exile) and voter registration forms (it was just days before Tibetans would be casting ballots for their Sikyong, the secular leader of the government in exile). A computer streaming live video from India of a debate between the two remaining candidates glowed beside him.

Not even religious artifacts had room to breathe. A wooden mask used in Tibetan "long life" dances, and an intricately painted throne that the Dalai Lama sat on during a July 2015 teaching he gave at the Jacob K. Javits Convention Center, rested in separate corners. Both would normally be venerated as holy relics, but in the cramped confines of the Tibetan clubhouse the mask lay atop a dusty filing cabinet, and the throne was covered with a cardboard box, some fraying fabric, and a lone loose screw.

The renovation of the twenty-six-thousand-square-foot former sock and apron factory—paid for through donations and a $1.6 million mortgage[9]—wasn't simply about building a space to host potluck dinners on the weekend. This was about managing Tibetans' next wave of migration.

"What we're seeing now is the second big transformation within the exile community, which for us is a massive movement of people, mostly to the West," said Kaydor Aukatsang, who was the Dalai Lama's representative to North America at the time. "I see this as both a positive and a negative. Positive in a sense that as we have a bigger and bigger diaspora in the West, that itself becomes a base for the future leaders, and new energy and new thinking in terms of how to both preserve and maintain our culture and identity as well as how to take the movement forward in terms of trying to resolve the Tibet issue."

The problem this presents is that there is no physical center. In India, Nepal, and Bhutan, refugee settlements were originally conceived as all-Tibetan towns governed by the Central Tibetan Administration through political appointees. "It was a very direct and strong relationship," Aukatsang said, where settlement officers looked after their flock with a parental sense of responsibility. "But now, as the community gets more scattered, it will require [the CTA in] Dharamsala to refashion a different kind of relationship and government structure." In time, Aukatsang added, the bonds that hold Tibetans together in the West will be social constructs and the physical centers like the one in Woodside that they build to host them.

Many of Tibetan Buddhism's greatest spiritual and political leaders are already embracing this shifting center of gravity. Sera Jey, one of Tibet's "great three" Gelug universities, has property in Woodside.[10] And as the flood of Tibetans has increased, so too has the number of Tibetan associations and organizations to meet their political and social needs. In early 2016 there were about three dozen Tibetan cultural and political organizations in the New York metro area, such as the Tibetan Women's Association, the Tibetan Youth Congress, the US Tibet Committee, and the Tibet Action Institute.

Groups representing Tibetans from historic parts of Tibet—Amdo, Kham, and Ü-Tsang—are also rapidly being formed. These *kyidugs*, as they are called, celebrate the geographically distinct traditions among people from cities like Lhasa, Kyirong, Nyalam, Tingri, and Shelkar. There are roughly two dozen *kyidugs* in New York already, with more on the way.

Scholars like Oxford University's Fiona McConnell have postulated that when the current Dalai Lama is gone, the refugees' political center of gravity could shift from India to the West, which is already benefitting from a Tibetan "brain drain" from Asia. She imagines a situation in which "the physical presence" of the Tibetan government in exile might even be downsized and "replaced by a networked-style structure that operates through globally scattered hubs and online forums." Though such a shift would likely be a long-term development, anything close would nonetheless "open up the question of how the legitimacy of the [Tibetan government in exile] might be retained and reconstituted in such circumstances."[11] It would also open up the question of how China would respond to a largely digital government with no true geographic center.

For now, though, it is social organizations that serve as the glue for Tibetans trying to rebuild their exile community, for a second time. "There's a real danger of total assimilation [in the West]," said Aukatsang. "We keep talking about the threats and difficulties that Tibetans in Tibet have," particularly because of China's policies. "But there it is institutionalized repression. That's just the policy, the environment. Whereas here [in the West], we have all the freedoms and rights, but then, just through modern-day realities, there is a real risk that the community . . . could also just disappear."

— — —

The Tibetan communities of South Asia are aging, shifting, shrinking, and being reimagined. As the numbers in Woodside make clear, many Tibetans are moving west amid the reshuffle.

But some are choosing to move east—to China and Chinese-controlled Tibet. Tibetan officials say they don't keep track of how many Tibetans return to the Middle Kingdom voluntarily, but anecdotal evidence suggests it is more than a trickle. In New Delhi in late 2015, hundreds of Tibetans cued along rows of brick and razor wire outside the Chinese embassy following the announcement of streamlined visas for Tibetan returnees.[12] Elsewhere, in Chinese consulates in New York, San Francisco, and Toronto, the Chinese government employs ethnic Tibetans to facilitate visa processing (and also, presumably, to spy on their brethren).

Perceived dysfunction within the exiled Tibetan political establishment, coupled with China's economic and political ascendance, has given Beijing a new narrative to lure Tibetan returnees—even if the Tibetan dysfunction is largely of China's making.[13] In 2010, a staff member at the China Tibetology Research Center named Liu Bin urged the United Front Work Department to increase its "targeted work" on Tibetan refugees (second- and third-generation refugees among them) in a bid to urge the return of overseas Chinese ethnic minorities.[14] Among the proposed "targeted work" propaganda activities—the idea of which drew condemnation online[15]—was the creation of an Overseas Tibetan Friendship Association, proposed for California, to promote China's version of life in Tibet. In 2012, officials in the Tibet Autonomous Region were also reported to be planning a dedicated office to "communicate with and serve overseas Tibetans."[16]

Tibetans from across the spectrum—from senior lamas to fresh arrivals unable to integrate into the exile economy—are responding to these calls in modest numbers.[17] Matthew Akester, who has spent years living among Tibetan refugees, says China uses all manner of enticement to cajole non-politically orientated Tibetans to return. After the April 2015 earthquake in

Nepal, for instance, "there was a flurry of movement" by China to encourage Tibetan returnees. "They did an exercise in Nepal where they suddenly opened that counter in the embassy in Nepal, and said anyone who lives in earthquake affected areas can come, no-questions-asked kind of thing, more or less as a PR exercise." It was the first time since 2008, when China abruptly halted the issuance of visit permits to Tibetans abroad, that the policy was reversed. China had essentially used a tragedy to encourage Tibetans to return to Chinese-controlled Tibet, possibly for good.

For many Tibetans in exile, some of whom have spent decades in legal or political limbo, China's calls of reunification—a key strategy for resolving the Tibetan issue—seem to resonate. Moreover, the Tibetan government in exile "doesn't have a policy discouraging people to visit," one Tibetan official told me. "In fact, the understanding is that it's good to go. We've got to keep those connections. Otherwise, the community outside Tibet is so small, and the longer we stay in our current situation, the ties become that much more tenuous."

But that doesn't mean a reverse Tibetan migration wouldn't cause huge policy challenges for Tibetan exile leaders. A Tibetan American or Tibetan Canadian applying for a visa must go through "a very invasive, complicated process," the same official said. "You really have to list [all] your relatives in Tibet, where are you visiting, and then they follow it up by actually contacting the individual people listed on the visa application form. So, it's a really big concern, because then that way they are able to track people, here and in Tibet. They know, in a certain village, Mr. Tashi or Mr. Tenzin has a relative in, say, Canada. That information is obviously used in ways [to monitor] that we know the Chinese government is capable of doing."

———

Like any refugees forcibly separated from their homeland, Tibetans are migrating for better lives, better education, and better opportunities. But unlike many ethnic minorities who have drawn xenophobic ire from hosts elsewhere—Syrians in France, Kurds in Turkey, or Palestinians in Israel, for example—Tibetans retain a high degree of support, especially in the United States. Online, American immigration lawyers almost brag about how easy it is for Tibetans to gain asylum if properly coached.[18] Lobsang Nyandak, who heads the Tibet Fund charity in New York, said that while he had seen a few cases in which Tibetans were not granted asylum to the United States, "these are a very small number . . . the majority of Tibetans, they seem to get asylum." (That was before the election of Donald Trump, however; how his policies affect immigration of all types, including Tibetan, remains to be seen.)

The day after my visit to Woodside, Tibetans gathered in a park near the United Nations to mark their failed March 10, 1959, uprising. Robert Thurman, a preeminent Buddhist scholar and Tibet House president, exhorted young Tibetans in the audience to "study hard, go see *geshe la* [a Tibetan religious teacher who has earned a degree in Buddhist studies], and learn your language." Many of the Tibetans who had set themselves alight inside Tibet had complained of China's restrictions on speaking their birth tongue, Thurman told the crowd. "So, therefore, you young people, keep studying your Tibetan in addition to economics and politics and whatever else you're studying in school."

Thurman's plea to "young people" may have fallen on deaf ears—many in the crowd gathered at Dag Hammarskjöld Plaza near the UN thumbed their cell phones or chatted among themselves as he spoke—but it captured a generational divide that Tibetans, academics, and even the US government fear could end the Tibetan refugee experiment. According to a 2008 State Department assessment of Tibetan settlements in India, a lack of opportunity and earning power is pushing younger Tibetans away, and adversely affecting the Dalai Lama's goal of cultural and traditional cohesion.[19] Settlement officers warned that because so many young Tibetans are leaving India, "Tibetan culture [in that country] may die out with this generation."

It could actually happen sooner. Annual growth rates across the five dozen Tibetan camps in India, Nepal, and Bhutan was a paltry 1.4 percent in the decade after 1998; some settlements, like the enclave in the once-bustling urban center of Kathmandu, saw a decline of 10 percent. And even in camps where population numbers appear to be holding steady, a closer look often reveals a more depressing reality. At the Lugsum Samdupling settlement in Bylakuppe, India, the numbers paint a mixed picture. Established in 1960 with an initial population of roughly 3,000, the settlement counted 9,200 Tibetans in 2009, up from 7,500 a decade earlier—an average annual growth rate of 1.9 percent.[20] But in the same settlement, deaths are outpacing births by 30 percent, unemployment hovers at 40 percent, only 9 percent of young people attend college, and nearly two-thirds—63 percent—report that they are migrating abroad or plan to do so soon.[21]

The bustling ethnic soup of Queens, in New York City, is where many of those who make good on their plans to leave end up. In Jackson Heights, two miles east of the Woodside community hall, Tibetan and Himalayan restaurants serve up plates of noodles and mugs of butter tea. Over the years the area once known for its Indian salons and sari shops has transformed into a "Little Tibet," where storefronts stuffed with Tibetan flags, Buddhist statues, and endless rows of incense share space with chefs hawking mounds of momos. It has even become a hipster destination for Tibetan cuisine: in November 2012, a local non-Tibetan foodie organized Jackson Heights's first-ever Tibetan Momo Crawl; the event has now been held four times.[22]

Kalsang Wangmo is among the thousands of Tibetans who navigate these cultural reinterpretations. Kalsang was born and raised in the Lugsum Sam-dupling settlement in Bylakuppe, to parents born and raised in Tibet. And like many of her peers in the West, she has worked hard to give her children a better life. Jackson Heights—not India, and certainly not Tibet—is now home.

I first met Kalsang in 2009, when I interviewed her for a documentary I was working on while at the Council on Foreign Relations. Another Tibetan friend—a former representative of the Tibetan government in exile in the United States—introduced us. She welcomed me into her home to speak about her life in India and the United States, and her fears of raising children in an America that unintentionally encourages cultural assimilation. From the looks of things, she was doing well: plush couches lined one wall of her bright three-bedroom flat, photos of her children in traditional Tibetan dress hung near the door, and an electronic keyboard—where her daughter Tenzin practices her singing—stood ready for rehearsal.

As a kid, Kalsang was poor. Her parents moved to India from Tibet just a few months after the Dalai Lama in 1959, and had been living in Bylakuppe ever since. Her early life was dictated by the weather. "In India we used to work as farmers. We'd plant the maize; we had two acres. You know, success depends on the rain. If it's good rain, then we get something. If there's no rain, everything is gone." (I'd seen this same crude calculus up close during my irrigation project in Phuntsokling.) Most years were mediocre. But no matter how fruitful the harvest, corn alone was never enough to financially sustain the family. During the winter months, Kalsang and her siblings hit the road to sell hand-knit sweaters. There were no off-season jobs in Bylakuppe, "so we'd go for sweater business for . . . three or four months. If it's cold, [we have] good business, but if it's not cold, then no business."

Kalsang grew tired of the sales life by the time she was in her mid-twenties, and tried her hand at another common job for young Tibetans in India: as a soldier in India's army. Just as families in Tibet have for centuries sent one family member to the monastery, today in India, especially in northern areas, most refugees have at least one family member serving in the Special Frontier Force, all-Tibetan units that guard the India-China border in the mountainous regions of Sikkim and Arunachal Pradesh.[23] Kalsang spent five years in the male-dominated SFF. "I volunteered for everything. I did parachuting. I did rock climbing. I did mountaineering. The first mountain I did was Bhagirathi. There is Bhagirathi One, Two, and Three. I did the second one. That's like twenty-two thousand feet. The next one I did is Satopanth. That's at twenty-four thousand feet. I'm the only girl who climbed to the top with the men."

But that adventure eventually grew old, too, and by late 2001 Kalsang made up her mind to leave the service and immigrate to North America. She settled on New York, and found someone in the United States willing to issue her an invitation letter for an outlandish sum of 250,000 rupees (about $4,000)—far more than she made selling sweaters in a year. She borrowed the cash from a local monastery, a common practice for Tibetans looking to migrate.

She arrived in New York a few months before 9/11 with just the clothes on her back and a few photographs of her family. After a year earning money as a live-in housekeeper to pay off the monastery loan, she presented her story to immigration officials. Facts mattered little to the Americans, she recalls, and even with little to back up her story, her application for residency was granted in less than 180 days. She was able to bring her children over in 2004, and eventually found work cooking and cleaning for a few families on the Upper East Side, including for a prominent US philanthropist who has invested heavily in China's education system (she told me his name, but because he still does work in China asked that I not publish it). In 2003 she got her own apartment, and the next year she had earned enough money to bring her children over, then her sister.

"Everybody wants to come to New York, not only me. All Tibetans want to come here. They are dying to come here, like line by line. America is like a totally different world.

"We paid money, but I don't care because we make that money here. Here we have such opportunity, the opportunity to work. We can prove who we are."

Today, Kalsang is raising her children to embrace their Tibetan culture. "It's my job to teach my own kids, because in the United States, Tibetans are a minority. We have a few thousand Tibetans, that's it. [We are] mixing with people from other countries. So it's very important for me to teach them who we are, where we come from. You know, we're Tibetan." As community centers like the one in Woodside open, Tibetans like her will have a place to learn from one another. In time, that may be enough to sustain them.

Had Kelsang sought asylum in another country, or chosen another time to flee India, she might still be without a home. America's approach to Tibetan immigration has not been perfect; despite a legacy of political and economic support, efforts to formalize the visa process for displaced Tibetans has stalled in Congress.[24] But it's far worse in parts of Europe, where places like Germany, Belgium, and Switzerland—countries that once provided agricultural and technical support to newly arrived refugees in India in the 1960s—are increasingly turning away Tibetan arrivals.[25]

Sonam Dorgee, the settlement officer in Dharamsala, said that as many as one thousand Tibetans in India were issued "black papers" by European countries in 2015, as immigration officials concluded that changes to Indian law (including the "rehabilitation" deal that the Indian minister of state for home affairs had boasted about) meant Tibetans could no longer claim political asylum in Europe.

——

Given the current state of affairs, Purang Dorjee's middle daughter, Dechen, was lucky to leave when she did. On October 27, 2013, after paying the equivalent of $15,000 to an "agent," Dechen, then thirty-four, boarded a flight at Indira Gandhi International Airport in New Delhi. She arrived in Paris with little more than a desire to see the world, to make money, and to leave the tedium and legal uncertainty of perpetual refuge in India behind her. A cousin met her at the airport and helped her get settled.

By September 2016, Dechen had found her way to a commuter town on the outskirts of the capital called Ivry-sur-Seine. According to the Tibetan government in exile, she was one of just five hundred Tibetans living in the country at the time, though Dechen suspects there are many more undocumented Tibetans who have arrived since the last official government survey was conducted. Within days of clearing customs she had found a job, a place to live, and a new lease on life. Dechen had experience as a beautician, and was quickly hired in a salon far from the city center, trimming the hair and painting the nails of Parisians in a bedroom community.

The unsettled nature of life in India is what pushed her to leave, she said. It was early 2013, and after breaking up with her boyfriend of a few years, she came to a realization: "India was useless for me."

But where would she go? "America is very tough, very difficult to go to." Unlike Kelsang and thousands of other Tibetans who had pointed their compasses to the United States over the years, Dechen thought she would have better luck in Europe. It was an admittedly risky move. At the time, immigrants from Syria, Iraq, and countries farther east were raising the ire of France's anti-immigrant politicians. China, meanwhile, would seem to have more sway over European decisions related to Tibetan immigration than it did over Washington.

Days before she arrived, as if to set the stage, police in another Paris suburb detained a young, undocumented Kosovar girl who was on an educational field trip with classmates. Leonarda Dibrani was swiftly deported to Kosovo, kicking off a flurry of student-led protests across the city. It was just one of an endless string of arrests and deportations of France's migrant population, any one of which might have put a young Tibetan women off from testing the route for herself.[26]

For Dechen, though, emigrating was miraculously straightforward. "Some people, they find it very hard to come here," she said. Tibetans, like other immigrants, "have to go to every country, to the border, and try to get in. Some have to cross water, through rivers. But I didn't face problems like that." As the daughter of a relatively successful Tibetan businessman, raising the funds for airfare and papers was not hard. She simply paid her "agent," secured her documents, and collected her luggage at baggage claim. "Maybe I am lucky," she says coyly. "I pray a lot."

Today she lives in a small one-bedroom on the banks of the Seine. She works ten-hour days, six days a week, Monday through Saturday, at the salon some ninety minutes away by train. Three other Tibetan transplants trim hair with her, along with four Sri Lankan ladies and two girls from Vietnam.

During her commute she sleeps, reads, or plays Candy Crush Saga on her cell phone.

And in between the hours spent staring at the French countryside slipping past the train window, she considers the alternative: during the three years before she left India for Europe she was unemployed, living with her parents, and knotted up with a Tibetan man in a relationship that she said had no future. It's a trap many Tibetans her age are unable to avoid, including members of her own family.

Despite being homesick, Dechen has settled well. Since arriving she has earned enough money to move into her own flat, has begun a new relationship with a Tibetan she met in Paris, and regularly sends money home to her parents to repay money she borrowed when she left. "Everything is different than in India, and life in France is easier," she says. "It's good. What we want, we get."

"India is very difficult for Tibetans."

———

Back in the parking lot of the community center in Woodside, Sonam finished our tour on a cautionary note. There may be no stopping the migratory wave of young Tibetans like Kalsang or Dechen moving to Western capitals, but what they find when they arrive—either cities of money and strangers, or communities committed to carrying on the traditions of their forefathers—is up to Tibetans themselves.

Distance from the Dalai Lama has made it easier for divisions to solidify, and Tibetans have in the relative freedom of expression grown increasingly fractured, especially on whether to call for independence from China or something far more compromising. Many outsiders consider the argument sterile anyway, given China's unwillingness to negotiate with His Holiness; but to Tibetans it is and will remain a serious topic of conversation, if not action.

One particularly messy spat made the rounds on social media in early 2015. During March 10 protests in New York City that year—a year before my visit to Woodside—Tibetans clashed angrily with each other on whether shouting "China out of Tibet" or waving "Free Tibet" signs violated the Dalai Lama's compromise middle-way strategy (which calls for a negotiated solution with China). A series of cell-phone videos posted to Facebook shows organizers of the protest, including the community center's Sonam, asking police to ban the "Free Tibet" advocates from marching. Police, citing the US Constitution, politely declined.

When I asked Sonam about this encounter, he said it was just a big misunderstanding. But he clearly believed that supporters of *rangzen*—"freedom" in Tibetan—had chosen the wrong day to raise their flags and sow discord.

"There was a little drama," he conceded sheepishly. The idea was not to ban free speech, but rather to speak with one voice. "Every year there has been a stage, and for five minutes one speaker will speak, saying 'We need to fight for the free Tibet, we need to fight for free Tibet.' Then, after five minutes, someone else speaks, shouting 'We are for the middle way.' Forget about the foreigners or Americans; the Tibetan audience themselves—the younger generation, the older generation—were confused. 'What are they talking about? What do they want us to do?' It's confusing.

"His Holiness has been explaining these things [the middle way] for many years now; people have to understand it. But people aren't getting it, especially the younger generation," he said.

Yet in this case it was Sonam who miscalculated. Calling on New York City police to prevent Tibetans from exercising their First Amendment rights backfired, and on social media, the response was brutal and swift.

"[I] think PRC is liking these discussions of our fellow Tibetans," wrote one observer from Darjeeling, India, as the videos of apparent censorship went viral within the Tibetan diaspora. "We give slogans like 'United we stand, divided we fall.' Yet we are dividing ourselves."

Another comment, posted by a protest participant, was more personal. "My heart broke today," the young woman wrote. "For the first time in my life my own people tried to ostracize me for simply standing up for a Free Tibet. I saw the unity of the Tibetan people and our struggle falling apart in front of my eyes." Her post was later shared nearly three hundred times.[27]

Going forward, it may not be the brick-and-mortar structures of community centers like the one taking form in Woodside that hold the Tibetan diaspora together, but rather, how the next generation of leaders navigates the chasms of discord that grow amid China's strategic silence.

My last walk with Pala was on a cold, crisp morning in November 2014. We met on the prayer path in McLeod Ganj, just as the sun was cresting over the Himalayan foothills in northern India. I found him near the giant incense urns where Tibetans incinerate juniper needles in offering to Buddhism's deities. We had no formal plan to meet that morning—one of his sons had told me when and where I could find him—but he didn't seem annoyed or surprised to have company. "Tashi delek," he said, smiling. "Good morning."

Even predawn Pala was upbeat, bubbly, focused, and faithful. He acknowledged me with a hearty "Hello, okay, okay, okay," followed by a slight bow and his familiar grin. Turning up the hill, he motioned for me to tag along. "Okay, okay, okay," he repeated again, then his go-to Tibetan catch phrase: "La-doh." Let's go.

We climbed the paved footpath in steady silence, just as we had nearly every morning when I stayed at his home seventeen years earlier. I studied his rhythmic thumbing on the wooden prayer beads that he clasped in his hands behind his back. Two decades earlier I had mimicked his devotion with my own set of beads, purchased in the market, to silently recite the *Om mani padme hum* mantra that Buddhists utter to the bodhisattva of compassion. But this time my *mala* stayed zipped in my coat pocket, and I was more interested in observing Pala's devotional stroll than zeroing in on my own (admittedly stalled) faith.

We inched slowly up the gravel footpath. Dozens of elderly Tibetan men and women, some spinning hand-held prayer wheels bigger than their heads, joined us in the slow lane on the highway of devotion. Pala stopped occasionally—to spin one of the prayer wheels fixed along the route, to catch his breath, or just to say hello to someone he knew from around town. With his easy smile and jovial style Pala exuded a mayoral air as he climbed.

By 8 a.m. we neared the top of the circuit, passing beneath the towering wire fence that circles the Dalai Lama's temple and living quarters. Tibetans seem to have a sixth sense about when His Holiness is in town (even at eighty-one he spends up to half the year traveling within India and abroad to Europe and North America). For everyone else, the positioning of armed Indian soldiers along the wire fence of the kora is the clearest signal that the Dalai Lama has returned from a trip. I continued climbing the hill behind Pala, staring uneasily at the half-dozen men and their rifles as we walked by (I had always found something contradictory about the world's best-known pacifist being guarded by heavily armed soldiers).

Just as we cleared the final incline, a few hundred feet before the taxi stand that serves as the route's terminus, Pala moved toward a turbaned, crippled beggar sitting crossed-kneed in the dirt. I had walked this route a few times in the days leading up to my encounter with Pala—mostly for exercise but also to reminisce—and had seen the middle-aged Indian man sitting there each time. But I had never stopped. I had long ago made a conscious choice not to give money to India's destitute, assuming that most beggars were running a scam or were indentured into someone else's service. India is notorious for tourist rackets and panhandler rip-offs, and I had been duped countless times before—by grungy children pretending to need money to buy milk for their sisters, by old men offering directions, by touts in train stations threatening to get rough unless they are paid. To me, the man on the ground was part of India's unfortunate, avoidable, reality.

But Pala saw a different man seated in the dirt. In his eyes the beggar, with his muddy prosthetic limbs and tin cup, was no different from the hundreds of Tibetan refugees who marched past him spinning their wheels every day. Just like the beggar, Tibetans had once been penniless and politically invisible, and were in many ways still trying to find their way in a country that had never fully embraced them. Moreover, the beggar—a local Gaddi tribesman, Pala's son told me later—had seen his ancestral homeland of mountains and valleys lost to foreigners, too. In Pala's case it was to the Chinese. For the beggar, it was to Tibetan refugees.

"My friend, my friend," said Pala, nodding and bowing in polite reverence to the man as he approached. "We," Pala continued, turning to me now. "We same. Same, same."

Pala leaned over and dropped a few coins in the man's empty tin cup, drawing a wide, toothless grin. "Namaste," I muttered, clasping my hands together, less at the man and more in awe of Pala's blind generosity.

Pala and I walked together for a while longer, plodding toward the taxi stand. I slowed my gait only slightly to accommodate his sprightly pace. Around a corner another beggar—this one looked to be Tibetan—awaited knowingly. Pala pulled more rupee coins from his bag and plopped them into the awaiting palm. He said he gives money to the same two men every morning, like clockwork. When I asked why, he smiled, nodded, and kept walking without saying a word. I assume it's just his way of spinning the karmic wheel.

Temple Road was just beginning to wake up as we approached the end of the path. A tea-and-egg seller was firing up his burner. Vendors with baskets of steaming potato momos were rolling their carts into place. Vegetable and prayer-bead sellers were laying out their wares for the day's transactions. Pausing near a grimy public toilet (proudly operated by the Department of Health, according to a sign painted on the wall), we had reached the end of the walk. Pala adjusted his sweater and knit hat. We had circled the path only once, and I was sweating, ready for breakfast. Pala—smiling and bouncy— was ready for his second clockwise rotation.

"Goodbye," I said, putting my hand on Pala's shoulder. "Thank you for the company."

"Okay, okay, okay" he muttered again, managing a crooked grin. "See you tomorrow," he said, before disappearing down the hill toward the circuit's leafy, cow-shit-strewn start. See you tomorrow.

Around the time that I made my final trip to McLeod Ganj to visit with my "Pala," I reconnected with two respected Tibet observers who have watched the Tibetan diaspora from different angles for many years: Robert Barnett and Matthew Akester. Just as I had before my first sojourn at the heart of

China's soft-power struggle, I reached out again, before and during my last, to share and validate what I had learned during nearly a decade of speaking with Tibetans navigating the front lines of an often invisible conflict.

Each was pessimistic about the Tibetan community's political trajectory, and each voiced doubts as to whether the current crop of leaders could lead the Tibetan community and its cause. In essence, they saw the Tibetan refugee community as symbolically important, but politically quiescent. "Dharamsala is by its nature an institution that it's difficult to reinvent and reimagine, in part because it's still based on memory and hope rather than initiative and output," Barnett said. That doesn't mean that Tibetans—both in exile and inside Tibet—don't still look to Dharamsala for political direction; they do. But what they find when they dig deeper are institutions that have "not excelled in terms of credibility, innovation, and so on, at least in terms of policies toward China." From a lack of vision and creativity to a devastating brain drain, "there are structural problems with the India Dharamsala project that would require really bold thinking to overcome."

Akester was even more circumspect. We met for tea in the garden at Norbulingka, in what had by then become an annual rite, a check-in with my geopolitical guru. His house, not far from where we sat, is a few miles from the complex that houses the Tibetan administration. I told him about my latest conversations with Tibetan refugees in New York, in South India, and in Nepal, and shared the sentiment of my host brother's seemingly undying faith in the direction being charted by the Tibetan leadership.

"I'm afraid that's the voice of many in the community up there," Akester said, nodding up the hill in the direction of McLeod Ganj. "There is either an inability or a refusal to think progressively about the future, especially on the part of the exile leadership. To think that there is more to their struggle than the world peace diplomacy of the Dalai Lama. Protest exploded in Tibet in 2008, but the exiles failed to catch that wind, to engage with the real issues, and the political debate here has degenerated into witch-hunting anyone accused of disloyalty. I am afraid that is a sign of desperation."

Amid such dire observations and downward trends it's impossible not to wonder what will become of the Tibetan diaspora when the Dalai Lama is gone—a question Akester says Tibetans have thought too little about. There is no doubt it will look different, but in what ways depends on so many factors (like where a Fifteenth Dalai Lama is recognized, and by whom, and whether international political support for Tibetans begins to wane in the power vacuum) that it's easy to see why exiled Tibetans would rather think about something else. Not even the Dalai Lama's private office seems interested in engaging in the debate; I made over a half dozen requests for a follow-up interview to our brief 2009 conversation, looking to speak either with His Holiness or a representative from his office, but was told that because of a busy schedule and advanced age, His Holiness wasn't able to accommodate.

"Much as we would have liked to arrange an interview, it is difficult for the time being due to His Holiness' very busy schedule with extended travels," Chhime Chhoekyapa, the private office's secretary, said by e-mail. "As you may know, His Holiness has spoken at length on Tibetan culture and related issues on many occasions, which are on record. You may like to consider looking into some of his statements for inclusion in your book."

Despite a desire to move away from the political spotlight, which he solidified in 2011 by stepping down as Tibetans' temporal leader, abandoning a four-century tradition of Dalai Lamas serving as Tibet's spiritual and political leader, there is no doubt that the institution of the Dalai Lama continues to carry the Tibetan torch in exile—at least in the minds of many Tibetans. And it is where that torch is being carried to that Tibetans like Purang Dorjee and his family must work out for themselves.

I once asked Pala what he thought his family's future looked like. We spoke through a translator at his house, in the same concrete courtyard where we had once huddled for warmth around steaming cups of tea and buckets of smoldering coal. Tenants came in and out, and his wife sat silently on a nearby stoop, knitting, preparing dinner, and refilling our mugs when they went dry. (During every one of my visits to Pala's house, either as a houseguest in the late 1990s or a writer in the 2010s, Pala's wife was present but largely silent. I never learned much about her beyond where she was raised and how she met her husband.) For over two hours we spoke as monkeys bounced from the rooftops and dogs howled aimlessly at the sky.

"Do you still hold out hope that you might see your homeland again, or at least that your children will?"

"I'm still hopeful, because His Holiness is working hard," Pala said, adding:

"I have hope for the Chinese government. . . . and I have faith in the Chinese people." He said he would return only to a free Tibet, suggesting that no one in his family would be taking the bait and moving to Tibet under Chinese control. (He also refused to discuss what family he still has in Tibet, fearful that doing so might bring them trouble.)

"What are some of the biggest changes to your adopted home?" I asked.

"Two things. The younger generation today has started moving to the West, and the new houses that are being built in Dharamsala are for Indians, not Tibetans."

"Do you wish more of your family could move to the West," like your daughter?

"I wish all of my family could stay together here, in Dharamsala. It will be easier, when we get freedom, for the whole family to move back to Tibet from here. But of course, if they want to go to the West, that's their choice."

"Did you ever try to leave McLeod Ganj and move to the West?" I asked.

"No, no," he said, chuckling. "India has the best roti. Why would I move to the West? Seriously, in India, we're all the same."

Shunning the translator for the moment, Pala moved into broken English. "Fifty-fifty [*pifty-pifty*]. I good. You good. Same same. In Dharamsala, Tibetans and Gaddi, half and half—Tibetans are benefiting, and the Gaddi are benefiting."

"Do you consider India your home?"

Returning to the translator, he continued. "I've built a house here . . . but it's hard to say. It doesn't feel like home. But it's up to the Tibetan government in exile or the CTA. Whatever they say, I want to listen. I don't want to express whether this place, India, feels like home."

"Do you feel lucky to be in Dharamsala?" I asked.

"It cannot be wrong; I am fortunate to be here, near to His Holiness the Dalai Lama. It's a privilege to be here. Because of His Holiness I always think about mutual benefits. Everyone wants happiness. Being a peaceful society and world is best and suitable for everybody. With His Holiness living here, there are more people coming here. More international people, and more Chinese."

By now the sun was beginning to wane, and Purang Dorjee, my Pala, was growing tired. Two hours of conversation through translation was pushing him to exhaustion. As I gathered my bag and closed up my notebook, I asked the patriarch one more question, something I imagined his own children asking him over the years as they grew to accept their place as stateless people in a world of countries.

"Are you still angry with the Chinese today, after all this time?" I asked. Pala replied quickly, and with a typical sense of hope, trust, and faith.

"The Dalai Lama is the manifestation of Chenraizig, the bodhisattva of compassion. He introduced this middle-way approach for dealing with China, a mutual means of benefiting both Tibetans and Chinese. If that happens, if China accepts this approach, it would be a wonderful thing. Tibetans could return to Tibet.

"But when it comes to China, it is like a sky—it's vast. There is nothing much we can do; it's too big. But I don't have any anger toward China. There is no use of anger. It's our karma. China has a billion people, and we only have six million Tibetans—there are big differences between the two. We can't do much about it. It's up to them."

EPILOGUE

As far as I know, Pala is still walking the kora, circling the temple complex that he and Tibetans like him have venerated for nearly six decades. If he makes it to March 2019—the sixtieth anniversary of Tibetans' flight—he will be eighty-four, just one year older than the man he followed over the icy Himalayas to freedom six decades earlier. But when he does die, his body will likely be taken to the local crematorium outside the North Indian village where he has made a life and raised a family. His flesh and bones will be burned on a pyre, and his ashes scattered to the wind above a home he never asked for, and certainly never wanted.

Unlike so many of the world's political and religious exiles whose suffering is only momentarily mourned globally, Tibetans have managed to stay in the spotlight far longer than even they might have expected. India and Western democracies—especially the United States, which first used Tibetans to further Washington's foreign policy goals and today maintains ties for more humanitarian reasons—deserve the credit for keeping them there, at least politically and financially. Tibetans have served as an exemplar that actors and musicians, pacifists and democracy denizens can attach themselves to with conviction. And Tibetans have captured the world's affection in spite of—or perhaps because of—China's insidious, persistent campaigning to drive them into irrelevance.

There is, of course, much to be discouraged about in the Tibetan exile struggle today, and much of this book has focused on those challenges. Tibetan refugees are squeezed from all sides—first and foremost by China's ever-present gaze, but also by their own internal fracturing, bickering, addictions, and political missteps. The hard slog and long wait for redemption have no doubt been complicated and made more painful by these and other challenges.

But there are also, much to China's dismay, bright spots seeping through the Tibetan refugee haze. During my earliest years of reporting on Beijing's "blessings," most Tibetans I spoke with cast blame for their woes elsewhere: on China's spying; on Nepal's border policies; on the weakening resolve of the international community. Today, though, such finger pointing appears to be subsiding, and is giving way to much-needed self-reflection by a new generation of young Tibetans who are committed to providing a counternarrative to China's vilification. In turn, fresh ideas and new energy are saturating a long-stifled, stultified political movement.

There are Tibetans like Tenzin Seldon, twenty-seven, who advises the United Nations on Tibet and other issues from Bangkok, and says that the slow "silencing of our cause" will be a wake-up call to Tibetan youth everywhere. Born in India and educated in the United States, she is a Rhodes scholar and the first-ever Tibetan to receive the Truman graduate scholarship for gifted US college juniors. Among her contributions to the Tibet conversation are Tibetan and Chinese student dialogue sessions that bring people from opposing poles to sit and discuss their mutual predicament.[1]

There are Tibetans like Namgyal Dolkar, vice president the GuChuSum Political Prisoners Movement of Tibet in Dharamsala, who sued the government of India to become an Indian citizen. When the Indian-born Tibetan won her case in 2011 at twenty-five years old, she became the first Tibetan living in exile to publicly secure this right through the courts.[2] "When Tibetans came here they did not need Indian citizenship. But now, society is changing, the community is changing," she reflected a few years after her victory. "More and more educated Tibetans are speaking from more platforms, and the majority of those platforms demand Indian citizenship in India, like any other country around the world."

And then there are Tibetans like Tsewang Namgyal, an investment banker in New York City who grew up in India's largest Tibetan settlement, Doeguling, in the South Indian town of Mundgod. Today he is spearheading an effort to "reimagine" the Tibetan settlement concept itself, to breathe new life into Tibetan communities in India that are suffering steep population declines, low birthrates, and the outmigration of young talent.[3] Tsewang believes his project, Reimagining Doeguling Tibetan Settlement, could reverse these trends by bringing jobs through eco- and religious-based tourism. Robert Thurman, a professor of Buddhist studies at Columbia University, says the idea is to lure visitors to India's isolated South by marketing Doeguling as "a focal point for rest and relaxation, Tibetan Medicine Buddha health restorative tourism, meditational tourism, and spiritual inspiration."[4]

Intrigued by Tsewang's vision for Doeguling—and impressed by the support it has received from scholars like Thurman—I arranged a visit to the sprawling settlement in late 2016, to see for myself if Tibetan communities in India could actually be "reimagined." To be honest, I was skeptical from the start. I've visited many Tibetan camps in India, and most are geographically isolated, lack basic amenities (like hot water and reliable electricity), and are closed to foreigners unless they obtain a Protected Area Permit from the Indian government. Failure to obtain one can bring hefty fines, and even jail time.

Yet once I finally did arrive, traveling from London to India via Abu Dhabi (with an entry permit secured with Tsewang's help), my initial skepticism become more conflicted. On the one hand, India's deep South offers fresh air, starry nights, purposeful isolation, and spiritual solitude—increasingly rare commodities in a hyper-connected planet. And after a week of exploring the half-dozen temples that line the road in the settlement's sprawling "lama camp," slurping bowls of homemade noodles with Tibetan bureaucrats, and chasing soccer balls with monks along dusty monastery lanes, it was easy to envision many more tourists engaging in the type of commoditized solitude Thurman suggests is possible.

On the other hand, any Tibetan seeking to challenge the status quo faces a long slog. Tibetan refugee officials could easily interpret the need to "reinvent" the Tibetan settlement concept as a suggestion that the original approach, spearheaded by the Dalai Lama, had failed. And as Tsewang had already discovered, such an implication hasn't been received well. At the moment, the CTA controls every aspect of settlement life through ministries in North India, acting similar to a top-down model employed by international aid organizations. Settlements—as neglected as some are—provide the CTA with its main source of political legitimacy through voting and ad hoc taxes. What Tibetans in settlements really need, Tsewang believes, is the ability to chart their own path forward, something his project has championed. That hasn't been an easy pill for Dharamsala to swallow.

"My argument to them is that the goal of CTA is really to bring freedom to Tibetans in Tibet; it's more of a political mission. If Tibetan settlements do well, they will become assets rather than liabilities to CTA."

While Tsewang has earned some support in Dharamsala, progress is slow and the challenges daunting. They include shoring up short-term land leases, raising capital investment, and figuring out how to suspend the Indian-mandated foreign entry permit to make it easier for non-Indian visitors to travel to the region.

During my visit I also uncovered a fourth challenge: convincing the thousands of monks and their crimson-clad administrators that Tibetan Buddhism—cloistered, mystical, and esoteric—*should* be commoditized. Doeguling houses some of the most vibrant and active monasteries outside of Tibet today, including the mighty Ganden and Drepung, two of the most important monasteries in the Dalai Lama's Yellow Hat sect. They are arguably more authentic than their present-day counterparts on the other side of the border, where Chinese control is ubiquitous. But Tibetan Buddhism is also notoriously complex, and difficult for non-monastic students to access. Monks can spend up to thirty years in deep contemplation and training—not to mention months at a time in solitary meditation. Whether busloads of tourists can or should see such serious study up close is a topic of great debate in communities like this one.

"Monastic institutes are like universities, where we produce professionals who could be able to teach and guide people in their spiritual journey," the abbot of Ganden, Khen Rinpoche Jangchup Choeden, said when I asked him about the reimagining project, which he advises as a board member. "Reimaging Doeguling will, in the long run, have a kind of very significant impact on the society, [and] make sure that there are a lot of positive changes and improvements. But it will take time."[5]

As young, educated Tibetan refugees explore new ways to challenge the status quo, longtime supporters are betting on their success—and against China's efforts to see them fail. Since 2013, Tibetans' lobbying efforts in the United States have resulted in a relative windfall of federal support for Tibetan refugees. In its 2015 appropriations bill, the US Congress, for the first time ever, allocated $3 million in USAID money "for programs to promote and preserve Tibetan culture, development, and the resilience of Tibetan communities in India and Nepal, and to assist in the education and development of the next generation of Tibetan leaders from such communities."

Before that earmark, US federal spending on Tibetans in South Asia had remained largely static since the 1980s, when Congress first directed the State Department to make money available to the Central Tibetan Administration. And for the most part, those funds stayed level—roughly $2 million annually to fund health care, education, and settlement reconstruction programs for refugees and new arrivals. While Congress has also authorized funds for Tibetan-language media (like Voice of America and Radio Free Asia programming), a Tibetan scholarship program called the Ngawang Choephel Fellowship, and several other one-off initiatives, the bulk of US funding over the last three decades went to projects inside Tibet.

The 2015 budget cycle marked a turning point in that strategy. By 2016, the refugee earmark doubled to $6 million, and it has remained steady since.[6] (President Trump's skeptical approach to foreign aid, however, could put a halt to the upward trajectory.)

Tibetans, Tibet lobbyists, scholars, and officials within the State Department differ on why the US government proportionally ratcheted up support for Tibetan refugees during the waning days of the Obama administration. Some say the Democratic president was using Tibetan refugees to reinforce his so-called Asia pivot. "We were shocked," one adviser close to the Tibetans told me. "No one expected it." Others point back to the Tibetans themselves. For decades the focus of the International Campaign for Tibet, which serves as the de facto lobbying arm of the CTA in Washington, was on democracy promotion, security, and development programs inside Tibet; infrastructure in settlements across India and Nepal were not given full funding priority. The uptick in settlement funding under Obama, therefore, may have signaled a shift in Tibetans' own thinking, a tacit acknowledgment that camps in India and Nepal dating to the 1960s will—regardless of what becomes of their freedom struggle—remain places of residence for Tibetans for many, many years to come.[7]

— — —

Tibetan refugees' ability to navigate Beijing's blessings (and Washington's politics) in the post–Dalai Lama era will require many more forms of reinvention. For one, their success in parrying China's relentless soft-power assault will depend on continual financial and political support from Western and European nations. It will also be guided by China's reaction to His Holiness's passing. Many speculate Beijing will move to enthrone its own Dalai Lama candidate, leading to a likely showdown between two "recognized" leaders. How Tibetan leaders chart a way through these issues without a global icon at the helm will be a true test of Tibetan resolve.

One of the best ways to understand why China would rather wait it out is to attend one of the public teachings the Dalai Lama gives to the Buddhist faithful each year in India. For up to two weeks between January and March, tens of thousands of Tibetan monks, nuns, laypeople, and tourists drag themselves to a different corner of Indian to sit cross-legged for hours and hang on the Tibetan spiritual leader's every word. It is this magnetism—and the Dalai Lama's ability to summon huge numbers of people for days on end—that present some of the most fundamental challenges to China's war on the Tibetan diaspora.

A few days after exploring the reinvention of Doeguling, I packed my bags and headed north to Bihar State and Bodh Gaya, the birthplace of the Buddha, to pay witness to how the Fourteenth Dalai Lama summons his flock. The biennial "wheel of time" teaching—an ancient rite known as the Kalachakra Initiation—was to be held that year in the shadows of the Bodi Tree, one of Buddhism's holiest sites. Local Indian officials expected crowds in excess of two hundred thousand—Buddhists from Taiwan, Australia, the United Kingdom, mainland China, and beyond.

Unlike in past years, when huge numbers of Tibetans from inside Tibet made the journey, the 2017 edition was light on Tibetans with Chinese passports. A few days before the Dalai Lama arrived, Communist Party authorities in Tibetan areas reportedly confiscated Tibetans passports, blocked Tibetans from boarding planes, and threatened jail time to families of those whose relatives ignored orders not to travel.[8] Chinese officials later denied pressuring Tibetans who had already traveled to return home, although one senior official in Beijing called the ritual a "political tool" held to propagate "hating the Chinese government."[9]

With Tibetans mixing so easily among throngs of global supporters, it was easy to forget that Tibetans remain a marginalized people, on both sides of the border. But at the Kalachakra, Tibetans were in charge. For twelve days in January 2017, colorfully clad devotees traipsed through a heaving cacophony of cattle, cars, beggars, and bicycles, inching along congested motorways for a glimpse of their living god. One young woman from the United States, a Buddhist and ethnic Kalmyk, told me that she attended the 2017 Kalachakra, at the site of the Buddha's enlightenment, to reap the extra karma that comes with receiving teachings in such a holy place (by her measure it was seven times more valuable). The line into the Mahabodhi Temple, where the Buddha is said to have entered his enlightened state, was so jammed with Tibetans one morning that it stretched at least a mile down the road.

As I wandered the streets that January, it was clear to me that China's strategy of "waiting it out" carries great risk—for both sides. Tibetan Buddhism is far bigger than any man or women; it is transcendent, and has been for centuries. Along just about every dirt alleyway outside the teaching grounds were stalls of monks collecting donations for temple projects, monasteries, and dharma centers being built in far-flung corners of the world. Plunking down cash and collecting colorful yellow or pink payment vouchers seemed like some holy scavenger hunt; Tibetan *momo-las* and *popo-las* (grandmothers and grandfathers), wrapped in traditional finery, shuffled through the throngs waving fistfuls of receipts like Wall Street traders buying stocks.

So disarmingly effective were the rows of smiling monks seated at the booths that even non-Buddhists were powerless to resist. Two monks caught my eye and wouldn't let go until I put down a few hundred rupees for a temple project under construction somewhere in rural Nepal. According to my own karmic golden ticket, "the 47-foot-tall" peace stupa and monastery was to be dedicated to "harmony generally in the world, and specifically in Nepal." The monks assured me that my donation would not be wasted, and that my act of kindness might even help me on the path toward achieving "Buddhahood." In exile, as in Tibet, money mixes with faith in a way that all but guarantees Tibetans' religion will persist long after their current patriarch cashes in.

Even so, keeping the issue of Tibet globally relevant for the next sixty years will require much more than money. When the Fourteenth Dalai Lama dies, the loss of such an important symbol of Tibetan unity will make it harder for Tibetans inside Tibet and those outside to find common ground (often unrecognized is how successful the current Dalai Lama has been in sewing together the religious and political factionalism of his own countrymen, on both sides of the border). While the Dalai Lama insists he will live for many more years (he has repeatedly predicted he will live to 113)[10] and is already playing a role in his reincarnation,[11] it is not too early for Tibetans both in and outside Tiber to start pondering how they will stay unified without him.

"For people like me that's the big issue. That's the number one sort of step we have to take, to say, 'Hey, these two groups are different,'" Columbia's Robert Barnett told me. For Tibetans in exile, "their future viability and credibility depends on them being able to promote, or even place themselves as secondary to, the Tibet Tibetans. Giving them real positions as leaders in their government, their society, and not looking down on them."

No matter where the Tibetan refugee experiment winds up, the most important factors in navigating Beijing's blessings effectively will be maintaining unity, tolerance, and peace within Tibetan ranks. Scholars like Barnett say that's not a given. In Paris, a suicide in early 2016 by a new arrival from Tibet underscored the sense of isolation that some Tibetans feel when they join the diaspora. And amid reports of Tibetan gang violence in Toronto,[12] stabbings and fights in settlements across India, and substance abuse by young Tibetans everywhere, it is clear that today's refugees—despite their bright spots—have many obstacles complicating the way forward.

The Dalai Lama has been pleading for his people's patience, compassion, and trust for almost as long as they have been displaced. On March 10, 1961, in the first of more than fifty annual statements marking his exile, His Holiness called on his countrymen in India, Nepal, and Bhutan to stay true to their Tibetan values while they prepared themselves to return, one day, to a freer country. "A heavy responsibility devolves on all of us to prepare ourselves for the day when we can return to our country and build a happier and greater independent Tibet," he said. "New Tibet will need thousands of trained and skilled men and women, necessary to bring Tibet in consonance with the spirit of democracy without losing our cultural and religious heritage or our soul."

So much has changed for Tibetans in exile since that initial message of patience. And yet, portions of it are repeated verbatim today, delivered to new legions of young refugees navigating their own paths through China's soft-power war.

Lobsang Nyandak, the Dalai Lama's former envoy to North America, once asked me what I thought was the Tibetan exile community's greatest strength, and its biggest weakness. My answer to both questions was the same. "Faith," I replied, in the belief that Tibetans' religious and political leadership might one day guide them home.

I explained my reasoning this way: After so many years of living with and writing about Tibetans in exile, and with China more powerful than ever, I could see no scenario in which Tibetans would return to govern their Land of Snows in any meaningful way, at least not anytime soon. And yet, so many of Tibet's refugees—people I've known for half my life and most of theirs—maintain an almost blind devotion in the proclamations of a Nobel Peace Prize–winning septuagenarian monk that their struggle will end favorably. To Lobsang's question I couldn't help replying with questions of my own: "Has Tibetans' faith in their future become blinded? And when the Fourteenth Dalai Lama dies, what becomes of these bonds formed of hope?"

Lobsang, leaning back in his chair slightly, nodded knowingly. "It's true," he said, surprising me. "From a Tibetan perspective, also we feel the same way."

When His Holiness dies, he went on, "no Tibetan, inside or outside Tibet, would agree to a new [single] religious leader because of our . . . complicated religious sects. Even within sect[s] it's really difficult to agree upon one leader. Having an individual—like His Holiness the Dalai Lama—in whom we all have faith, it's very, very difficult. Under the current circumstances, the only institution that can unite Tibetans, in the absence of His Holiness, is the democratic institution, our own political leadership. That is why we are all struggling toward preserving and promoting that way. We're not talking about individuals. We're talking about the institution [of democracy]."[13]

This sentiment is, in a nutshell, why China cares so deeply about what happens within the Tibetan exile community today: the institutions of a functioning yet unrecognized state have enabled Tibetans to nurture, outside the borders of their abandoned land, a system that could one day be replicated or relocated to the other side of the border. Oxford's Fiona McConnell calls it a rehearsal for the real deal; although unrecognized by any state as a legitimate government, the Tibetan government in exile has nonetheless managed to establish a de facto state—one that has a constitution, collects taxes, manages land, holds elections, and sees to the welfare of its "citizens." Although the Tibetan government in exile lacks a monopoly of force, a requirement that the great German sociologist Max Weber defined as the defining aspect of a modern nation-state, it does have legitimacy in the eyes of its people. And as unlikely as it may seem, the Tibetan government in exile is both symbolically and actually a challenge to China itself. It is not dependent on a single figurehead, and even in the Dalai Lama's absence it has the potential to continue to serve as a focal point for Tibetan ambitions, aspirations, and self-determination. Tibetans' exile institutions are, in short, the wild cards of China's Tibet project.

That is why Beijing's blessings will continue to be bestowed long after the Fourteenth Dalai Lama is gone, long after new, young religious and political leaders rise through the ranks of a cultural and political experiment unrivaled in recent memory. And it is why Tibetans everywhere, men like Pala—Purang Dorjee—and his children, despite the long odds, have hope and faith that their struggle will not be a fruitless one.

INTRODUCTION

1. Much of this work focuses on the challenges facing the Tibetan diaspora today, but it must be noted at the outset that Tibetans' current predicament follows decades of past success. As the anthropologist Christoph von Fürer-Haimendorf once observed, "The ability of homeless and impoverished groups of refugees to build and fund in foreign lands numerous monasteries of a remarkably high architectural standard and their success in developing viable monastic communities similar to those of Tibet is one of the miracles of the twentieth century." See Christoph von Fürer-Haimendorf, *The Renaissance of Tibetan Civilization* (Santa Fe, NM: Synergetic, 1990).

2. Egil Aarvik, "Award Ceremony Speech" by the chairman of the Norwegian Nobel Committee, delivered on December 10, 1989, http://www.nobelprize.org/nobel _prizes/peace/laureates/1989/presentation-speech.html.

3. Nicholas Kristof, "The World; How Tiananmen Square Helped Rally Support for Tibetans," *New York Times*, August 18, 1991, http://www.nytimes.com/1991/08/18 /weekinreview/the-world-how-tiananmen-square-helped-rally-support-for-tibet. html.

4. "International Olympic Committee Sets Precedent with Reprimand for Tibet Party Boss," International Campaign for Tibet, June 26, 2008, https://www.savetibet .org/international-olympic-committee-sets-precedent-with-reprimand-for-tibet -party-boss/.

5. That year, protests in Tibet began when a few hundred monks staged a small demonstration against China's detention of Tibetans celebrating the Dalai Lama's receipt of the Nobel Prize. Within days, the dissent had mushroomed into the largest mass mobilization of Tibetans in decades, reaching all three of the historical

provinces of Tibet. As the International Center on Nonviolent Conflict noted in a 2015 summary of Tibet's nonviolent struggle, the uprising took many in Beijing and Dharamsala by surprise. China's violent crackdown inside Tibet, and its aggressive stance beyond its border, therefore must be understood in this context. See https://www.nonviolent-conflict.org/wp-content/uploads/2016/03/TibetMonograph FinalApril.pdf.

6. Hillary Clinton, "Closing Remarks for U.S.-China Strategic and Economic Dialogue," US Department of State, Washington, DC, July 28, 2009, https://www.realclearpolitics.com/articles/2009/07/28/closing_remarks_for_us-china_strategic _and_economic_dialogue_97671.html.

7. "China Faces More Diverse, Complex Security Challenges: White Paper," Xinhua, March 31, 2011, http://en.people.cn/90001/90776/90785/7336220.html.

8. Zhang Wenmu, "Sea Power and China's Strategic Choices," *China Security*, Summer 2006: 17–31.

9. In 2005, a former Chinese diplomat produced an internal PRC document that outlined five groups China believed posed a serious threat to internal stability. The so-called poisonous groups included Falun Gong members, Uighur separatists, Taiwan pro-independence activists, prodemocracy activists, and Tibetan separatists. See US-China Economic and Security Review Commission, *2009 Annual Report to Congress*, 163.

10. "Chinese Government Asks Corvallis to Take Down Mural," Fox 12 Oregon, http://www.kptv.com/story/19519205/corvallis-mural-chinese-government.

11. Xing Zhigang and Li Xiaokun, "Envoy Brief on Sarkozy-Dalai Meet Dismissed," *China Daily*, December 12, 2008, http://www.chinadaily.com.cn/china/2008-12/12 /content_7296768.htm.

12. "France Seeks to Repair Relations with China," *China Daily*, February 7, 2009, http://news.xinhuanet.com/english/2009–02/07/content_10778176.htm.

13. "Report on Tibet Negotiations," US Department of State, August 19, 2016, https://www.savetibet.org/wp-content/uploads/2016/10/20160819_State-Report -on-Tibet-Negotiations-copy.pdf.

14. "Tibet Website Says Dalai Lama's Clique Is Falling Apart," *Global Times*, January 6, 2016.

ONE BLESSINGS FROM BEIJING

1. Melvyn C. Goldstein, *The Snow Lion and the Dragon: China, Tibet, and the Dalai Lama* (Berkeley: University of California Press, 1995), 44.

2. Bates Gill, *Rising Star: China's New Security Diplomacy* (Washington, DC: Brookings Institution Press, 2010).

3. Dean Nelson, "Dalai Lama Reveals Warning of Chinese Plot to Kill Him," *Telegraph*, May 12, 2012, http://www.telegraph.co.uk/news/worldnews/asia/tibet/9261729/Dalai-Lama-reveals-warning-of-Chinese-plot-to-kill-him.html.

4. "Dalai Assassination Claims Mind-Boggling," *Global Times*, May 14, 2012 http://www.globaltimes.cn/content/709252.shtml.

5. Anand Bodh, "Himachal Police Arrest Eight Chinese Nationals," *Times of India*, June 13, 2012, http://timesofindia.indiatimes.com/india/Himachal-police-arrest-eight-Chinese-nationals/articleshow/14083678.cms.

6. "Eight Chinese Spies Arrested in Himachal Pradesh," *Press Trust of India*, June 13, 2012, http://zeenews.india.com/news/nation/eight-chinese-spies-arrested-in-himachal-pradesh_781485.html.

7. A 2009 report from the University of Toronto's Citizen Lab suggests that Chinese-affiliated interests have been spying on Tibetans' digital communications since at least 2002.

8. "Tracking Ghostnet: Investigating a Cyber Espionage Network," Information Warfare Monitor, University of Toronto, Munk Centre for International Studies, March 29, 2009.

9. H. E. Richardson, *A Corpus of Early Tibetan Inscriptions* (London: Royal Asiatic Society, 1985), 107.

10. Goldstein, *Snow Lion*, 10.

11. Ibid., 14.

12. "The Dalai Clique's Separatist Activities and the Central Government's Policy," *People's Daily*, http://english.peopledaily.com.cn/whitepaper/6%283%29.html.

13. John Kenneth Knaus, *Orphans of the Cold War: America and the Tibetan Struggle for Survival* (New York: PublicAffairs, 2000).

14. John Roberts and Elizabeth Roberts, *Freeing Tibet: 50 Years of Struggle, Resilience, and Hope* (New York: AMACOM, 2009).

15. Barbara Demick, "Tibetan-Muslim Tensions Roil China," *Los Angeles Times*, June 23, 2008, http://articles.latimes.com/2008/jun/23/world/fg-muslims23.

16. Warren Smith, "Origins of the Middle Way Policy," from *Trails of the Tibetan Tradition: Papers for Elliot Sperling*," ed. Roberto Vitale (New Delhi: Amnye Machen Institute, 2015).

17. "Statement of His Holiness the Dalai Lama on the 52nd Anniversary of the Tibetan National Uprising Day," Office of His Holiness the 14th Dalai Lama, March 10, 2011, http://www.dalailama.com/messages/retirement/52-anniversary-tibetan-uprising-statement.

18. Jamyang Norbu, comment on the Dalai Lama's devolution decision, "Ending to Begin (Part 1)," *Shadow Tibet*, July 14, 2011, http://www.jamyangnorbu.com/blog/2011/07/14/ending-to-begin-part-i/.

19. Tenzin Nyinjey, "Censorship and the Struggle for Tibetan Freedom," *Tibet Sun*, July 27, 2012, https://www.tibetsun.com/opinions/2012/07/27/censorship-and-the-struggle-for-tibetan-freedom.

20. Peter Wonacott, "Tibetan Youth Challenge Beijing, and Dalai Lama," *Wall Street Journal*, March 20, 2008, http://www.wsj.com/articles/SB120596094739349681.

21. "TYC, a Terror Group Worse Than Bin Laden's," *China Daily*, April 11, 2008, http://en.people.cn/90001/90780/91342/6390946.html.

22. "White Paper: Tibet's Path of Development Is Driven by an Irresistible Historical Tide," China's State Council Information Office, April 2015, http://english.gov.cn/archive/white_paper/2015/04/15/content_281475089444218.htm.

23. Rituparna Bhowmik, "Young Tibet Up in Arms," *Statesman*, July 4, 2003, http://www.phayul.com/news/article.aspx?id=4491&t=1.

24. Mark Owen, "Preparing for the Future: Reassessing the Possibility of Violence Emanating from Tibetan Exile Communities in India," *India Review* 13, no. 2 (2014): 149–169.

TWO CRUSHING LITTLE LHASA

1. Planning Commission, Central Tibetan Administration, *Demographic Survey of Tibetans in Exile—2009*, Household Ownership of Assets, 65.

2. John Roberts and Elizabeth Roberts, *Freeing Tibet: 50 Years of Struggle, Resilience, and Hope* (New York: AMACOM, 2009).

3. Which is not to imply that Nehru ignored China in his calculations. Jan Magnusson, a Swedish sociologist, suggests that the selection of South Indian land for locating the Tibetans was made in large part to appease Beijing. Tibetans were a "delicate issue for the Indian government. A refugee community near the border could serve as a base for resistance fighters thus creating a risk and reason for Chinese troops to make pre-emptive strikes on Indian territory, or it could serve as a cover for Tibetans working in India as Chinese spies." Pushing Tibetans into India's deep South, or its undeveloped North, was meant to avoid such concern.

4. Fiona McConnell, *Rehearsing the State: The Political Practices of the Tibetan Government-in-Exile* (West Sussex, UK: Wiley Blackwell, 2016), 65.

5. Ibid.

6. The figure of 128,000 is drawn from the Planning Commission's 2009 *Demographic Survey of Tibetans in Exile*. Unofficial estimates put the number closer to 150,000, which includes Tibetans not registered with the CTA.

7. David Shambaugh, "China's Soft-Power Push: The Search for Respect," *Foreign Affairs*, July/August 2015, https://www.foreignaffairs.com/articles/china/2015-06-16/china-s-soft-power-push.

8. Anne-Marie Brady, "We Are All Part of the Same Family: China's Ethnic Propaganda," *Journal of Current Chinese Affairs* 41, no. 4 (2012): 159–181.

9. For a discussion of the history of the Central Tibetan Administration see Stephanie Roemer, *The Tibetan Government-in-Exile: Politics at Large*, Routledge Advances in South Asian Studies (London: Routledge, 2008).

10. As Tibetans in exile prepared to vote in March 2016 for a new prime minister, China's Foreign Ministry reiterated that it has never recognized the CTA. "You must be quite clear about the position of Chinese government, that we have never recognized this so-called government-in-exile," Foreign Ministry spokesman Lu Kang said. "We also hope that countries around the world, especially those which have friendly relations with us will not provide any stage for Tibetan independence separatist activities." See "China Tells Nations Not to Give Any 'Stage' to Tibetans," *Press Trust of India*, March 17, 2016, http://www.business-standard.com/article/pti-stories/china-tells-nations-not-to-give-any-stage-to-tibetans-116031701239_1.html.

11. According to the CTA's 2009 census of Tibetans in exile, 78 percent of households in India, Nepal, and Bhutan have televisions.

12. Gary King, Jennifer Pan, and Margaret E. Roberts, "How the Chinese Government Fabricates Social Media Posts for Strategic Distraction, Not Engaged Argument," *American Political Science Review*, forthcoming 2017, http://gking.harvard.edu/50c.

13. Brady, "We Are All Part of the Same Family," 159–181.

14. Anne-Marie Brady, "The Beijing Olympics as a Campaign of Mass Distraction," *China Quarterly* 197 (March 2009): 1–24.

15. "Pew Global Attitudes and Trends Question Database," Pew Research Center, http://www.pewglobal.org/question-search/?qid=1513&cntIDs=&stdIDs=.

16. Isaac Stone Fish, "Blame Norway: Why Is Oslo Kowtowing to Beijing and Stiff-Arming the Dalai Lama?," *Foreign Policy*, May 6, 2014, http://foreignpolicy.com/2014/05/06/blame-norway/.

17. Sui-Lee Wee and Stephanie Nebehay, "At U.N., China Uses Intimidation Tactics to Silence Its Critics," Reuters, October 5, 2015, http://www.reuters.com/investigates/special-report/china-softpower-rights/.

18. Although the film is intensely critical of China's policies inside Tibet, it also shines a light on Tibetan refugees themselves, exploring the deep divisions between those supporting total independence from China, known as *rangzen*, and the political compromise advocated by the Dalai Lama, which he refers to as the middle way.

19. "Chinese Government Fails to Block Tibet Film Screening at Major Festival in US," International Campaign for Tibet, January 7, 2010, http://www.savetibet.org/chinese-government-fails-to-block-tibet-film-screening-at-major-festival-in-us/.

20. Timothy McGrath, "No One Likes the Dalai Lama Anymore," *Global Post*,

September 5, 2014, https://www.pri.org/stories/2014-09-04/no-one-likes-dalai-lama
-anymore.

21. Anthea Lipsett, "Dalai Lama Receives PhD from London Metropolitan,"
Guardian, May 20, 2008, https://www.theguardian.com/education/2008/may/20
/highereducation.uk1.

22. Aislinn Simpson, "British University Sparks Protest over Apology to China for
Dalai Lama Degree," *Telegraph*, July 9, 2008, http://www.telegraph.co.uk/news/world
news/asia/china/2274496/British-university-sparks-protest-over-apology-to-China
-for-Dalai-Lama-degree.html.

23. Melanie Newman, "'Regret at Unhappiness' over Dalai Lama's Degree," *Times
Higher Education*, July 9, 2008, https://www.timeshighereducation.com/news/regret
-at-unhappiness-over-dalai-lamas-degree/402720.article.

24. Tim Johnson, *Tragedy in Crimson: How the Dalai Lama Conquered the World
but Lost the Battle with China* (New York: Nation Books, 2011), 251.

25. Avani Dias, "Chinese Whispers: The Dalai Lama and Sydney University," *Honi
Soit*, April 21, 2013, http://honisoit.com/2013/04/chinese-whispers-the-dalai-lama
-and-sydney-university/.

26. "University Cancels Dalai Lama's Degree," ABC News Australia, August 11, 2009.

27. Philip Pullella, "Vatican Denies Dalai Lama Papal Audience over China
Concern," Reuters, December 12, 2014, http://www.reuters.com/article/us-vatican
-dalailama-idUSKBN0JQ1DC20141212.

28. Ivan Watson and Pamela Boykoff, "No Escape? China's Crackdown on Dissent
Goes Global," CNN, February 4, 2016, http://www.cnn.com/2016/02/04/asia/china
-dissident-crackdown-goes-global/.

29. Sui-Lee Wee and Stephanie Nebehay, "At UN, China Uses Intimidation Tactics
to Silence Its Critics," Reuters, October 5, 2015, http://www.reuters.com/investigates
/special-report/china-softpower-rights/.

30. Nargiza Salidjanova, *Going Out: An Overview of China's Outward Foreign
Direct Investment* (Washington, DC: USCC Staff Research Report, March 30, 2011),
https://www.uscc.gov/sites/default/files/Research/GoingOut.pdf.

31. "China Denies 'Money Diplomacy' with Sao Tome and Principe," Xinhua,
December 22, 2016, http://www.globaltimes.cn/content/1025206.shtml.

32. "China Plans to Build a Deep Water Port in Sao Tome," china.aiddata.org, 2013,
http://china.aiddata.org/projects/30727.

33. James Mann, *About Face: A History of America's Curious Relationship with
China, from Nixon to Clinton* (New York: Knopf, 1999).

34. US-China Economic and Security Review Commission, *2009 Annual Report to
Congress*, 163.

35. "China Has 'Vast, Dark Spy Network': Defector," Agence France-Presse, March
20, 2009, http://www.abc.net.au/news/stories/2009/03/20/2521919.htm.

36. Peter Navarro and Greg Autry, *Death by China: Confronting the Dragon—a Global Call to Action* (Upper Saddle River, NJ: Pearson FT, 2011), 130.

37. Adam Yuet Chau, "The Politics of Legitimation and the Revival of Popular Religion in Shaanbei, North-Central China," *Modern China* 31, no. 2 (2005): 236–278.

38. US House of Representatives, Joint Hearing before the Subcommittee on Africa, Global Human Rights and International Operations, "Falun Gong and China's Continuing War on Human Rights," July 21, 2005, http://www.gpo.gov/fdsys/pkg /CHRG-109hhrg22579/pdf/CHRG-109hhrg22579.pdf, p. 40.

39. "Leaked PRC Statement on 'Tibet-Related External Propaganda,'" June 12, 2000, statement from Zhao Qizheng at the meeting on national research in Tibetology and external propaganda on Tibet, translated from Chinese by the International Campaign for Tibet, https://www.savetibet.org/leaked-prc-statement-on-tibet-related -external-propaganda/.

40. Lobsang Sangay, the Tibetan prime minister, earns just $400 a month. See Stephanie Schorow, "Harvard-Trained Tibetan Leader," *Harvard Gazette*, April 27, 2011, http://news.harvard.edu/gazette/story/2011/04/harvard-trained-tibetan -leader/. Choyang resigned her post in 2016, citing political reasons.

THREE THE HORSE MAN FROM PURANG

1. Melvyn C. Goldstein, *History of Modern Tibet*, vol. 2, *The Calm before the Storm, 1951–1955* (Berkeley: University of California Press, 2009), 283.

2. *The Writings of Mao Zedong, 1949–1976: September 1945–December 1955*, ed. John K. Leung and Michael Y. M. Kau (Armonk, NY: M. E. Sharpe, 1986), 255.

3. Colin Thubron, *To a Mountain in Tibet* (New York: HarperCollins, 2011), 110.

FOUR TO KILL A GOOSE, CUT OFF ITS HEAD

1. In April 2015, Kodari's prominence as a trade and transit hub was shattered when a 7.8 magnitude earthquake rocked the Himalayan nation. As of late 2017, the Friendship Highway and bridge connecting Kodari with the Tibetan capital of Lhasa remained closed. A second key trade route with China, the Rasuwagadhi-Kerung border crossing, which was also damaged during the quake, was closed for six months before reopening in October 2015.

2. International Campaign for Tibet, *Dangerous Crossing: Conditions Impacting the Flight of Tibetan Refugees, 2009 Update*, https://www.savetibet.org/wp-content /uploads/2013/05/Dangerous-Crossing-2009.pdf.

3. Jonathan Green, *Murder in the High Himalaya: Loyalty, Tragedy, and Escape from Tibet* (New York: PublicAffairs, 2010).

4. "17 Tibetans Held for Entering Nepal 'Illegally,'" *Himalayan Times*, February 27,

2010, http://thehimalayantimes.com/kathmandu/17-tibetans-held-for-entering-nepal
-illegally/.

5. Human Rights Watch, *Under China's Shadow: Mistreatment of Tibetans in Nepal*,
April 1, 2014, https://www.hrw.org/report/2014/04/01/under-chinas-shadow/mistreat
ment-tibetans-nepal.

6. Ramesh Khatiwada, "China Ups the Ante following Tibetans' Arrest," *Republica*,
February 28, 2010, http://www.tibet.ca/en/library/wtn/8826.

7. "Agreement on Trade, Intercourse and Related Questions between Tibet Autonomous Region of China and Nepal," signed in Beijing on May 2, 1966, http://saf-7.org
/saf/safdic/bilaterals/chinanepal/chinanepal11.asp.

8. Ramesh Raj Kunwar, "Paganism and Spiritism: A Study of Religion and Ritual
in the Sherpa Society," *Ancient Nepal, Journal of the Department of Archaeology* 103
(1988): 1–18, http://himalaya.socanth.cam.ac.uk/collections/journals/ancientnepal
/pdf/ancient_nepal_104_01.pdf.

9. Jonathan Holslag, *China and India: Prospects for Peace* (New York: Columbia
University Press, 2010), 149–50.

10. "Delhi Diary, January 30–February 19, 2010," US government cable, February
22, 2010, WikiLeaks, https://wikileaks.org/plusd/cables/10NEWDELHI321_a.html.

11. "Nepal-China Relations," Embassy of the People's Republic of China in the Federal Democratic Republic of Nepal, http://np.china-embassy.org/eng/ChinaNepal
/t362330.htm.

12. "Delhi Diary, January 30–February 19, 2010."

13. Although I hadn't seen the seventeen in prison, I am aware of the conditions
in which they had been jailed. A few weeks after the Lamabagar Tibetans were
released, the same humanitarian group that sprung them—the Human Rights Organization of Nepal—invited me on a legal aid mission to search for Tibetans arrested
in the Kathmandu Valley. Over the course of twelve hours we bounced through the
back streets of the capital in a red Tata Sumo SUV, sipping tea with district police
chiefs, interviewing patrolmen, and visiting men and women holed up in a half
dozen dark and urine-stained prisons on the hunt for Tibetan refugees detained
under similar circumstances.

FIVE **THE WALMART OF LITTLE LHASA**

1. Dalai Lama, *Freedom in Exile: The Autobiography of the Dalai Lama* (New York:
Harper Perennial, 1991), 158.

2. Ibid.

3. Stephanie Roemer, *The Tibetan Government-in-Exile: Politics at Large*, Routledge
Advances in South Asian Studies (London: Routledge, 2008), 64.

4. H. C. Heda, "Dalai Lama and India: Indian Public and Prime Minister on Tibetan Crisis," Institute of National Affairs, 1959.

5. Roemer, *Tibetan Government-in-Exile*, 64.

6. Fiona McConnell, "A State within a State? Exploring Relations between the Indian State and the Tibetan Community and Government-in-Exile," *Contemporary South Asia* 19, no. 3 (2011): 297–313.

7. *Prime Minister on Sino-Indian Relations*, vol. 2, *Press Conferences*, External Publicity Division, Ministry of External Affairs, Government of India, 1962, 16.

8. Ibid.

9. Roemer, *Tibetan Government-in-Exile*, 62–63.

10. McConnell, "State within a State?"

11. India was not a signatory to the United Nations' 1951 Convention Relating to the Status of Refugees or its 1967 Protocol, and the nation's policies toward refugee groups is ad hoc and at times discriminatory. Tibetans, despite enjoying few legal protections in India, are nonetheless considered as among the best-protected "refugee" groups in the country.

12. Geeta Anand, "Modi's Cash Ban Brings Pain, but Corruption-Weary India Grits Its Teeth," *New York Times*, January 2, 2017.

13. S. Manasi, K. C. Smitha, R. G. Nadadur, N. Sivanna, and P. G. Chengappa, "Urban Property Ownership Records in Karnataka: Computerized Land Registration System for Urban Properties," Institute for Social and Economic Change, Bangalore, Working Paper 308, 2013.

14. In February 2011 the state government in Himachal Pradesh seized one prominent monastery's property after police accused a senior Tibetan lama, the Seventeenth Karmapa Ogyen Trinley Dorje, of using it to hide millions in illegally acquired funds. According to press reports, some $112,000 in Chinese and other currency was stashed in the temples. The case was later dropped, but the seizure refocused attention on the practice of benami land transfers, according to Indian media. See "HP Govt Acquires Gyuto Monastery Land," *India Today*, February 15, 2011, http://indiatoday.intoday.in/story/hp-govt-acquires-gyuto-monastery-land/1/129928.html.

15. D. M. deVoe, "Keeping Refugee Status: A Tibetan Perspective," in *People in Upheaval*, ed. Scott M. Morgan and Elizabeth Colson (New York: Center for Migration Studies, 1987), 54–64.

16. "Fire Rips through Tibetan Area of Dharamsala," Radio Free Asia, December 21, 2004, http://www.rfa.org/english/news/tibetan_fire-20041221.html.

17. "10 Shops, Hotel Gutted in Mcleodganj," *Tribune News Service*, December 21, 2004, http://www.tribuneindia.com/2004/20041221/himachal.htm#10.

18. Topden Tsering, "Demise of a Place: An Obituary," Phayul.com, December 23, 2004, http://www.phayul.com/news/article.aspx?id=8639&t=1&c=4.

19. The total amount of aid distributed by the Central Tibetan Administration was 160,000 rupees, or about $2,400. The regional Indian shopkeepers' association contributed 100,000 rupees ($1,500), and a local taxi union chipped in another 21,000 rupees ($314). For many of those affected, the fire took a heavy dent out of personal savings. See http://tibet.net/2004/12/kashag-atpd-provides-relief-money-to-fire-affected/.

SIX BEADY EYES AND A DEAD LAMA

1. Planning Commission, Central Tibetan Administration, *Demographic Survey of Tibetans in Exile—2009*, Household Ownership of Assets.

2. Tibetans have not always prayed to the same enlightened being. The institution of the Dalai Lama—which is part of the Gelug tradition (known as the Yellow Hats)—is a relatively recent one. Founded in the fourteenth century, the Gelug sect is the youngest of the four major traditions. The Nyingma, which means "ancient," is the oldest, and has historical roots dating to the seventh century. And despite Buddhism's installation as the official state religion of Tibet in the eighth century by King Trisong Detsen, it wasn't until the sixteenth century that the title of "Dalai Lama" was bestowed. It was even later that the holder of the crown was considered a reincarnation of the Buddhist bodhisattva of compassion.

3. Dolgyal Shugden Research Society, *Dolgyal Shugden: A History* (New York: Tibet House US, 2014).

4. L. G. McCune, "Tales of Intrigue from Tibet's Holy City: The Historical Underpinnings of a Modern Buddhist Crisis" (MA thesis, Florida State University College of Arts and Sciences, 2007), 57.

5. Carole McGranahan, *Arrested Histories: Tibet, the CIA, and Memories of a Forgotten War* (Durham, NC: Duke University Press, 2010), 98–99.

6. "Kashag's Statement concerning Dolgyal," *Cabinet of the Tibetan Government in Exile,* May 31, 1996, http://tibet.net/important-issues/dolgyal-related-statements -and-resolutions/6/.

7. Manjeet Sehgal, "His Holiness Seeks Southern Comfort: Dalai Lama May Spend Two Months a Year in Karnataka for Health Reasons," *Mail Today*, August 3, 2013, http://www.dailymail.co.uk/indiahome/indianews/article-2384177/His-Holiness -seeks-southern-comfort-Dalai-Lama-spend-months-year-Mysore-health-reasons. html.

8. S. Gopal Puril, "China May Use Dissident Sect against Dalai Lama: Tibet," *Times of India*, May 15, 2012.

9. Jane Macartney, "Interpol on Trail of Buddhist Killers," *Australian*, June 22, 2007, http://www.theaustralian.com.au/news/world/interpol-on-trail-of-buddhist -killers/story-e6frg6so-1111113803569.

10. "Dalai Lama 'Supporters' Violently Oppress Buddhist Monks in Mundgod,

India," *Deccan Herald*, September 11, 2000, http://www.dorjeshugden.com/all-articles
/the-controversy/dalai-lama-supporters-violently-oppress-buddhist-monks-in
-mundgod-india/.

11. For a list of Shugden-affiliated monasteries and temples see Dorje Shugden,
http://www.dorjeshugden.com.

12. "An interview with Geshe Kelsang Gyatso," *tricycle*, Spring 1998, https://tricycle
.org/magazine/interview-geshe-kelsang-gyatso/.

13. "New Kadampa Tradition-International Kadampa Buddhist Union Financial
Statements," December 31, 2011, filed with the UK Charities Commission (Charity
Number 1015054).

14. "Return of Organization Exempt from Income Tax, Form 900 for Tax Year
2008," filed by the Kadampa Meditation Center New York, Glen Spey, NY, on August
18, 2009.

15. Robert Thurman, "The Dalai Lama and the Cult of Dolgyal Shugden," *Huffington Post*, May 5, 2014, http://www.huffingtonpost.com/entry/the-dalai-lama-cult-of
-dolgyal-shugden_b_4903441.html.

16. David Lague, Paul Mooney, and Benjamin Kang Lim, "China Co-opts a Buddhist Sect in Global Effort to Smear Dalai Lama," Reuters, December 21, 2015, http://
www.reuters.com/investigates/special-report/china-dalailama/.

17. Ben Hillman, "Monastic Politics and the Local State in China: Authority and
Autonomy in an Ethnically Tibetan Prefecture," *China Journal* 54 (2005): 29–51.

18. Communist Party Committee of the Tibet Autonomous Region, "Some Opin-
ions on Dealing Correctly with the 'Gyalchen Shugden' Issue," February 20, 2014,
translated from Tibetan by the International Campaign for Tibet, http://www
.savetibet.org/the-official-line-on-shugden-translation/.

19. "Elderly Tibetan Is Jailed for Discouraging Worship of Controversial Deity,"
Radio Free Asia, December 12, 2014, http://www.rfa.org/english/news/tibet/worship
-12122014152106.html.

20. "Another Tibetan Is Jailed for Discouraging Worship of Controversial Deity,"
Radio Free Asia, December 17, 2014, http://www.rfa.org/english/news/tibet/more
-12172014142131.html.

21. Embassy of the People's Republic of China in the Federal Democratic Republic
of Nepal, "H.E. Ambassador Yang Houlan Visited Tibetan Community in Kathmandu," press release dated August 22, 2011, http://www.fmprc.gov.cn/ce/cenp/eng
/EmbassyInfo/asaa/t852601.htm.

22. "'Every Picture Tells a Story': Shugden Devotees and Their Chinese 'Friends,'"
Dalai Lama Protesters Info, http://www.dalailamaprotesters.info/?p=1304.

23. Lague, Mooney, and Kang Lim, "China Co-opts a Buddhist Sect."

24. "Beyond Belief," *South China Morning Post*, September 4, 2011, http://www
.scmp.com/article/977990/beyond-belief.

25. Enrica Mazzi, "The Miracle of Gangchen," Lama Gangchen Peace Times blog entry, undated, http://www.lgpt.net/News/13/07_13en.htm.

SEVEN THE POLITICS OF REBIRTH

1. As Vincent Goossaert and David A. Palmer observe in their seminal work *The Religious Question in Modern China* (Chicago: University of Chicago Press, 2011), China's leaders have come to terms with religion as a necessary evil; it is no longer dismissed simply as dangerous, but rather is viewed as a tool that can be nurtured carefully. Faith is generally tolerated, rather than fully embraced by the party. And if adequately controlled, religion can even offer the Communist Party "positive contributions . . . for the execution of social plans." See Goossaert and Palmer, *Religious Question*, 2.

2. Jamil Anderlini, "The Rise of Christianity in China," *Financial Times*, November 7, 2014, https://www.ft.com/content/a6d2a690-6545-11e4-91b1-00144feabdc0?mhq5j=e1.

3. Emma Finamore, "The Chinese Communist Party Cracks Down on Religion: All Party Members Must Be Atheist," *Independent*, February 4, 2015, http://www.independent.co.uk/news/world/asia/the-chinese-communist-party-cracks-down-on-religion-all-party-members-must-be-atheist-10024034.html.

4. Melvyn C. Goldstein and Matthew T. Kapstein, *Buddhism in Contemporary Tibet: Religious Revival and Cultural Identity* (Berkeley: University of California Press, 1998), 6.

5. Tsering Topgyal, "The Securitization of Tibetan Buddhism in Communist China," *Politics and Religion in Contemporary China* 6, no. 2 (2012): 230.

6. Ibid.

7. Goossaert and Palmer, *Religious Question*, 365.

8. "Reincarnation and Enthronement of the 17th Living Buddha Karmapa," Xinhuanet, China Tibet Online, April 14, 2009, http://chinatibet.people.com.cn/6636399.html.

9. "China's Register of Reincarnations," Free Tibet, January 19, 2016, https://freetibet.org/news-media/na/china-launches-list-authorised-living-buddhas.

10. David Van Biema, "The World's Next Top Lama," *Time*, May 15, 2008, http://content.time.com/time/world/article/0,8599,1807103,00.html.

11. Mick Brown, *The Dance of 17 Lives: The Incredible True Story of Tibet's 17th Karmapa* (London: Bloomsbury, 2010), 7.

12. "The Boy Lama's Long and Mysterious Journey," *Economist*, January 13, 2000, http://www.economist.com/node/273440.

13. Tien-sze Fang, Asymmetrical Threat Perceptions in India-China Relations (New Delhi: Oxford University Press, 2014), 69.

14. Ishaan Tharoor, "Why India Is Investigating a Reincarnated Tibetan Lama,"

Time, February 3, 2011, http://content.time.com/time/world/article/0,8599,2046124,00.html.

15. Ashis Ray, "The Karmapa Greets the World," *Asian Affairs*, June 2017, http://www.asianaffairs.in/2017/06/the-karmapa-greets-the-world/#.WWStqBPytE4.

16. Sanjay Kapoor, "'Tawang Is a Beautiful Part of India': Karmapa Lama," *Hard News*, May 12, 2017, http://www.hardnewsmedia.com/2017/05/tawang-beautiful-part-india-karmapa-lama.

EIGHT PALA AND THE "FOREIGN" PLUMBER

1. Carey Reich, "A New Generation of Buddhist: The Views and Practice of Tibetan Youth," 2014, Independent Study Project (ISP) Collection, Paper 1971, http://digitalcollections.sit.edu/isp_collection/1971/.

2. "Dharamshala to Get Ropeway Link," *Times of India*, January 16, 2016, http://timesofindia.indiatimes.com/city/shimla/Dharamshala-to-get-ropeway-link/articleshow/50633895.cms.

3. Fiona McConnell, "A State within a State? Exploring Relations between the Indian State and the Tibetan Community and Government-in-Exile," *Contemporary South Asia* 19, no. 3 (2011): 297–313.

4. Ibid.

5. "Background on Tibetan Refugees," Tibetan Innovation Challenge, University of Rochester, www.rochester.edu/tibetchallenge/wp-content/uploads/2015/04/BACKGROUND-ON-TIBETAN-REFUGEES.docx.

6. Lalit Mohan, "Tibetan Showman to Get Indian Passport," *Tribune*, September 24, 2016, http://www.tribuneindia.com/news/himachal/community/tibetan-showman-to-get-indian-passport/299806.html.

7. Vijay Arora, "'Encroachments' over Forest Land: HC Issues Notice to State, CTA," *Tribune*, April 14, 2012, www.tribuneindia.com/2012/20120415/himachal.htm#12.

8. It was not the first case Mr. Kumar had filed against Tibetans in McLeod Ganj. In 2010, he filed papers challenging Tibetan land leasing arrangements, and also for the removal of all Tibetan flags from Indian soil. Unlike the 2012 suit, that petition was later dismissed without cause.

9. Naresh Kumar, "HC Orders Eviction of Land Encroachments in 1,090 Cases in Dharamsala," *Hindustan Times*, August 28, 2012, http://www.hindustantimes.com/chandigarh/hc-orders-eviction-of-land-encroachements-in-1-090-cases-in-dharamsala/story-IRSRgR10pUS2kpSBbYc48J.html.

10. "Himachal Pradesh Not to Evict Bonafide Tibetans," *Times of India*, February 26, 2015, http://timesofindia.indiatimes.com/city/chandigarh/Himachal-Pradesh-not-to-evict-bonafide-Tibetans/articleshow/46376405.cms.

11. Pratibha Chauhan, "Govt to Drop Eviction Proceedings against Tibetan

Refugees," *Tribune*, April 2, 2015, http://www.tribuneindia.com/news/himachal/govt
-to-drop-eviction-proceedings-against-tibetan-refugees/61579.html.

NINE A FIERY SPLIT

1. Rong Ma, "Population Structure Changes in the Tibet Autonomous Region,"
China Tibetology, no. 3 (2008): 167–182.

2. "Escalation in Ngaba following Self-Immolation: Two Tibetans Shot," International Campaign for Tibet, January 14, 2012, https://www.savetibet.org/escalation
-in-ngaba-following-self-immolation-two-tibetans-shot-updated-jan-16/.

3. A video of Lobsang Jamyang's self-immolation was posted to YouTube by Free
Tibet, a UK-based human rights advocacy group, on April 20, 2012, and is accessible
at https://www.youtube.com/watch?v=1BFAiO8TMac.

4. Tenzin Norbu is a pseudonym. I have changed his name to protect family members who still live in Chinese-controlled Tibet.

5. Congressional-Executive Commission on China, *Special Report: Tibetan Self-
Immolation—Rising Frequency, Wider Spread, Great Diversity*, August 22, 2012, http://
www.cecc.gov/publications/issue-papers/special-report-tibetan-self-immolation
-rising-frequency-wider-spread; Greg Bruno, "Tibetan Suicides Are Tinder for
Future Unrest in China," *National*, February 27, 2012, http://www.thenational.ae
/thenationalconversation/comment/tibetan-suicides-are-tinder-for-future-unrest-in
-china; Simon Denyer, "Self-Immolations Reflect Rising Tibetan Anger," *Washington
Post*, April 1, 2012, https://www.washingtonpost.com/world/asia_pacific/self-immo
lations-reflect-rising-tibetan-anger/2012/04/01/gIQA2szapS_story.html?utm_term=
.ba81eb87a744; "New Footage Depicts Self-Immolation in Tibet," *Voice of America*,
April 16, 2012, http://www.voanews.com/content/new-footage-depicts-self-immola
tion-in-tibet-147744485/180157.html.

6. Kham, one of three regions that make up historic Tibet, is today mostly cen-
tered in Sichuan Province (with portions extending to Gansu, Qinghai, and Yunnan);
it is separate from the Tibet Autonomous Region, the geopolitical boundary drawn
by China after occupation. The two other regions of historic Tibet are Ü-Tsang
(which corresponds approximately to the present-day TAR) and Amdo (covering
most of Qinghai and portions of Gansu and Sichuan Provinces). See map, p. viii.

7. Parameswaran Ponnudurai, "Four Tibetans Self-Immolate," Radio Free Asia,
November 26, 2012, http://www.rfa.org/english/news/tibet/protest-11262012131404.
html.

8. "New Video Footage of Latest Tibet Self-Immolation Incident," Central Tibetan
Administration, June 23, 2012, http://tibet.net/2012/06/new-video-footage-of-latest
-self-immolation-incident/. According to this account, Ngawang survived.

9. Constitution of the People's Republic of China, adopted December 4, 1982, pub-

lished in English by *People's Daily*, http://en.people.cn/constitution/constitution
.html.

10. Mary S. Erbaugh, review of *China's Assimilationist Language Policy: The Impact on Indigenous/Minority Literacy and Social Harmony*, by Gulbahar H. Beckett and Gerard A. Postiglione, *China Quarterly* 210 (2012): 527–528.

11. Ibid.

12. June T. Dreyer, *China's Forty Millions: Minority Nationalities and National Integration in the People's Republic of China* (Cambridge, MA: Harvard University Press, 1976), 160–161.

13. Matt Adler, "Interview with Dr. Robert Barnett: 'Tibetan Language: Policy and Practice,'" *Culturally Curious*, January 20, 2015, https://culturallycuriousblog.wordpress.com/2015/01/20/interview-with-dr-robert-barnett-tibetan-language-policy -and-practice/.

14. Edward Wong, "Tibetans Fight to Salvage Fading Culture in China," *New York Times*, November 28, 2015, https://www.nytimes.com/2015/11/29/world/asia/china -tibet-language-education.html.

15. "Self-Immolations by Tibetans," fact sheet, International Campaign for Tibet, https://www.savetibet.org/resources/fact-sheets/self-immolations-by-tibetans/.

16. "Self-Immolation at Tibet's Labrang Monastery," International Campaign for Tibet, October 22, 2012, https://www.savetibet.org/self-immolation-at-tibets -labrang-monastery/.

17. James Verini, "A Terrible Act of Reason: When Did Self-Immolation Become the Paramount Form of Protest?," *New Yorker*, May 16, 2012, http://www.newyorker .com/culture/culture-desk/a-terrible-act-of-reason-when-did-self-immolation -become-the-paramount-form-of-protest.

18. Jenny Chan and Pun Ngai, "Suicide as Protest for the New Generation of Chinese Migrant Workers: Foxconn, Global Capital, and the State," *Asia-Pacific Journal* 8, issue 37, no. 2 (2010).

19. Verini, "A Terrible Act of Reason."

20. Warren W. Smith Jr., *China's Tibet? Autonomy or Assimilation* (Lanham, MD: Rowman & Littlefield, 2008), 38.

21. Ibid., 37.

22. Carole McGranahan, *Arrested Histories: Tibet, the CIA, and Memories of a Forgotten War* (Durham, NC: Duke University Press, 2010), 75.

23. Smith, *China's Tibet?*, 38.

24. McGranahan, *Arrested Histories*, 102.

25. A. Tom Grunfeld, *The Making of Modern Tibet* (London: Routledge, 1996), 185.

26. Ibid., 188.

27. Michael Weisskopf, "Dalai Lama: Sacred to Tibet, a Thorn in China's Side," *Washington Post*, August 28, 1983.

28. Grunfeld, *Making of Modern Tibet*, 232.

29. "Central Gov't Spends 310 Bln Yuan Bolstering Tibet's Development," Xinhua, January 25, 2010.

30. Cui Jia and Hou Liqiang, "Himalayan Rail Route Endorsed," *China Daily*, August 5, 2016, http://europe.chinadaily.com.cn/business/2016-08/05/content_26350829.htm.

31. "China's Tibetan Delegation Starts Britain Visit," Xinhua, April 1, 2017, http://news.xinhuanet.com/english/2017-03/25/c_136157564.htm.

32. "Tibet: Growing Frustration after Latest Round of Talks between Beijing and the Dalai Lama's Envoys," US government cable, February 11, 2010, WikiLeaks, https://search.wikileaks.org/plusd/cables/10NEWDELHI290_a.html.

33. "Delhi Diary, January 30–February 19, 2010," US government cable, February 22, 2010, WikiLeaks, https://wikileaks.org/plusd/cables/10NEWDELHI321_a.html.

34. Dalai Lama, *Freedom in Exile: The Autobiography of the Dalai Lama* (New York: Harper Perennial, 1991).

TEN KINGFISHER STRONG

1. Ngodup Gyatso is a pseudonym; see preface for explanation.

2. Helen Sowey, "Are Refugees at Increased Risk of Substance Misuse?" *Drug and Alcohol Multicultural Education Centre*, 2005 (ed. 1). See http://library.bsl.org.au/jspui/bitstream/1/747/1/Refugee_Drug_Alcohol_Vulnerability.pdf.

3. Gauri Bhattacharya, "Drug Use among Asian-Indian Adolescents: Identifying Protective/Risk Factors," *Adolescence* 33, no. 129 (Spring 1998): 169–184.

4. Warren W. Smith Jr., "Origins of the Middle Way Policy," in *Trails of the Tibetan Tradition: Papers for Elliot Sperling*, ed. Roberto Vitale (New Delhi: Amnye Machen Institute, 2015): 385–399.

5. Maura Moynihan, "The High Cost of Protracted Refugee Syndrome," Rangzen Alliance, September 13, 2012, http://www.rangzen.net/2012/09/13/the-high-cost-of-protracted-refugee-syndrome/.

6. Conference on "Craving, Desire, and Addiction," held at the Dalai Lama's residence in Dharamsala, India, October 28 to November 1, 2013. See https://www.dalailama.com/videos/mind-and-life-xxvii-craving-desire-and-addiction. See also "Talking to the Dalia Lama about Addiction Science," National Institute on Drug Abuse, November 12, 2013, https://www.drugabuse.gov/about-nida/noras-blog/2013/11/talking-to-dalai-lama-about-addiction-science.

7. In particular, Kunphen's owner, local businessman Dawa Tsering, has come under scrutiny in the past for questionable financial dealings. See Lobsang Wangyal, "Yongling School—MP Dawa Tsering Accused of Corruption," *Tibet Sun*, July 22,

2013, https://www.tibetsun.com/news/2013/07/22/yongling-school-mp-dawa-tsering
-accused-of-corruption.

8. "Tibetan NGO CHOICE HIV/AIDS to Dissolve, Releases Executive Report,"
Phayul.com, May 30, 2013, http://www.phayul.com/news/article.aspx?id=33517.

ELEVEN POTSHOTS AT PHUNTSOKLING

1. For a description of Tibetan life in the road camps see Dervla Murphy, *Tibetan Foothold* (London: John Murray, 1966).

2. Jan Magnusson, Subramanya Nagarajarao, and Geoff Childs, "South Indian Tibetans: Development Dynamics in the Early Stages of the Tibetan Refugee Settlement Lugs zung bsam grub gling, Bylakuppe," *Journal of the International Association of Tibetan Studies* 4 (2008).

3. George Woodcock, "Tibetan Refugees in a Decade of Exile," *Pacific Affairs* 43 (1970): 410–420.

4. Other anthropologists conducting research on the earliest settlements noted a similar economic miracle unfolding in Bylakuppe, notably Melvyn C. Goldstein, who arrived in January 1966 and found that the Tibetans had "became a tremendous economic success" in record time, with "very little manifestation of the dysfunctional behavior commonly associated with the 'refugee' syndrome," such as alcoholism. See Goldstein, "Ethnogenesis and Resource Competition among Tibetan Refugees in South India: A New Face to the Indo-Tibetan Interface," in *Himalayan Anthropology: The Indo-Tibetan Interface*, ed. James Fisher (The Hague: Mouton, 1978), 399.

5. Magnusson, Nagarajarao, and Childs, "South Indian Tibetans."

6. Rainfall patterns in Orissa are highly variable, but according to one study, in 2009, overall rainfall totals in the coastal state were actually increasing because of a later onset of monsoon rains, coupled with a greater amount of pre-monsoon precipitation. See Surendranath Pasupalak, "Climate Change and Agriculture in Orissa," *Orissa Review*, April–May 2009: 49–52.

7. Despite the crop's limitations, Orissa and other agriculture-dependent states have in recent years sought to increase corn cultivation, a push being driven by major seed companies and India's increasing demand for animal feedstock.

8. "Tribal People 'Occupy' Land," *Hindu*, May 28, 2012, http://www.thehindu.com/todays-paper/tp-national/tp-otherstates/tribal-people-occupy-land/article3464102.ece.

9. Magnusson, Nagarajarao, and Childs, "South Indian Tibetans."

10. "Tribal People Up in Arms against Landgrab," *Hindu*, February 11, 2013, http://www.thehindu.com/todays-paper/tp-national/tp-otherstates/tribal-people-up-in-arms-against-landgrab/article4402301.ece.

11. Communist Party of India (Marxist), Orissa State Committee leadership list, http://www.cpimodisha.org/leadership.

12. "Tribal Families Seek Intervention of Revenue Officials," *Hindu*, December 24, 2013, http://www.thehindu.com/news/national/other-states/tribal-families-seek -intervention-of-revenue-officials/article5497217.ece.

13. "Tibetan Settlers Asked to Surrender 'Occupied' Land," *Indian Express*, November 7, 2012, http://www.newindianexpress.com/states/orissa/article1330685.ece.

14. "Statement on Land Case in Phuntsokling Settlement," Central Tibetan Administration, May 10, 2013, http://tibet.net/2013/05/statement-on-land-case-in-phuntsok ling-settlement/.

15. T. C. Palakshappa, *Tibetans in India: A Case Study of the Mundgod Tibetans* (New Delhi, 1978).

16. Girija Saklaini, *The Uprooted Tibetans in India: A Sociological Study of Continuity and Change* (New Delhi: Cosmo, 1984).

17. In *Sh. Visharad Sood v. Election Commission of Himachal Pradesh and Others*, CWP No. 2898 of 2014-J.

18. Niranjan Kaggere, "Karnataka to Allow Tibetan Refugees to Lease Land in Their Own Names," *Bangalore Mirror*, November 4, 2015, http://www.bangaloremirror.com /bangalore/others/Karnataka-to-allow-Tibetan-refugees-to-lease-land-in-their-own -names/articleshow/49651214.cms.

19. Namgyal Choedup, "From Tibetan Refugees to Transmigrants: Negotiating Cultural Continuity and Economic Mobility through Migration," Arts & Sciences Electronic Theses and Dissertations, Paper 643, 2015, 151.

20. "Indians Demand Tibet Exiles Leave Dharamsala," Associated Press, April 25, 1994.

21. "Irate Mob Burns Tibetan Market," *Tribune*, July 6, 1999, http://www.tribune india.com/1999/99jul06/himachal.htm#2.

22. Some longtime members of the Tibetan diaspora suspect the violence was instigated by corrupt local officials looking to shake down Tibetan businesses, possibly for protection money, but the allegations remain unfounded.

23. Maura Moynihan, "Tibetans in Exile—Passports or RC's: Who Gets What?" Rangzen.net, October 28, 2012, http://www.rangzen.net/2012/10/28/tibetans-in-exile -%E2%80%93-passports-or-rc%E2%80%99s-who-gets-what/.

24. Tenzin Dharpo, "Tibetan Youth Murdered in McLeod Ganj," Phayul.com, October 31, 2015, http://www.phayul.com/news/article.aspx?id=36677.

25. Mila Rangzen, "Is Dharamshala Safe for Tibetans?," *Tibet Telegraph*, June 12, 2014, http://www.tibettelegraph.com/2014/06/is-dharamshala-safe-for-tibetans.html.

26. *The Tibetan Rehabilitation Policy—2014*, Government of India Ministry of Home Affairs (Dharamsala: H.H. the Dalai Lama's Central Tibetan Relief Committee, 2015), http://www.centraltibetanreliefcommittee.org/ctrc/trp-2014/tibetan-rehab -policy-2014-final-copy.pdf.

1. Planning Commission, Central Tibetan Administration, *Demographic Survey of Tibetans in Exile—2009*, 60.

2. Tibetan Community of NY & NJ, Phuntsok Deshi project website, http://tcnynj .org/tach-hall/.

3. Perhaps the most infamous example of the fictional liberties taken by Hollywood to romanticize Tibet was Frank Capra's 1937 rendition of James Hilton's 1933 novel, *Lost Horizon*. The book and film tell the story of a British diplomat who finds love and inner peace at a monastery deep in the mountains of Tibet. Among the tale's lasting achievements is the term "Shangri-La." *Lost Horizon* forever positioned Tibet as the prototypical Shangri-La in the world's imagination.

4. Melvyn C. Goldstein, "Serfdom and Mobility: An Examination of the Institution of 'Human Lease' in Traditional Tibetan Society," *Journal of Asian Studies* 3 (1971).

5. Heidi Fjeld, *Commoners and Nobles: Hereditary Divisions in Tibet* (Copenhagen: Nordic Institute of Asian Studies, 2005), 5.

6. Stephanie Roemer, *The Tibetan Government-in-Exile: Politics at Large*, Routledge Advances in South Asian Studies (London: Routledge, 2008), 67.

7. Dawa Norbu, *Red Star over Tibet* (London: Collins, 1974), 246.

8. Dibyesh Anand, "A Contemporary Story of Diaspora: The Tibetan Version," *Diaspora* 12, no. 2 (2003): 211–229.

9. New York City Department of Finance, Mortgage document, https://a836-acris .nyc.gov/DS/DocumentSearch/DocumentImageView?doc_id=2012121100422002.

10. Established in 2009 as a US nonprofit, the Sera Jey Buddhist Culture Center appointed a full-time residential lama in June 2012 but didn't move into a permanent space until March 2016. According to the center's website, prayer sessions and cultural events before then were conducted in private homes, in public parks, at board members' apartments, "and even at McDonald's restaurants." See http://www.serajey.org/.

11. Fiona McConnell, *Rehearsing the State: The Political Practices of the Tibetan Government-in-Exile* (West Sussex, UK: Wiley Blackwell, 2016), 173.

12. Photos of the lineup posted to social media showed hundreds of Tibetans—men and women, monks and laypeople—waiting under cold, gray skies to enter the consulate to submit application forms. Among the details required for a visa: the name, age, occupation, address, and phone number of "major family members" inside Tibet.

13. "Tibet Website Says Dalai Lama's Clique Is Falling Apart," *Global Times*, January 6, 2016, http://www.globaltimes.cn/content/962033.shtml.

14. Elena Barabantseva, "Who Are 'Overseas Chinese Ethnic Minorities'? China's Search for Transnational Ethnic Unity," *Modern China* 38, no. 1 (2012): 78–109.

15. Woeser, "'Tibetans' Center of the Tibet Autonomous Region," *Invisible Tibet*, November 22, 2010, http://woeser.middle-way.net/2010/11/blog-post_19.html.

16. Guo Kai, "China Woos Overseas Tibetans," *Global Times*, October 9, 2012, http://www.globaltimes.cn/content/732077.shtml.

17. Pauline MacDonald, *Dharamsala Days, Dharamsala Nights: The Unexpected World of the Refugees from Tibet* (self-published, 2013).

18. While immigration lawyers—and Tibetan leaders—exude confidence in the process, immigrating to the United States remains costly, complex, and time consuming (and after the election of Donald Trump highly unpredictable). According to the United States–based Tibet Justice Center, which provides resources for lawyers in Tibetan immigration cases, there are many instances of Tibetans in India and Nepal who don't meet the legal criteria for political asylum, and just as many people are rejected as are admitted. See http://www.tibetjustice.org/?page_id=68.

19. "U.S. Embassy Cables: 'Widening Generational Divide' between Tibet's Leaders and Youth," *Guardian*, December 16, 2010, http://www.theguardian.com/world/us-embassy-cables-documents/160094.

20. Initial population figures according to Central Tibet Administration Department of Home estimates, http://centraltibetanreliefcommittee.org/doh/settlements/india/south/lugsung-samdupling.html.

21. Planning Commission, Central Tibetan Administration, *Demographic Survey of Tibetans in Exile—2009*.

22. Alanna Schubach, "A Feast of Tibetan Dumplings at the Momo Crawl in Jackson Heights," *Village Voice*, November 16, 2015, http://www.villagevoice.com/restaurants/a-feast-of-tibetan-dumplings-at-the-momo-crawl-in-jackson-heights-7921921.

23. "U.S. Embassy Cables: 'Widening Generational Divide.'"

24. In 2013 and again in 2015, US lawmakers debating immigration reform introduced legislation paving the way for thousands of new visas to be made available for Tibetan refugees. In both cases the bills never made it out of committee. See https://www.govtrack.us/congress/bills/114/hr2679/text.

25. For examples see "Tibetans in India, Nepal Cautioned against Traveling to Europe for Asylum," *Tibetan Review*, July 2014, http://www.tibetanreview.net/tibetans-in-india-nepal-cautioned-against-traveling-to-europe-for-asylum/, and "Switzerland 'Revised' Tibet Policy to Boost Ties: Chinese Media," *Press Trust of India*, February 19, 2017, http://www.india.com/news/agencies/switzerland-revised-tibet-policy-to-boost-tieschinese-media-1853889/.

26. "French Schoolchildren Protest at Migrant Expulsions with Paris March," Associated Press, October 17, 2013, https://www.theguardian.com/world/2013/oct/17/french-schoolchildren-protest-migrant-explusions-paris-kosovar.

27. Pema Yoko, "'Free Tibet' Banned at March 10, NYC," March 11, 2015, https://www.facebook.com/notes/pema-yoko/free-tibet-banned-at-march-10-nyc/10153158350457743.

EPILOGUE

1. Leslie Nguyen-Okwu, "The Dalai Lama's Right-Hand Woman," ozy.com, January 15, 2016, http://www.ozy.com/rising-stars/the-dalai-lamas-right-hand-woman/65381.

2. Anand Bodh, "25-Yr-Old First Tibetan to Be Indian Citizen," *Times of India*, January 20, 2011, http://timesofindia.indiatimes.com/india/25-yr-old-first-Tibetan-to -be-Indian-citizen/articleshow/7323090.cms.

3. For settlement-specific data see Planning Commission, Central Tibetan Administration, *Demographic Survey of Tibetans in Exile—2009*.

4. For an overview of the "Reimaging Doeguling Tibetan Settlement" project see http://www.doeguling.com/.

5. While leaders of Ganden seem circumspect about welcoming non-Buddhist visitors to join them in South Indian, Drepung has gone all out. A massive new research center is being built adjacent to the Drepung Loseling Monastery in Mungod, in partnership with Emory University. When it opens, it will have study and living space for up to 125 students and 50 faculty members. Research will focus on the intersection of science and Buddhism, especially how "contemplative sciences," like meditation, affect the brain. A similar research partnership is already under way at Emory's Atlanta campus.

6. "US Sanctions Massive Six Million Dollars for Tibetans in Nepal and India for Fiscal Year 2016," Tibet.net, December 21, 2015, http://tibet.net/2015/12/us-sanctions -massive-six-million-dollars-for-tibetans-in-nepal-and-india-for-fiscal-year-2016/. At the time of this writing, it was unclear what might become of US support to Tibetan refugees under President Trump.

7. The US government apparently accepts this reality, too. In January 2016 the Office of the Special Coordinator of Tibet organized an outreach effort to entice governments that have historically supported Tibetan refugees to reinvigorate their funding streams.

8. Richard Finney, "China Calls Dalai Lama's Kalachakra 'Illegal,' Threatens Punishment for Those Taking Part," Radio Free Asia, January 5, 2017, http://www.rfa.org /english/news/tibet/illegal-01052017151431.html.

9. Chen Heying, "Dalai Lama Ritual a 'Political Tool,'" *Global Times*, January 5, 2017, http://www.globaltimes.cn/content/1027367.shtml.

10. Tenzin Dharpo, "His Holiness Reaffirmed to Live 113 Years: Senior Gelug Leaders," Phayul.com, April 17, 2016.

11. On September 24, 2011, the Fourteenth Dalai Lama issued a statement declaring that when he is "about ninety," which would be on July 6, 2025, he will consult with the tradition's highest lamas to "re-evaluate whether the institution of the Dalai Lama should continue or not." If it is decided that it should continue, heads of the

various traditions will consult on identifying a successor. "I shall leave clear written instructions about this," he wrote. "Bear in mind that, apart from the reincarnation recognized through such legitimate methods, no recognition or acceptance should be given to a candidate chosen for political ends by anyone, including those in the People's Republic of China." For the full statement see http://dalailama.com/messages /statement-of-his-holiness-the-fourteenth-dalai-lama-tenzin-gyatso-on-the-issue-of -his-reincarnation.

12. Sarah Boesveld, "3 Students Stabbed after Schoolyard Sports Fight," *Toronto Star*, April 26, 2008.

13. China undoubtedly understands this, too, which is one reason the Communist Party has sought to control the reincarnation of lamas and enshrined its own religious leaders inside Tibet.

BIBLIOGRAPHY

AFP. "China Has 'Vast, Dark Spy Network': Defector." Agence France-Presse, March 20, 2009.

Alexandrowicz, C. H. "India and the Tibetan Tragedy." *Foreign Affairs*, April 1953.

Arora, Vijay. "'Encroachments' over Forest Land: HC Issues Notice to State, CTA." *Tribune*, April 14, 2012.

Associated Press. "Indians Demand Tibet Exiles Leave Dharamsala." April 25, 1994.

Avedon, John F. *In Exile from the Land of Snows: The Definitive Account of the Dalai Lama and Tibet since the Chinese Conquest.* New York: Vintage Books, 1986.

Barabantseva, Elena. "Who Are 'Overseas Chinese Ethnic Minorities'? China's Search for Transnational Ethnic Unity." *Modern China* 38, no. 1 (January 2012): 78–109.

Bhattacharya, Abanti. "Chinese Nationalism and the Fate of Tibet: Implications for India and Future Scenarios." *Strategic Analysis* 31, no. 2 (2007): 237–266.

Bhattacharya, Gauri. "Drug Use among Asian-Indian Adolescents: Identifying Protective/Risk Factors." *Adolescence* 33 (1998): 169–184.

Bodh, Anand. "Himachal Police Arrest Eight Chinese Nationals." *Times of India*, June 13, 2012.

———. "25-Yr-Old First Tibetan to Be Indian Citizen." *Times of India*, January 20, 2011.

Brown, Kerry. 2010. "China's Soft Power Diplomacy in the 21st Century." In *A Handbook of China's International Relations*, edited by Shaun Breslin, 85–93. London: Routledge, 2010.

Bruno, Greg. "China's Nationalism Is a Threat, but It's No Longer Personal." *National*, February 18, 2011.

———. "The Monocropping Dilemma." School for International Training. Independent Study Project, 1998.

———. "Pushed by China, Tibetans Leave Nepal." *Global Post*, April 12, 2010.

———. "Tibetan Suicides Are Tinder for Future Unrest in China." *National*, February 27, 2012.

Callahan, William A. *China Dreams: 20 Visions of the Future*. New York: Oxford University Press, 2015.

Carlson, Catherine. "Substance Abuse among Second-Generation Tibetan Refugees Living in India." Diss., Emory-IBD Tibetan Studies Program, 2003.

Chauhan, Pratibha. "Govt to Drop Eviction Proceedings against Tibetan Refugees." *Tribune*, April 2, 2015.

Childs, Geoff. *Tibetan Diary: From Birth to Death and Beyond in a Himalayan Valley of Nepal*. Berkeley: University of California Press, 2004.

Childs, Geoff, Melvyn C. Goldstein, Ben Jiao, and Cynthia M. Beall. "Tibetan Fertility Transitions in China and South Asia." *Population and Development Review* 31, no. 2 (2005): 337–349.

Congressional-Executive Commission on China. *Special Report: Tibetan Self-Immolation—Rising Frequency, Wider Spread, Great Diversity*. Washington, DC: CECC, 2012.

Cuervo, Ivy. "Fight outside Tibetan Cultural Centre Leaves 1 Dead, 1 Hurt." CBC News, March 9, 2014.

Dalai Lama. *Freedom in Exile: The Autobiography of the Dalai Lama*. New York: Harper Perennial, 1991.

———. *My Land and My People: The Original Autobiography of His Holiness the Dalai Lama of Tibet*. New York: Grand Central, 2008.

Denyer, Simon. "Self-Immolations Reflect Rising Tibetan Anger." *Washington Post*, April 1, 2012.

Department of Home. "Agriculture Development Project for Phuntsokling Tibetan Settlements, Chandragiri, Gajapati District, Orissa." Central Tibetan Administration, Gangchen Kyishong, August 1996.

Dharpo, Tenzin. "Tibetan Youth Murdered in McLeod Ganj." Phayul.com, October 31, 2015.

Directorate of Soil Conservation. "Project Report on Soil and Land Capability Survey of Phuntsokling Tibetan Settlement Area." Vol. 1. Government of Orissa, Bhubaneswar, India. May 1996.

Dorjee, Tenzin. "6 Things You Should Know about the Anti–Dalai Lama Protesters." *Huffington Post*, November 5, 2014.

Famularo, Julia. "Spinning the Wheel: Policy Implications of the Dalai Lama's Reincarnation." Project 2049 Institute, January 30, 2012.

Fish, Isaac Stone. "Blame Norway: Why Is Oslo Kowtowing to Beijing and Stiff-Arming the Dalai Lama?" *Foreign Policy*, May 6, 2014.

Fuchs, Andreas, and Nil-Hendrik Klann. "Pay a Visit: The Dalai Lama Effect on International Trade." Center for European Governance and Economic Development Research. CEGE Discussion Papers, 113, October 2013.

Fürer-Haimendorf, Christoph von. *The Renaissance of Tibetan Civilization*. Santa Fe, NM: Synergetic, 1990.

Garnaut, John. "China Spreads Its Watching Web of Surveillance across Australia." *Sydney Morning Herald*, April 26, 2014.

Garratt, Kevin. "Tibetan Refugees, Asylum Seekers, Returnees and the Refugees Convention: Predicaments, Problems and Prospects." *Tibet Journal* 22, no. 3 (Autumn 1997): 18–56.

Gill, Bates. *Rising Star: China's New Security Diplomacy*. Washington, DC: Brookings Institution Press, 2010.

Gill, Bates, and Yanzhong Huang. "Sources and Limits of Chinese 'Soft Power.'" *Survival* 48, no. 2 (2006): 17–36.

Global Times. "Dalai Assassination Claims Mind-Boggling." May 14, 2012.

———. "Tibet Website Says Dalai Lama's Clique Is Falling Apart." January 6, 2016.

Goldstein, Melvyn C. *History of Modern Tibet*. Vol. 2, *The Calm before the Storm, 1951–1955*. Berkeley: University of California Press, 2009.

Goossaert, Vincent, and David A. Palmer. *The Religious Question in Modern China*. Chicago: University of Chicago Press, 2011.

Green, Jonathan. *Murder in the High Himalaya: Loyalty, Tragedy, and Escape from Tibet*. New York: PublicAffairs, 2010.

Gross, Ernest A. "Tibetans Plan for Tomorrow." *Foreign Affairs*, October 1961.

Guodong, Du. "France Seeks to Repair Relations with China." *China Daily*, February 7, 2009.

Gyatso, Soepa. "Another Tibetan Is Jailed for Discouraging Worship of Controversial Deity." Radio Free Asia Tibetan Service, December 17, 2014.

Halper, Lezlee Brown, and Stefan Halper. *Tibet: An Unfinished Story*. New York: Oxford University Press, 2014.

Hillman, Ben. "Monastic Politics and the Local State in China: Authority and Autonomy in an Ethnically Tibetan Prefecture." *China Journal* 54 (2005): 29–51.

Hindu. "Tribal Families Seek Intervention of Revenue Officials." December 24, 2013.

——— "Tribal People 'Occupy' Land." May 28, 2012.

———. "Tribal People Up in Arms against Land Grab." February 11, 2013.

His Holiness the Fourteenth Dalai Lama, Private Office. "His Holiness the Dalai Lama's Advice concerning Dolgyal (Shugden)." https://www.dalailama.com /messages/dolgyal-shugden/statements-announcements/his-holiness-advice.

Huber, Toni. *The Holy Land Reborn: Pilgrimage and the Tibetan Reinvention of Buddhist India*. Chicago: University of Chicago Press, 2008.

Human Rights Watch. *Appeasing China: Restricting the Rights of Tibetans in Nepal*. New York, 2008.

———. *Under China's Shadow: Mistreatment of Tibetans in Nepal.* Washington, DC, 2014.

Hutt, Michael. *Himalayan 'People's War': Nepal's Maoist Rebellion.* London: C. Hurst & Co., 2004.

Indian Express. "Tibetan Settlers Asked to Surrender 'Occupied' Land." Express News Service, November 7, 2012.

Information Warfare Monitor. "Tracking GhostNet: Investigating a Cyber Espionage Network." March 29, 2009.

Institute for Defense Studies and Analyses. *Tibet and India's Security: Himalayan Region, Refugees, and Sino-Indian Relations.* IDSA Task Force Report. New Delhi, 2012.

International Campaign for Tibet. *Dangerous Crossing: Conditions Impacting the Flight of Tibetan Refugees in 2001.* Washington, DC, 2002.

———. *Dangerous Crossing: Conditions Impacting the Flight of Tibetan Refugees, 2007–2008 Report.* Washington, DC, 2008.

———. *Dangerous Crossing: Conditions Impacting the Flight of Tibetan Refugees, 2009 Update.* Washington, DC, 2010.

———. *Dangerous Crossing: Conditions Impacting the Flight of Tibetan Refugees, 2010 Update.* Washington, 2010.

———. "Escalation in Ngaba following Self-Immolation: Two Tibetans Shot." January 14, 2012.

———. "A Fragile Welcome: China's Influence on Nepal and Its Impact on Tibetans." Washington, DC, June 19, 2010.

———. "Self-Immolations by Tibetans." Washington, DC, 2015.

———. "Storm in the Grasslands: Self-Immolations in Tibet and Chinese Policy." Washington, DC, December 2008.

———. "An Uncertain Welcome: How China's Influence Impacts Tibetans in Nepal." Washington, DC, 2009.

Jakobson, Linda, and Dean Knox. "New Foreign Policy Actors in China." Stockholm International Peace Research Institute. SIPRI Policy Paper no. 26, September 2010.

Johnson, Tim. *Tragedy in Crimson: How the Dalai Lama Conquered the World but Lost the Battle with China.* New York: Nation Books, 2011.

Kaggere, Niranjan. "Karnataka to Allow Tibetan Refugees to Lease Land in Their Own Names." *Bangalore Mirror*, November 4, 2015.

Kai, Guo. "China Woos Overseas Tibetans." *Global Times*, October 9, 2012.

Khatiwada, Ramesh. "China Ups the Ante Following Tibetans' Arrest." *Republica*, February 28, 2010.

Knaus, John Kenneth. *Orphans of the Cold War: America and the Tibetan Struggle for Survival.* New York: PublicAffairs, 2000.

Kranti, Vijay. "How Tibetans Are Losing Their Focus and Unity." Phayul.com, February 6, 2013.

Kumar, Naresh. "HC Orders Eviction of Land Encroachments in 1,090 Cases in Dharamsala." *Hindustan Times*, August 28, 2012.

Kunwar, Ramesh Raj. "Paganism and Spiritism: A Study of Religion and Ritual in the Sherpa Society." *Ancient Nepal, Journal of the Department of Archaeology* 103 (1988): 1–18.

Li, Jianglin. *Tibet in Agony: Lhasa 1959.* Cambridge, MA: Harvard University Press, 2016.

Ma, Rong. "Population Structure Changes in the Tibet Autonomous Region." *China Tibetology* 3 (2008): 167–182.

Macartney, Jane. "Interpol on Trail of Buddhist Killers." *Australian*, June 22, 2007.

MacDonald, Pauline. *Dharamsala Days, Dharamsala Nights: The Unexpected World of the Refugees from Tibet.* Self-published, 2013.

MacLeod-Bluver, Caitlin. "I Didn't Feel Like Living: The Prevalence, Perceptions, and Prevention of HIV/AIDS among Tibetan Refugees in Kathmandu." School for International Training. Independent Study Project (ISP) Collection, Paper 807, 2009.

Magnusson, Jan, Subramanya Nagarajarao, and Geoff Childs. "South Indian Tibetans: Development Dynamics in the Early Stages of the Tibetan Refugee Settlement Lugs zung bsam grub gling, Bylakuppe." *Journal of the International Association of Tibetan Studies* 4 (2008): 1–31.

Mazzi, Enrica. "The Miracle of Gangchen." *Lama Gangchen Peace Times*, blog entry, undated.

McConnell, Fiona. *Rehearsing the State: The Political Practices of the Tibetan Government-in-Exile.* West Sussex, UK: Wiley Blackwell, 2016.

McGrath, Timothy. "No One Likes the Dalai Lama Anymore." *Global Post*, September 5, 2014.

Mechling, Katherine. "Know Your Enemy: Tibetan Perceptions of and Approaches to Chinese Studies in Exile." School for International Training. Independent Study Project (ISP) Collection, Paper 808, 2009.

Ministry of Finance. The Benami Transactions (Prohibition) Act, 1988. Union Government of India. New Delhi, 1988.

Ministry of Foreign Affairs. "H.E. Ambassador Yang Houlan Visited Tibetan Community in Kathmandu." Embassy of the People's Republic of China in the Federal Democratic Republic of Nepal, press release, August 22, 2011.

Ministry of Home Affairs. The Tibetan Rehabilitation Policy—2014. Union Government of India. New Delhi, 2014.

Mishra, Pankaj. "The Last Dalai Lama?" *New York Times*, December 1, 2015.

Mooney, Paul. "Beyond Belief." *South China Morning Post*, September 4, 2011.

Moynihan, Maura. "Tibetans in Exile—Passports or RC's: Who Gets What?" Rangzen.net, October 28, 2012.

Murphy, Dervla. *Tibetan Foothold*. London: John Murray, 1966.

Navarro, Peter, and Greg Autry. *Death by China: Confronting the Dragon—a Global Call to Action*. Upper Saddle River, NJ: Pearson FT, 2011.

Nelson, Dean. "Dalai Lama Reveals Warning of Chinese Plot to Kill Him." *Telegraph*, May 12, 2012.

Norbu, Dawa. "Tibetan Refugees in South Asia: Implications for Security." Paper presented at Seminar on Refugees and Internal Security in South Asia, Colombo, Sri Lanka, July 10–11, 1994.

Norbu, Jamyang. *Shadow Tibet*. http://www.jamyangnorbu.com.

Nyinjey, Tenzin. "Censorship and the Struggle for Tibetan Freedom." *Tibet Sun*, July 27, 2012.

Palakshappa, T. C. *Tibetans in India: A Case Study of the Mundgod Tibetans*. New Delhi: Sterling, 1978.

Pew Research Center. "U.S.-China Security Perceptions Project 2012 General Public Survey Data." US general public survey conducted April 30, 2012, to May 13, 2012.

Phayul. "Tibetan NGO CHOICE HIV/AIDS to Dissolve, Releases Executive Report." Phayul.com, May 30, 2013.

Planning Commission. *Demographic Survey of Tibetans in Exile—2009*. Central Tibetan Administration, Gangchen Kyishong, Dharamsala, India, 2010.

Planning Commission. *Tibetan Demographic Survey 1998*. Central Tibetan Administration, Gangchen Kyishong, Dharamsala, India. 2000.

Ponnudurai, Parameswaran. "Four Tibetans Self-Immolate." Radio Free Asia, November 26, 2012.

Radio Free Asia. "Elderly Tibetan Is Jailed for Discouraging Worship of Controversial Deity." Radio Free Asia Tibetan Service, December 12, 2014.

———. "Fire Rips through Tibetan Area of Dharamsala." December 21, 2004.

Rangzen, Mile. "Is Dharamshala Safe for Tibetans?" *Tibet Telegraph*, June 12, 2014.

Reich, Carey. "A New Generation of Buddhist: The Views and Practice of Tibetan Youth." School for International Training. Independent Study Project, 2014.

Rigzin, Tsewang. "A Survey Research on Tibetan Entrepreneurs in India." MDP diss., Emory University, 2015.

Roberts, John, and Elizabeth Roberts. *Freeing Tibet: 50 Years of Struggle, Resilience, and Hope*. New York: AMACOM, 2009.

Roemer, Stephanie. *The Tibetan Government-in-Exile: Politics at Large*. Routledge Advances in South Asian Studies. Edited by Subrata K. Mitra. London: Routledge, 2008.

Rozeboom, Annelie. *Waiting for the Dalai Lama: Stories from All Sides of the Tibetan Debate*. Hong Kong: Blacksmith Books, 2011.

Saklaini, Girija. *The Uprooted Tibetans in India: A Sociological Study of Continuity and Change*. New Delhi: Cosmo, 1984.

Salidjanova, Nargiza. *Going Out: Overview of China's Outward Foreign Direct Investment*. US-China Economic and Security Review Commission, Staff Research Report, March 30, 2011.

Schubach, Alanna. "A Feast of Tibetan Dumplings at the Momo Crawl in Jackson Heights." *Village Voice*, November 16, 2015.

Sehgal, Manjeet. "His Holiness Seeks Southern Comfort: Dalai Lama May Spend Two Months a Year in Karnataka for Health Reasons." *Mail Today*, August 3, 2013.

Shambaugh, David. *China Goes Global: The Partial Power*. New York: Oxford University Press, 2014.

Sheridan, Michael. "Chinese Embassy Blitzed by NATO Was Hiding Serbs." *Sunday Times*, February 13, 2011.

Shih, Shani. "Beyond Ramaluk: Towards a More Inclusive View of Identity in the Tibetan Diaspora." School for International Training. Independent Study Project (ISP) Collection, Paper 1740, 2013.

Smith, Warren W. *Tibet's Last Stand? The Tibetan Uprising of 2008 and China's Response*. Lanham, MD: Rowman & Littlefield, 2009.

South Asia Foundation. "Agreement on Trade, Intercourse and Related Questions between Tibet Autonomous Region of China and Nepal." Bilateral trade agreement signed between the People's Republic of China and His Majesty's Government of Nepal, May 2, 1966.

Sowey, Helen. *Are Refugees at Increased Risk of Substance Misuse?* Drug and Alcohol Multicultural Education Centre, 2005.

Stein, Jeff. "How China Keeps Tabs on Tibetan Exiles." *Newsweek*, March 5, 2014.

Swaine, Michael D. "China's Assertive Behavior; Part One: On 'Core Interests.'" *China Leadership Monitor*, Carnegie Endowment for International Peace, no. 34, 2010.

Tharoor, Ishaan. "Why India Is Investigating a Reincarnated Tibetan Lama." *Time*, February 3, 2011.

Thondup, Gyalo. *The Noodle Maker of Kalimpong: The Untold Story of My Struggle for Tibet*. New York: PublicAffairs, 2015.

Thuborn, Colin. *To a Mountain in Tibet*. New York: HarperCollins, 2011.

Tibet Justice Center. "Tibet's Stateless Nationals II: Tibetan Refugees in India." September 2011.

———. "Tibet's Stateless Nationals II: Tibetan Refugees in India—2014 Update." June 30, 2015.

Tibetan Review. "Tibetans in India, Nepal Cautioned against Traveling to Europe for Asylum." July 2014.

Tribune. "Irate Mob Burns Tibetan Market." July 6, 1999.

Tricycle. "An Interview with Geshe Kelsang Gyatso." *Tricycle Magazine*, Spring 1998.

Tsering, Topden. "Demise of a Place: An Obituary." Phayul.com, December 23, 2004.

US-China Economic and Security Review Commission. *2009 Annual Report to Congress*. Washington, DC: USCC, 2009.

———. *Report to Congress*. 2011. Washington, DC: USCC, 2011.

US Department of State. "Congressional Budget Justification: Fiscal Year 2016." Foreign Operations and Related Programs. February 2015.

US House of Representatives. "Falun Gong and China's Continuing War on Human Rights." Joint Hearing before the Subcommittee on Africa, Global Human Rights and International Operations. Washington, DC, July 21, 2005.

US State Department. "Widening Generational Divide between Tibet's Leaders and Youth." US Embassy, New Delhi, cables published by the *Guardian*, December 16, 2010.

Vaughn, Bruce. "Nepal: Background and U.S. Relations." US Congressional Research Service, July 30, 2007.

Verini, James. "A Terrible Act of Reason: When Did Self-Immolation Become the Paramount Form of Protest?" *New Yorker*, May 16, 2012.

VOA. "New Footage Depicts Self-Immolation in Tibet." Voice of America, April 16, 2012.

Wang Lixiong, "Last-Words Analysis: Why Tibetans Self-Immolate?" *Invisible Tibet*, December 29, 2012, translated from Chinese by Ogyen Kyab.

Watson, Ivan, and Pamela Boykoff. "No Escape? China's Crackdown on Dissent Goes Global." CNN, February 4, 2016.

Watts, Jonathan, and Ken Macfarlane. "Inside Tibet's Heart of Protest." *Guardian*, February 10, 2012.

Wee, Sui-Lee, and Stephanie Nebehay. "At UN, China Uses Intimidation Tactics to Silence Its Critics." Reuters, October 5, 2015.

Woodcock, George. "Tibetan Refugees in a Decade of Exile." *Pacific Affairs* 43 (1970): 410–420.

Xinhua. "Central Gov't Spends 310 Bln Yuan Bolstering Tibet's Development." January 25, 2010.

———. "A New Tibet through Homecomers' Eyes." September 8, 2015.

———. "Reincarnation of Living Buddha Needs Gov't Approval." August 4, 2007.

Yoko, Pema. "'Free Tibet' Banned at March 10, NYC." Blog posted to Facebook March 11, 2015. https://www.facebook.com/notes/pema-yoko/free-tibet-banned-at-march-10-nyc/10153158350457743.

Zhigang, Xing, and Li Xiaokun. "Envoy Brief on Sarkozy-Dalai Meet Dismissed." *China Daily*, December 12, 2008.

Zhu, Guobin. "Prosecuting 'Evil Cults': A Critical Examination of Law regarding Freedom of Religious Belief in Mainland China." *Human Rights Quarterly* 32, no. 3 (2010): 471–501.

INDEX

Page numbers in *italics* refer to maps;
those followed by *n* refer to notes, with note number.

in Nepal, 60; strategy to await death of, 136, 178, 179; support of Dorje Shugden sect against, 80, 81–82, 83, 84; surveillance of, 5–6

China, and India: support for independent Tibet, pressure to drop, 67–68; trade agreements, 67

China, and religion: Communist Party's policies on, 37, 89–91, 121–22, 194n1; history of, before Communist Party, 89

China's Long March, 11

Chinese aggression against Tibetans: author's interest in, 42; author's research on, 3, 43; Beijing Olympics as turning point in, 2–3; efforts to divide Tibetan community, 5, 7–9; global interest as damper on, 18; increase in, ix, 4; Internet surveillance and attacks, 5, 13–14; kidnappings of activists in China, 5; media propaganda and, 29, 30–31; pressure on foreign supporters, 4, 33; pressure on scholars studying Tibet, 6–7; pressure on supportive nations, 5–6, 32, 35–36; pressure on universities to isolate Tibetan activists, 33–34; refusal to acknowledge Tibetan issues, 6; and scholarship as propaganda, 38–39; as soft-power war, 28; strategies employed in, 4–7, 38–39; Tibetan responses to, 21, 39–40

Chinese economic power: and isolation of Taiwan, 36; and Nepal, influence in, 53, 56, 59–60, 61, 62; and pressuring of Tibet supporters, 33–36; and spending in Tibet, failure to pacify populace by, 123–24

Chinese foreign policy: core interests declared by, 3–4; increasing aggressiveness of, 3–4, 35

Chinese negotiations with Tibetan government in exile: and Chinese strategy to wait for Dalai Lama's death, 136; history of, 6, 17, 18, 20, 120, 122; hope for success of, xii; refusal to continue, 6, 18, 109, 135–36; and Seventeen-Point Agreement, 120

Chinese occupation, Tibetan resistance to: armed resistance in 1950s–60s, 17, 21, 46, 57, 65, 76, 120–21; Chinese suppression of protests, 2–3, 183–84n5; crackdown on activists after 1989, 17, 91, 122; Dalai Lama's rejection of violence in, 23; growing support for violent action, 10, 19–20, 22–23; and martial law, declaration of (1989), 91, (2008) 123; and potential violence after death of Dalai Lama, 23–24; protests of 1987, 122; protests of 2008, 2, 31–32, 50–51, 112, 114–15, 123, 183–84n5. *See also* self-immolation protests by Tibetans

Chinese occupation of Tibet, *viii*; abuses perpetrated during, 119–24; assimilation policies and, 17, 115–17, 120; author's visit and, 122–23; and ban on Tibetan language, 110, 113, 114–17; China's narrative on, 153; and Chinese education, 125; Chinese fear of US influence and, 57; claimed historical legitimacy of, 17–18; and Cultural Revolution, attacks on Tibetan culture in, 89–90, 116, 122; early efforts to woo Tibetans, 11–12, 16–17; and fracturing of historic Tibet, 120; international communities' acceptance of, 120; nationalist backlash against, 120–22; number fleeing, 125; Purang Dorjee's experience of, 45–46; relaxing of control after death of Mao, 17; and surveillance and intimidation, 5, 123, 126; and Tibetan flight, 46; tightening of control after 1959, 17, 90, 121–22; violent clashes with Muslims, 21

Chinese propaganda: broad reach of, 29; image of ethnic harmony projected by, 29, 30–31; increasing sophistication of, 31; isolation of dissidents by, 29; in Nepal, against Dalai Lama, 60; response to Tibetan unrest of 2008, 31–32; rewriting of Tibetan history in, 120; social media and, 31, 32; on Tibetan TV, 29, 30–31; use of scholarly work for, 38–39

Chinese spies: and Falun Gong, campaign against, 37–38; large number across globe, 37; in McLeod Ganj, 10, 13; tactics used by, 38

Choephal, Tenzin (son of Purang Dorjee): author's friendship with, 98; career path of, 100–101; as CTA employee, 98, 99, 101, 108–9; described, 99; faith in Dalai Lama's leadership, 102, 105, 109; on future of Tibetans in India, 109; home of, 99; on hopes for children, 108; on Indian citizenship, 102; interviews of, 100–102, 105, 108–9; marriage of, 66, 101; pride in Dharamsala, 102; on refugee status, 98, 102

Choice (NGO), 138

Chonor Samdup, 146

Chopel, Sonam, 76

Chushi Gangdruk Committee, 65

CIA, and Tibetan resistance, 21, 57, 121

Communist Party of India, 145–46

CTA. See Central Tibetan Administration

Dai Bingguo, 3–4

Dalai Lama, death of: Chinese strategy of waiting for, 136, 178, 179; and fate of Tibetan exiles, 109, 169–70, 178, 179–80, 181; potential for violent revolt against Chinese following, 23–24

Dalai Lama, Fifth (Ngawang Lobsang Gyatso): and Gelug school schism, 75–76; unification of four sects of Tibetan Buddhism by, 75

Dalai Lama, flight from Tibet, 17, 27, 121; anniversary celebrations in Nepal, Chinese-led suppression of, 53, 61–62; and Chinese crackdown on Tibetans, 90; Tibetans following, 46, 50

Dalai Lama, Fourteenth: and anti-Tibetan violence, 149; author's efforts to interview, 170; author's group meeting with, 9–11; biennial Kalachakra Initiation, 178–79; calls for patience of Tibetan exiles, 180; dampening of Tibetan factionalism by, 180; Dorje Shugden sect opposition to, x, 5, 75, 78–79, 81; on education, 137; as embodiment of Avalokiteshvara, 1, 192n2; health-related cancellations in 2016, 98; history of position, 192n2; Indian legal restrictions on, 68; influence in global community, 178–79; Internet's amplification of negative voices and, 7; Nobel Peace Prize for, 2, 26, 183n5; number of Twitter followers, xii; promise of return to Tibet in his lifetime, 102, 109; retirement from political leadership, 22, 170; security surrounding, 5, 10, 13, 95, 167; on substance abuse, 137; Tibetan factions opposed to, x, 5, 75, 78–79, 81; Tibetans' faith in leadership of, 102, 105, 109, 171, 181; Tibetans' frustration with lack of effective action by, 10, 20–21; as unquestioned leader of Tibetans in

lessness and, 135–36; and shunning of abusers, 139; and treatment options, 137–38

The Sun behind the Clouds (film), 33, 187n18

Taiwan, China and, 36, 37, 184n9

Tenzing, Tsepak, 149

Thich Quang Duc, 118

Third National Forum on Work in Tibet, 92

Thurman, Robert, 159, 175

Tiananmen Square protests (1989), 2, 17, 37, 91, 122

Tibet: history of, 14–16, 153; and Nepal, 54–55

Tibetan Buddhism: Chinese efforts to subjugate, 5, 90–93; four schools of, 75, 192n2; and Mount Kailash, 44–45

Tibetan education: as free for Tibetans in India, 125; Tibetan's desire for, 124

Tibetan government in exile. *See* Central Tibetan Administration

Tibetan language: author and, 77–78; Chinese ban on, 110, 113, 114–17

Tibetan news sites, 72

Tibetan refugees: accomplishments of, xi–xii; and assimilation, efforts to avoid, 154, 156–57; author's experience with, x, xi, 2, 3; challenges faced by, xi, 173–74; China's fear of, 37, 38–39, 40, 184n9; class tensions among, 153–54; dispersion of, ix, 3, 28, 155–56; emerging social problems in, x, 180; experiences of Tibetan-born versus Indian-born, 131, 140; hope of return, 1–2, 102, 109; length of exile, x, xii, 1, 2; migration to West, 156, 171; new arrivals, problems of, 139–41, 180; number of, 28; return to China by,

157–58, 201n12; success in building culture in exile, 183n1; and Tibetan identity, 154. *See also* Europe; future of Tibetan refugees; India, Tibetans in; Nepal; United States

Tibetan refugees, division within: as Chinese strategy, 5, 7; Dalai Lama's "Middle Way" plan and, 22, 39–40, 165–66; struggle to maintain cohesion, x, 154, 180

Tibetan Rehabilitation Policy (2014), 104, 149–50

Tibetans in China. *See* Chinese occupation of Tibet

Tibetan Youth Congress (TYC), 22–23

Tibet Autonomous Region (TAR), *viii*; as Chinese-imposed entity, 58. *See also* Chinese occupation of Tibet

Tibet Fund, 9

Tibet Justice Center (TJC), 68–69, 70, 106, 202n18, 202n24

Topgyal, Tsering, 91

Trijang Rinpoche, 76, 81, 83

Trisong Detsen (king of Tibet), 192n2

Trump, Donald J., 36, 159, 177, 202n18

Tsering, Jamyang, 82

Tsering, Penpa, 61

Tsuglagkhang Temple, ix, 10, 13, 167

Tulkus, selection of, 91–92

United Nations, Chinese intimidation tactics and, 35

United States: and Chinese pressure on Tibet, 4, 36; Dorje Shugden sect in, 80–81; ease of gaining asylum in, 158–59, 162; support for Tibetan refugees, 32, 176–77, 203n7; Tibetan fear of assimilation in, 159–62, 164; Tibetan migration to, 151–52, 155, 202n18. *See also* New York, Tibetan refugees in

universities, and Chinese pressure on
Tibetan issues, 33–34

Uyak Tulku Lobsang Tenzin, 82

Wang Lixiong, 24, 118

Wangmo, Kalsang, 160–62

Wangmo, Samdup, 78–79

Wangyal, Lobsang, 103–4

Wen Jiabao, 6, 84

West, Tibetan migration to, xiii, 156, 171;
challenges of, 140–41, 180

Woodcock, George, 142, 143

Yang Houlan, 83, 87

Yeshi, Jamphel, 117–18

Yongyal Rinpoche, 81